Managing
Ignatius

Dining on Bourbon, by Paul Lewis

Managing Ignatius

The Lunacy of
Lucky Dogs and
Life in the Quarter

JERRY E. STRAHAN

BROADWAY BOOKS   New York

BROADWAY

A hardcover edition of this book was originally published in 1998 by Louisiana State University Press. It is here reprinted by arrangement with Louisiana State University.

Broadway Books titles may be purchased for business or promotional use or for special sale For information, please write to: Special Markets Department, Random House, Inc., 1540 Broadway, New York, NY 10036.

BROADWAY BOOKS and its logo, a letter B bisected on the diagonal, are trademarks of Broadway Books, a division of Random House, Inc.

First Broadway Books trade paperback edition published 1999.

Designed by Michele Myatt Quinn

Library of Congress Cataloging-in-Publication Data

Strahan, Jerry E., 1951–
    Managing Ignatius : the lunacy of Lucky Dogs and life in the
Quarter / Jerry E. Strahan.
      p. cm.
    ISBN 0-7679-0324-2 (pbk.)
     1. Lucky Dogs, Inc.—History. 2. Hog dog stands—Louisiana—New
Orleans. 3. New Orleans (La.)—Social life and customs.
    4. Strahan, Jerry E., 1951– . 5. Talbot, Doug. I. Title.
[HF5459.U6S77 1998]
647.95763'35—dc21   98-40500
                                                          CIP

99 00 01 02 03 10 9 8 7 6 5 4 3 2 1

For Irene and Robert, with love

Clearly an area like the French Quarter is not the proper environment for a clean-living, chaste, prudent, and impressionable young Working Boy. Did Edison, Ford, and Rockefeller have to struggle against such odds?

—Ignatius J. Reilly, in *A Confederacy of Dunces*

Contents

Illustrations

Foreword

Stephen E. Ambrose

In January, 1955, I was a nineteen-year-old student at the University of Wisconsin. I was between semesters, and it was 40 degrees below zero. With some friends I hitchhiked to New Orleans. This is something all midwestern boys dream of doing, going to New Orleans (Abe Lincoln traveled there by raft when he was twenty years old).

For midwesterners, New Orleans is that fabled city at the end of the river. Its appeals are many: warm winter weather, live oaks, Spanish moss, mansions, a bustling port, and world-renowned food. And there is the exotic French Quarter with its balconies and iron grillwork, bars that never close, stripteasers, hustlers, pimps, and street characters of every imaginable type. None of this exists in the small towns of Wisconsin or Illinois, nor for that matter in Milwaukee or Chicago either. Those cities have plenty of sin, to be sure, but only behind closed doors. On Bourbon Street in the Quarter, the sin is right in front of your eyes, wherever you turn.

I took one look at the French Quarter, made one walking trip down Bourbon, and was hooked for life.

Jerry Strahan describes perfectly the scene and milieu that had such an immediate and powerful impact on me. He was one of my first and best students at the University of New Orleans and has been my friend for nearly a quarter of a century. He would have made an excellent historian—he wrote an outstanding biography of Andrew Higgins, the man who made the landing craft for D-Day. But instead, he went to, of all things, selling hot dogs in the French Quarter.

Now, one has to wonder about the good judgment of a man who goes into business selling wienies in the Quarter, home of more great restaurants per block than any other big city in America has in the whole of its downtown. I thought he was making a big mistake. But he was right, as *Managing Ignatius* makes clear.

I love this book. It catches perfectly the sights, sounds, smells, and sins of the Quarter. From now on, whenever I'm asked what is the single best book to read for an introduction to the spirit of New Orleans, I'll reply, *Managing Ignatius*.

Preface

In the 1960s, John Kennedy Toole penned the Pulitzer Prize–winning novel *A Confederacy of Dunces*. This brilliant comic masterpiece follows the hilarious misadventures of one Ignatius J. Reilly. Reilly, an overweight, gas-emitting, genius misfit, contends that life is controlled by the Roman goddess Fortuna, who spins our fates on a wheel. He pleads with her, "Oh, Fortuna, blind, heedless goddess, I am strapped to your wheel. Do not crush me beneath your spokes. Raise me on high divinity."

Instead of having his prayer answered, when Fortuna's wheel stops Ignatius finds himself relegated to the position of a hot dog vendor in New Orleans' French Quarter. Thus begins his fictitious adventures at Paradise Vendors, which those who have visited the Quarter will recognize as Lucky Dogs, Incorporated.

Ignatius came from the fertile mind of Toole. The characters and events that I write about in the following pages have come from my daily contact with real street vendors as manager of Lucky Dogs. Our crew is still made up of the same sorts of eccentric individuals that Toole must have met while doing research at Lucky Dogs during the 1960s. Since today's vendors are similar to the bizarre drifters that Toole studied in developing his main character, I chose to title this book *Managing Ignatius*. I had considered calling it "A Hundred and One People I Wish I Had Never Met," but I couldn't narrow down the list. I also thought about calling it "I'm OK, You're Not"; but after working twenty years in the Quarter, I wasn't so certain that I was OK.

My research for this book has been underway since the early 1970s, though until recent years I did not think of it as research. Accordingly, there are scores of people that I need to thank; however, many have requested that their real names not be used. They probably have loved ones whom they prefer not to embarrass, or more than likely, they don't want their creditors or ex-spouses to know where they are. P.J., Jim Stafford, Kevin Russo, David Garcia, Barbara Huggins, Julie Hutchins, and Dan Myers, you all know who you really are; and I thank you for spending hours with me reliving your good, bad, and humorous times hawking dogs on Bourbon Street.

There are also those whose actual names are used with their permission in this book, and I would like to thank them publicly for their candid videotaped interviews: Paul Hager, Kenneth Schmitt, Jim Campbell, Joe Mayfield, Larry Griffiths, Alice Knight, Pepper, Bill McCarty, Chester and Maggie Anderson, James Lott, Larry Simmons, James Hudson, and Tom Strahan. Just remember, all of you had your chance to assume an alias.

I am deeply indebted to Stephen and Moira Ambrose, who encouraged me to write this book and who were kind enough to read the initial draft with its thousands of mistakes. In spite of its faults, they gave me the moral support that I needed in order to continue writing. Also, I wish to thank Joseph Logsdon, who read a later version and pointed out that sometimes less is not such a bad thing. Following his advice I pared down my manuscript by a third.

I owe a special thanks to my mom and dad, Irene and Robert, for their guidance during my youth. Because of their influence, I have had the strength necessary to remain an observer of the Quarter's craziness rather than become one of its participants.

I would be remiss if I didn't thank Doug Talbot, Lucky Dogs' owner. Doug and I have worked together longer than most people stay married. He, too, encouraged me to go forward with this project.

A special thanks to my loving wife, Jane, and our sons, Chris and Jeff, for their support. They're the ones who take the vendors' wacky telephone calls when I am not home. I also want to remind my sons,

"Stay out of the Quarter! You can't fool me—I know what goes on down there."

Last but not least, I would like to thank Louisiana State University Press for having enough faith in my manuscript to publish it. And at the Press I am especially grateful to Les Phillabaum, Maureen Hewitt, and Catherine Landry. All have been exceedingly helpful and understanding throughout this project. Also, I am deeply grateful to Donna Perreault for the countless contributions she made as copy editor. Her effort and advice have been invaluable.

It wasn't until eleven years after Toole's tragic suicide that his work finally found its way into print. I never contemplated committing such a drastic act if I failed to find a publisher. I did, however, consider sacrificing a vendor a month until I received a firm commitment from an editor. LSU, our crew thanks you.

Untitled piece by Philip Sage

1

Nudity, Nooses, and the Supreme Court

Planned and partially built in the 1700s, the French Quarter is the soul of the city of New Orleans. Within its boundaries the Louisiana Purchase was signed, Marie Laveau practiced voodoo, legendary pirate Jean Lafitte fenced his plunder, jazz grew from infancy, and Tennessee Williams penned early drafts of *A Streetcar Named Desire*. Three- and four-story brick buildings adorned with decorative wrought-iron latticework balconies crowd narrow sidewalks, gaslights illuminate arched doorways, picturesque courtyards offer privacy amid subtropical gardens, and streets bear the names of early French and Spanish rulers.

During the 1950s and 1960s the number of tourists visiting the Quarter continually increased. It was not only the architecture, antique shops, elegant restaurants, art galleries, and museums that lured them.

It was also the vice: gaudy strip clubs, back-room gambling joints, never-closing bars, and hordes of hookers.

The constant influx of visitors in 1968 convinced Doug Talbot, Pete Simonson, and Lee Merhoff to open an Orange Julius fast-food franchise in the Quarter. Located in the five hundred block of Bourbon Street, it was next to exotic dancer Chris Owens' 809 Club and across from world-renowned trumpeter Al Hirt's night spot—a far different setting from the partners' first location in quiet, suburban Lakeside Mall on the western outskirts of New Orleans.

In the fall of 1968 I was a young, naïve high-school junior who spent his evenings grilling hot dogs in the O.J. stand in the center of Lakeside. There, I was surrounded by Thom McAn Shoes, Gordon's Jewelers, J. C. Penney's, Walgreens, and a variety of other family-oriented shops and stores. Our customers were housewives pushing kids in strollers and gray-haired grandmothers with curlers in their hair. For me, life was simple, calm, and wholesome; but it wouldn't remain that way for long. I was assigned to assist in the grand opening of the new French Quarter Orange Julius. Suddenly, I was thrust into an area that, according to Ignatius J. Reilly, housed "every vice that man has ever conceived in his wildest aberrations, including several modern variants made possible through the wonders of science."

In Lakeside I had been surrounded by nationally recognized retail outlets. On Bourbon Street I was close to Chris Owens, Al Hirt, Pete Fountain, Linda Brigette (the Cupid Doll), Allouette (billed as the world's greatest tassel dancer), and Rita Alexander (the Champagne Girl). Alexander was a gorgeous 6-foot 2-inch stripper with long blond hair, shapely legs, and a 42/24/38 figure. If her life-size photo displayed outside the Sho Bar didn't lure passers-by into the club, then the raspy-voiced barker standing in the doorway usually succeeded with his pitch, "See da world's most unique way to drink champagne." It was the kind of line that played with a man's mind.

I was fascinated by my new surroundings. Especially intriguing, after the strippers, were the characters who worked on Bourbon and those who roamed the street. There were anti-Vietnam protesters, budding gay-rights activists, religious fanatics, free-love advocates, drug pushers, pimps, undercover narcotics agents, artists, poets, novelists, photographers, lost souls, sidewalk con artists, peddlers, and persons simply drawn to the Quarter because of its carefree life style and Old World atmosphere. Many of the characters went by nicknames, others simply by initials.

People wanting to lose their past found the Quarter ideal. With the right connections and an ample supply of cash, one could obtain everything from fake birth certificates to forged passports. This atmosphere created an unwritten code of discretion: "Don't ask about my past and I won't ask you about yours." Yesterdays didn't matter. It was live and let live.

From this environment Orange Julius on Bourbon drew most of its employees. Those of us who had been transferred from the suburbs were the exceptions. Such a mixture of personalities resulted in interesting, often humorous, and on a few occasions even dangerous situations.

During one Saturday lunch rush, as impatient tourists filled our dining area and overflowed onto the brick enclosed patio, two New Orleans police officers calmly walked behind the counter and handcuffed my co-worker. Clean-cut, in his mid-thirties, Greg was an extremely likable guy. None of his Quarter friends ever suspected him of being a criminal, let alone a murderer. Nevertheless, one afternoon he had apparently returned home unexpectedly and discovered his wife and best friend in more than a friendly embrace. Losing control, he grabbed his .38 Smith and Wesson and ended both the affair and the life of his friend.

Greg had managed to avoid the law for years by using assorted aliases and by staying on the move. Settling in the Quarter in his case proved to be a mistake. An old hometown acquaintance vacationing in New Orleans spotted him and notified the authorities. The NOPD moved in swiftly. In fact, too swiftly. Had they waited just another hour, justice still could have been served and so could have a building full of hungry tourists.

Several months later, on the then-popular Sunday night television series "FBI," another co-worker, Sal, was given national exposure. At the conclusion of each episode the nation's ten most-wanted fugitives were flashed across the screen. Filling the number nine slot was our very own lovable Sal. The announcer referred to him by another name, but unmistakably it was our guy. The first line below his picture read "AWOL from the Army." A crime, I thought, but certainly not serious enough to warrant making J. Edgar Hoover's top ten. The second line gave the key charge: "arson of a government building."

After Sal had been apprehended in Oklahoma, he managed to set the local police station on fire, escaping as the flames raged. Afterward, the U.S. Army, the Oklahoma State Police, and the FBI were all in pursuit. A few moments after the photo flashed across the screen, Talbot called. We concluded that we had seen the last of Sal. We weren't wrong. His last payroll check remains unclaimed.

Another less serious incident involved Jeanne, a petite twenty-year-old stripper from the Fallen Angel. Jeanne became infatuated with Danny, Sal's replacement. Danny was eighteen, a student, a transplanted golden-haired California surfer who had moved to New Orleans when his father was transferred. However, like me, he was incredibly naïve. Jeanne, on the other hand, was mature, very attractive, a woman of the world, perhaps even of the evening. She was friendly, but no more so than anyone else who worked in the Quarter. There was a certain camaraderie that existed amongst those of us employed on the street.

Early one Sunday morning she sat at our counter sipping an Orange Julius. Danny was slicing oranges nearby. Rushing to prepare for the expected onslaught at lunch, he unintentionally ignored her. Perturbed by this unaccustomed lack of attention, Jeanne rose from her stool then disappeared behind the small pine-paneled partition that hid the entrances to the restrooms. Reappearing completely nude, she shouted, "Now do you notice me?" Danny, a bartender who had stopped in for a cup of freshly brewed coffee, and I certainly gave our undivided attention.

Hers was the type of body that graces the pages of *Playboy:* the kind that men love and envious women scorn. After a few seconds she again vanished behind the partition, returning in a matter of moments wearing her navy blue sweater and tight-fitting jeans. Sauntering by the counter, she smiled at Danny then strolled out the door. After gulping down his coffee, the bartender followed in quick pursuit.

Bartenders, not bound by an oath of secrecy, find it difficult to be discreet. Word of the incident spread rapidly down the street. In minutes Karl, the Fallen Angel's muscular bouncer, appeared wanting to discuss his potential girlfriend's recently revealing experience. Leaning over our red Formica counter, Karl quietly threatened Danny and occasionally thrust his right index finger into my co-worker's quivering chest. I gathered from Danny's expression that he would not be asking Jeanne to the senior prom.

Jeanne might be off-limits, but Randi was unattached and ready to rumba. Unfortunately, Randi was the flamboyant gay cook at the Scoop and Skillet grease emporium located diagonally across the street. At noon on Saturdays and Sundays, Randi religiously left a large platter of crispy fried chicken on the counter of our takeout window. It was the kind of mouth-watering chicken that only southern cooks can prepare.

Danny and I diligently tried to convince Randi that we were unwavering heterosexuals, but to no avail. His advances became more and more obvious and at times proved to be quite embarrassing. Finally, Tinkerbell, self-proclaimed Queen of the Quarter and a sometime Lucky Dog vendor, agreed to intercede on our behalf. Several months earlier he had reluctantly come to the conclusion that Danny and I were hopelessly straight. With Tinkerbell's help, Randi also learned to accept the fact that ours would be a purely platonic relationship. Sadly, platonic relationships didn't warrant gifts of crispy southern fried chicken.

Neither my parents nor Harry Garland, East Jefferson High School's principal, approved of my working in the Quarter. I tried to comfort my mom and dad by focusing on the historical elements that made up my surroundings, the interesting tourists that frequented our establishment, and the fact that Orange Julius was a family-oriented restaurant. I avoided mentioning Jeanne, Randi, Tinkerbell, or any of the risqué experiences that occurred at work.

Garland required a different approach. He was upset because late one fall evening in 1969, as he and his wife were showing out-of-town guests the sights of the city, he saw the newly elected student body president of his high school selling hamburgers, hot dogs, and draft beer through a takeout window on one of the world's bawdiest streets. Discreetly he pointed to me and whispered, "Monday morning, my office."

The situation occurred at a most inopportune time. The previous week Garland had removed the president of my high school's Key Club chapter because he had, with his parents' permission, missed a day of school to play in a local amateur golf tournament. Garland firmly believed that any absence for a noneducational and non-health-related reason was inexcusable and set an example unworthy of a student leader. However unjust it might have seemed, his decision was in keeping with his strict personal standards.

Early in his career Garland had established the reputation of being the Wyatt Earp of the New Orleans educational system. While serving as principal, he had tamed some of the city's rougher schools. Jefferson Parish, therefore, hired him to help guide East Jefferson High School through the turbulent integration process of the sixties. In the fall of 1969 ours was an all-boy public high school with an enrollment of 4,200 students. Garland was principal, and I was student body president, of a school larger than many U.S. cities.

Monday morning, as I entered his office, my thoughts were on Garland's recent disciplinary action. I was nervous, expected the worst, but was prepared to plead my case. As an avid Perry Mason fan, I knew that Mason always prevailed over Hamilton Burger because his defense was flawless and well planned. I tried to imitate Mason's thinking and figure out how to handle my situation. After lengthy consideration, I concluded that Mason would base my defense on duty and obligation.

Following this strategy, I pointed out to Garland that I had been transferred from the Metairie location to Bourbon Street; I had not gone by choice. I had been selected because I was the only student employee who had already turned eighteen—the legal age limit for employment at an establishment selling alcohol. The French Quarter position, as it happened, increased my hours and thus increased my income: a key point since I was trying to save enough money to attend college in the fall. My parents simply couldn't cover the costs.

Garland listened, occasionally asked for minor clarification of facts, but showed no outward sign of emotion. At the conclusion of my closing argument, he leaned back in his black high-back swivel chair and for several minutes sat quietly in deep thought, gazing upward. Then, looking me directly in the eyes, he rendered his decision. I could remain student body president and continue my employment at my present location, but I had to promise to stay out of the takeout window as much as possible. Mason would have been proud.

By early 1970 the hippie movement and drug culture had mushroomed in New Orleans as elsewhere. Flower children were moving into the Quarter in increasing numbers. The California look of our restaurant attracted colorful clientele with their tie-dyed shirts, torn jeans, musk oil perfume, and empty pockets. Five or six hippies would gather at a table sharing one drink and taking up the space of potential cash customers. We tried to counter their influx by switching to stand-up tables. This move simply resulted in more hippies fitting into the building. At times they were sprawled all over the floor lighting incense, strumming guitars, and reading the "New Orleans Free Press." Rapidly we were becoming the indoor counterpart to Woodstock. We resorted to numerous rules and regulations, but mine was a generation that tended to ignore authority. What it couldn't ignore was a mop and a wet floor.

The daily hassles became great and the profits small. Merhoff and Simonson had earlier sold their interest in the Bourbon Street franchise to their partner, and now Talbot decided that he, too, wanted to divest himself of the business. A want ad in the New Orleans *States-Item* featured a hot dog street-vending company for sale. After investigating the opportunity, Talbot sold Orange Julius and along with a friend, Peter Briant, purchased Lucky Dogs Novelty Carts, Incorporated.

Lucky Dogs, too, had its problems, but the new partnership felt confident that they could rejuvenate the old firm. Of major concern was the board of health's decision that Lucky Dogs had to precook and prepackage its product. For twenty-three years the vending company had steamed its hot dogs and buns in its unique hot dog–shaped carts. Never had a single complaint of food poisoning ever been levied against the operation. But some bureaucrat, in the name of progress and safety, rewrote the Orleans Parish health code, permitting only prepackaged foods to be sold on city streets. As a result, Lucky Dogs ended up serving a godawful product. The new regulation was one of the primary reasons that Stephen Loyacano wanted to sell the business. It was also one of the main reasons that no one other than Talbot and Briant showed any interest in Lucky Dogs. In late 1970 a deal was consummated.

After a short period of operating under the new health restrictions, sales plummeted and the company almost closed its doors. Extensive negotiations with the board of health resulted in a sneeze guard and a portable handwash system being added to each cart. The sneeze guard was intended to help protect the food from airborne contamination, thereby reducing the possibility of harmful bacteria contaminating the meat. The handwash system was installed to help ensure that vendors' hands remained clean. With these new modifications, the company was once again allowed to steam the dogs on the carts. Sales rapidly improved and the business survived.

Unfortunately, Talbot's sale of Orange Julius and purchase of Lucky Dogs altered my employment situation. I chose not to remain under O.J.'s new ownership, and the hours of a street-vending company were not compatible with my freshman schedule at the University of New Orleans. Merhoff and Simonson remained the owners of the Lakeside franchise, but they already had a full staff. Talbot helped me get a job with his friend Carmen Byrd, owner of a local Dunkin Donuts outlet.

However, in the spring of 1971 Talbot called and asked if I would be interested in serving as Lucky Dogs' relief manager for two days a week. He desperately needed someone that he could trust to fill in for his full-time managers, Sammy and Bill, and he knew that I was only working part-time for Carmen. Sammy, a seventy-year-old former trapeze artist, was in charge of the day shift. His duties included cart maintenance, vendor assignments, and the issuing of supplies. He did those jobs extremely well. But what he was an absolute master at was handling the conglomerate of eccentric personalities that comprised the street-vending crew. His years of circus experience had served as ideal training.

Bill, the sixty-three-year-old gray-haired night supervisor, had until recently been the relief manager. He took over the full-time position when his predecessor disappeared with the company's old red pickup and the night's receipts. The Ford truck was later found broken down in Arizona, but the man and the money had forever vanished. Bill's responsibilities included resupplying the vendors with hot dogs, buns, chili, onions, and also with kerosene for their pump Coleman burners. Additionally, he made frequent money collections from each cart, checked the vendors in at the end of their shifts, made the night deposit, and balanced the day's sales against the inventory.

Because Sammy and Bill were so desperate for a day off, they arranged their hours around my courseload and Dunkin Donuts work schedule. On a trial basis, I reported for training the afternoon following Talbot's request. Bill rapidly ran through a condensed thirty-five-minute management course, gave me the keys to the shop, the combination to the safe, a list of things to do, assurances that all would be fine, and then quickly headed out the door. All in all, the entire process seemed rather peculiar.

My first night started out well. The vendors were hawking their product in the French Quarter, and I was spending time between supply runs repairing broken hot dog carts in the warehouse at 1304 St. Charles Avenue. Then at 1:15 A.M. someone started to pound on the garage's barnlike doors. Before unbolting the heavy metal latch, I shouted, "Who's there?" "Bill," a gruff voice responded. I felt comforted knowing that Bill had stopped by to check on me.

As I pulled open the large wooden door, I realized that I had made a grave mistake. It wasn't Bill, but a giant of a man who had been calling out for Bill to open the door. His face was rugged and stern, and down his back to his broad shoulders draped a grayish pony tail. Stitched to the front of his faded denim jacket were patches bearing the names of police departments from across the nation. Looking through me to a darkened corner of the shop, he muttered, "I want you shud gimme da bikes."

"What bikes?" I nervously asked. "Da Harleys," he responded as he pushed past me and stepped into the shop. Impatiently, he informed me that Bill had promised him the two old broken-down Harley-Davidson triwheeled motorcycles leaning against the rear wall of the warehouse. I diplomatically explained that I had no knowledge of such an arrangement. Ignoring this response he continued toward the bikes.

I tried to explain that I had no authority to give anything away. I had to get the owners' approval. "Call 'um," he uttered. "I got time. I ain't goin' nowhere." It was 1:25 A.M., but I wasn't about to argue. I dialed Talbot's number. There was no answer. Where the hell could he and Judi be at this time of the morning? I then reached Peter Briant. Desperately, I tried to convince Briant that I had no alternative but to give up the junk motorcycles. The biker stood next to me and caught only my side of the conversation, which I delivered as eloquently as I knew how. However, my employer on the other end of the line, unhappy about being waked in the middle of the night and not conscious enough to be swayed by my oratorical abilities, responded, "Throw the son-of-a-bitch out. We need those bikes for spare parts. Good night."

I stand maybe five feet eleven inches on my toes. Before me stood the reincarnation of Attila the Hun. Every scenario I could conceive of ended grimly. With the expectation of excruciating pain prevailing, I chose the least honorable but most promising course of action. I lied. I explained that my employer wanted to turn over the bikes in the morning, along with an assortment of spare parts. But the biker was adamant: he wanted them now. I countered with an irresistible carrot, the bikes' titles. If he would be willing to wait and return in the morning, the owner could unlock the file cabinet where he stored the titles and sign them over. Legal ownership proved to be the convincing enticement.

As Attila drifted out onto the sidewalk, I quickly closed the door and pushed the heavy slide bolt back into place. The "Rider from Hell" was to return at 11 A.M., a time when I would be safely seated in Stephen

Ambrose's modern military history class at the University of New Orleans.

Bill obviously had left the shop in a hurry earlier in the day so as to avoid the biker and to pass the problem on to me. I, in turn, passed it on to Mr. Briant. Later that morning I called Lucky Dogs under the pretense of seeing if my closing inventory had been correct. Briant asserted that the paperwork was fine. However, he added, less than an hour before a lunatic had created havoc in the warehouse. The moose had insisted that a young twerp on the night shift had promised him that, if he returned in the morning, he could have the broken triwheeled Harleys, their titles, and a variety of spare parts.

I assured Briant that I had no idea how such a misunderstanding could have occurred. Ten hours earlier I had made it emphatically clear to the ill-mannered Neanderthal that he couldn't have the bikes. Obviously, he was trying to pull a fast one since I wasn't there. I remarked to my boss that I bet he had thrown the son-of-a-bitch out. "Not exactly," Briant responded. After closely reexamining the old, broken-down Harleys, he discovered that they were really nothing more than trash. So he and a few vendors helped load the worthless motorcycles into the biker's beat-up Chevy truck.

After six weeks as relief manager, I realized that getting off at 6 A.M. and attending class two hours later simply wasn't going to work. I was too tired to concentrate on the professors' lectures. Therefore, I left the Lucky Dog staff. During the next few years I continued my education while working for Carmen at the relatively peaceful Dunkin Donuts. On various occasions, Talbot would call and ask that I work a Lucky Dog cart for him at a private party or at a charity event. Additionally, an arrangement had been made with Carmen that allowed me to spend the last five hectic days of Carnival each year working as an assistant manager for Lucky Dogs.

As I met new challenges, so did Talbot. Shortly after I resigned as relief manager, he purchased Peter Briant's interest in the company and then moved the operation into the French Quarter at 211 Decatur Street. Also, Louisiana Concessions arrived on the scene. Lucky Dogs for years had been the sole hot dog vendor operating on the

French Quarter's narrow, tourist-filled streets. Dressed in red-and-white striped shirts and overseas-styled paper caps, serving products from hot dog–shaped carts, Lucky Dogs' salesmen had dominated the New Orleans hot dog business. Nancy Dukes and Frank Silliker had seen the company's success and decided that they, too, wanted to capture a piece of the street-vending trade. With a homemade cart, they began selling snacks and drinks in Jackson Square.

The Quarter during this period had fallen under a siege of panhandlers, shoeshine boys, and hippies selling underground newspapers. In addition, slick-haired, fast-talking land brokers were trapping unsuspecting tourists on almost ever corner, trying to sell them a piece of the glorious West. In 1972, in an attempt to save the French Quarter's tourist industry as well as its historical character, the New Orleans City Council passed an ordinance limiting street vending in the Quarter and in the central business district to those companies who had been operating there prior to 1964. This grandfather clause in essence gave Lucky Dogs a monopoly on the hot dog business in the restricted area, and Oliver Roberts exclusivity in vending ice cream.

Nancy Dukes challenged the ordinance, charging economic discrimination and violation of her rights under the Fourteenth Amendment. She contended that the ordinance created a monopoly since only one hot dog company, Lucky Dogs, Inc., had been operating in the Quarter before 1964. Previously, in 1957, the U.S. Supreme Court had ruled the use of grandfather clauses unconstitutional. Dukes felt that this precedent strongly favored her case, and the American Civil Liberties Union supported her. But federal district judge Jack M. Gordon ruled in the city's favor. Duke's attorneys immediately appealed the decision to the U.S. Fifth Circuit Court of Appeals.

In 1973, as Dukes persevered in her suit against the city, I pursued my education at the University of New Orleans. I also continued my part-time Mardi Gras work for Lucky Dogs. I enjoyed doing it because of the zaniness of Carnival, a celebration unlike any other in North America. It was transported to the Crescent City by early French settlers as part of their Old World culture. Literally translated, the French words "Mardi Gras" mean "Fat Tuesday" and make reference to the

Tuesday prior to Ash Wednesday: the last day of the pre-Lenten carnival season beginning on Twelfth Night, January 6.

During this period the city is host to elaborate formal balls, glamorous festivities, over fifty colorful parades, and rampant partying in the streets. In the Quarter the people are wild, but basically they're just fun seekers out trying to have a good time. Some wear elaborate feathered costumes. Others dress as monsters, political figures, clowns, ballerinas, or as historical characters. Then you have the guys with water pistols shaped like penises, men dressed as pregnant nuns, women barely clothed, lots of people in not so lots of leather: rich, poor, black, and white all partaking in the world's largest free party. The crowds are friendly. Instead of violence, people are focused on wine, sex, and revelry.

It was during the carnival season of 1973 that I met Jim Harvey and Eddie Vinterella. Harvey was Lucky Dogs' night manager and Vinterella was in charge of its day shift, but during the last five days of Mardi Gras there really are no distinct shifts. Crowds party on the street around the clock, and vendors hire helpers so that their carts can operate twenty-four hours a day. Days run into nights and nights into days. Once this party and work marathon is over, the mind and body need at least two weeks to fully recuperate.

Harvey had started with Lucky Dogs as a vendor and taken over the night manager's position when the previous manager, Bob Alexander, was found murdered in the company's office on January 2, 1973. Alexander had been shot in the back. The huge, old-fashioned iron safe was open and the cash box was found sitting empty on the office desk. At the time of the killing, the police found few clues and no prime suspects.

Harvey generally stayed in the office while Eddie and I made the twenty-two-block supply run on foot four times a night, pushing an old, beat-up, green tamale wagon that had been converted into the company's supply cart. We dropped off hot dogs, chili, napkins, mustard, and diced onions; and we picked up money generated from sales. This practice was based on the principle that the company would pay the vendor his commission and refund any overcollection at the end of the night. It was really the only practical method to use. If we allowed the vendor to hold the cash generated from his sales, there was the possibility that he might not return to the shop at all. Over the years, workers had abandoned carts in dark alleys or between cars in parking lots. By the time we recovered a vendor's cart, he had long since boarded some bus out of town or hitched a ride down the highway. It didn't matter that we were holding his driver's license as collateral. Vendors basically are creatures of impulse. They don't think of their actions' consequences; they simply react to the moment.

As Eddie and I spent hour after hour making supply runs down Bourbon Street, I began to realize that he was far tougher than I had imagined. He was then in his mid-twenties, approximately five feet ten inches, lean, and always neat and well dressed. Having grown up in Harlem, he had a distinctly New York accent and an inner strength derived from spending his youth in the streets. As a white kid in Harlem, he had overcome considerable obstacles in order to survive. But managing Lucky Dogs tested even his mettle.

Late one afternoon, as vendors were preparing their carts for the evening shift, a vendor named Charles Allen sat at the cutting table in the rear of the shop quietly dicing his onions, unaware that Frenchy had walked up behind him. Frenchy, a punch-drunk ex-heavyweight Canadian boxer, was one of the local street characters and had once even worked as a Lucky Dog vendor. But his uncontrollable temper had gotten him fired. During his last night on the job, he had become so frustrated at his lack of sales that he had gone berserk on his corner and started throwing steamed hot dogs at pedestrians. By the time the night manager arrived on the scene, the sidewalks and street were littered with smashed and broken wienies. Tourists and locals alike had taken refuge in doorways and behind parked cars to avoid the mad bomber and his deadly dogs. A few had taken direct hits and bore grease splotches on their clothes, but there had been no serious casualties. Once Frenchy's steamer was depleted of ammunition, he surrendered to the manager and pushed his cart back to the shop. A two-man crew armed with brooms and buckets of water was dispatched to clean up the mess.

In his mid-forties, Frenchy was a heavy drinker but still solidly built with broad shoulders, firm chest, massive arms, and quick fists. The aging fighter seldom spoke, but when he did he expected a response. Frenchy had mumbled hello. Allen, unaware that the greeting was directed at him, continued silently to work. The ex-boxer took the lack of response as a personal insult and picked up a butcher knife off the kitchen counter. Seeing this, Eddie instinctively grabbed the bottom half of a pool cue that was leaning against the rear wall of the kitchen. As Frenchy thrust the knife toward Allen's back, Eddie intercepted the boxer's arm with a powerful blow, forcing the knife to miss its mark and jab a pile of onions on the wooden table. Eddie then made two quick strikes to the Canadian's head and chest, stunning but never dropping him.

As the stars cleared from Frenchy's brain, we stood out of arm's reach and tried to convince him that Allen had meant no disrespect. He hadn't answered because he was unaware that the greeting was meant for him. Still trembling, Allen nervously apologized for the unintended insult. Eddie then moved closer and confessed that he felt awful about having to club such a good friend; but if he hadn't, he insisted, his friend would have had to do hard time for murder. Frenchy, feeling ashamed for almost killing Allen, stood silent for a moment. Then he announced that he was going to buy everyone a beer at the Pair-of-Dice bar on the corner. No one had the courage to refuse. As we sat on the bar stools drinking our drafts, all was forgiven; and in the world of the Quarter, life went on.

During Mardi Gras of 1974 I again worked for Lucky Dogs. That spring I received my B.A. in education, and in the fall I began working toward a master's degree in history at Louisiana State University in Baton Rouge.

As I began graduate school, the U.S. Fifth Circuit Court of Appeals reversed Judge Gordon's ruling limiting street vending in the Quarter. In striking down the city ordinance, Judge Irving L. Goldberg of Dallas, Texas, countered New Orleans' argument that business in the Vieux Carré must be regulated so as to maintain the district's charms with the decision that the city "cannot support its favoring a venerable hot dog dealer with the skins of eight seasons over franks of a more recent vintage." In overturning the earlier federal ruling, Goldberg concluded that the city's ordinance provided no proof that eight years in the hot dog–vending business instilled in a company a greater appreciation for the conservation of the Quarter's tradition than would be felt by a more recent vendor.

The city, stalling for a time while it tried to write a new ordinance, appealed "The Great New Orleans Hot Dog Case" to the U.S. Supreme Court. The high court unexpectedly agreed to hear arguments on the decision of the U.S. Fifth Circuit Court of Appeals.

As the city prepared its case for the high court, New Orleans detectives continued to investigate the murder of Lucky Dogs' manager Bob Alexander. In April, 1975, to everyone's astonishment, Jim Harvey, his girlfriend Barbara Hooper, and their friend Diane Lawrenson were arrested as suspects in Alexander's murder. The crime had remained unsolved for over two years when in March, 1975, Frank Ruiz, an investigator assigned to the district attorney's office, received confidential information that led the police to Lawrenson.

Lawrenson, arrested for conspiracy to commit murder, turned state's evidence. Harvey and Hooper were implicated, but the trigger man was identified as Rennie Atwell, formerly a Lucky Dog vendor. During her emotional testimony, Lawrenson confessed that she and Atwell had gone to the warehouse to see Bob while Harvey waited outside. "We were laughing and joking with Bob and he said to stick around, that he'd go have a drink with us. . . . A few minutes later, [Atwell] nodded his head and I heard a shot. . . . He killed Bob."

Lawrenson then testified that after the robbery, she, Atwell, and Harvey went to a nearby bar where Atwell tipped a cocktail waitress one hundred dollars. Several hours later she boarded a plane for New York along with Atwell and another friend. To avoid raising suspicions, Harvey and Hooper remained in New Orleans. During the trial, Hooper swore that Harvey "didn't believe there was going to be any violence."

Two weeks after the slaying, Doug Talbot, unaware of Harvey's involvement, promoted him from vendor to manager. The police had never mentioned Harvey as a suspect, and Talbot had no reason to believe that he was involved. At the time of his arrest, Harvey was no longer a Lucky Dogs employee.

Bob had been killed for less than three thousand dollars. During the two Mardi Gras seasons that Harvey and I had worked together, we often had more than that in the safe. It wasn't a comforting thought. In recent years, armed guards have been hired during Carnival, and special arrangements have been made to ensure that there is never a large accumulation of cash on our premises.

In June, 1976, the U.S. Supreme Court reached its decision, ruling in favor of the City of New Orleans. The Court rejected Louisiana Concessions' argument that it had been the victim of economic discrimination. Instead, the justices agreed with the city that the rights of the community outweighed those of the individual.

Joel Loeffelholz, a brilliant young city attorney, had argued that if Dukes's one cart was allowed to operate in the Vieux Carré, then the door would be opened for others to follow. Loeffelholz maintained that the Court had properly protected the character and charm of the city's most historic district.

Joseph N. Marcal III, who had replaced the American Civil Liberties Union as Dukes's attorney, claimed that protecting the Quarter's charm was a "bogus issue." According to an article in the New York *Times*, Marcal believed that "the City Council had engaged in 'legislative chicanery' with the clear intention of helping a political friend, the Lucky Dogs concern."

Actually, Talbot had no political friends in high places and no knowledge of the city's case until it was already underway. Certainly, the company benefited from the decision; but the basis for the city's action was not to protect Lucky Dogs, Inc., but to protect the French Quarter—the heart of New Orleans' budding tourist industry. The U.S. Supreme Court justices in their decision had agreed with Loeffelholz, ruling that Lucky Dogs "had themselves become part of the distinctive character and charm that distinguishes the Vieux Carré." The press had a field day with the decision. Headlines such as "Vendor Doesn't Relish

Ruling" and "New Vendor Doesn't Cut the Mustard" appeared not only in the local papers, but also in such publications as the New York *Times* and the Washington *Post*.

During the summer of 1976, when the Supreme Court handed down its decision in the Dukes case, I was completing my requirements for a master's degree at the University of New Orleans. I had transferred from LSU back to UNO after my first year of graduate study. An American history professor at LSU for whom I served as a graduate assistant during the spring of 1975 had suggested over lunch one day that I consider changing programs from history to sociology or anthropology. In his opinion, I would find greater success in one of the alternate fields. Before rising from the table, I had made up my mind to transfer back to UNO. I could hardly remain at LSU and have this authority sit on my orals committee deciding whether or not I would receive an M.A. in history.

After I completed my final graduate course at UNO, my wife Jane and I (we were married in the summer of 1973) loaded our new Chevy Chevette and headed west to Lemhi Pass, Montana. We were to rendezvous atop the Continental Divide on the Fourth of July with Professor Ambrose, his wife Moira, their family, and a few other students as part of an expedition retracing the Lewis and Clark trail. Camping under the stars, cooking over an open fire, and hiking in Montana and then through fifty miles of the Bitterroot Range in Idaho proved to be an incredible experience.

In late August, a few weeks after returning from this western trek, I was again called into service at Lucky Dogs. Talbot wanted me to deposit the company's daily receipts while he and his family were spending a week vacationing in Florida. He wasn't certain that he could trust that task to his present manager.

After Bob's death, managerial stability had collapsed at the firm. Subsequent managers seldom lasted more than a month. Most could not distance themselves from the partying that filled the Quarter. Others found it frustrating and mentally draining to work with a transient labor force that scorned authority and held little respect for property. Most vendors exhibited an "I don't give a damn" attitude. If something displeased them, they simply packed their bags and left town—without notice or reason. They had no roots, no obligations, so the loss of a job meant nothing to them. Trying to manage a business under such conditions created enormous stress and resulted in rapid burnout among managers.

Talbot tried one avenue after another in search of reliable managers. Newspaper ads brought new applicants, but these, too, quickly departed. Tinkerbell had even served as Lucky Dogs' manager for a brief period but resigned and disappeared after he fell in love with a blond-haired, broad-shouldered Norwegian seaman. Street gossip had it that the sailor had taken Tinkerbell home to Scandinavia.

After Lucky Dogs had moved from its original location at 1304 St. Charles Avenue, it occupied the bottom floor of a four-story white brick building at 211 Decatur Street. The warehouse was long and rectangular with the kitchen located in the rear and the office located in the front left of the building. The ceiling of the shop was approximately sixteen feet high with large, exposed cypress beams. The timbers, once white, were now yellowish and peeling. Rusted four-tube fluorescent light fixtures hung by chains from the ceiling. Most were inoperative, and as a result, the shop always appeared dimly lit. The upper floors had a separate entrance, but it was seldom used. Generally, we were the building's only tenant.

From the St. Charles site it was fourteen blocks to the closest western or upriver boundary of the French Quarter—a considerable distance for someone pushing a seven-foot-long hot dog cart. Moreover, it was a twenty-four-block push to the farthest corner that the company worked on the eastern or downriver side of the Quarter. The new shop's location at the upriver side of the Quarter lessened the latter trip by fifteen blocks. However, though more convenient, Decatur Street increased the business' human diversity problems. In 1976 the two hundred block of Decatur was filled with seamen's bars: rowdy joints with rough men and tough women. Greek and Cuban clubs lined the street and offered blaring music, native foods, and an interesting time to those brave enough to enter. Brawls were common. Hookers, pimps, pushers, and sailors looking for excitement considered the clubs a favorite haunt. Tourists occasionally drifted in but exited more quickly than they had entered.

The first time I walked into Lucky Dogs' big new warehouse, it took my eyes a moment to adjust. Outside it was sunny and bright; inside it appeared dark and cavernous. The malfunctioning fluorescent fixtures accounted only partly for the gloom. In addition, the planked wood floor and the bottom half of the warehouse's walls were painted battle-ship gray, causing the interior to reflect little of the meager light. The large walk-in cooler positioned centrally in the rear of the shop also had been rolled with the same drab color. Obviously, the navy had had a great influence on someone.

As my eyes adjusted I glanced about the building, seeing nobody. I walked into the main office. It, too, was deserted. Next I headed toward the rear of the warehouse, past the twenty-two neatly angled hot dog–shaped carts, around the walk-in cooler, and then through the open kitchen door. There, sitting in the middle of the room on a wooden bar stool was an attractive, petite blond in her mid-twenties with wavy shoulder-length hair, blue eyes, faded jeans, a partially unbuttoned blouse, and a hangman's noose secured to her neck. The large one-half-inch-thick rope ran down her back and lay coiled harmlessly on the dirty brown linoleum floor.

I wasn't sure what I had walked into—a suicide, a murder, a practical joke? I quickly scanned the kitchen. There was no sign of danger. So I calmly asked her about the noose. As she gazed up at the dingy grayish drop ceiling she softly replied, "Some guys put it there." Obviously, she was high on drugs. I tried to loosen the noose, but to no avail. I then picked up one of the knives used by the vendors to dice their onions and carefully cut the rope.

Once the noose was eliminated, I inquired as to the whereabouts of the day manager. "He's on his way to California," she replied as she swayed back and forth on the stool.

"Does the night manager know this?"

"I think so," she said giggling. "They left together in his car."

I immediately opened the old cast-iron combination safe. It was empty, except for a note from the departed duo recording the exact amount that they had taken. Just as I put the paper down, the pay phone hanging on the wood paneled wall next to the office door began ringing. It was Doug Talbot.

He cheerfully asked how everything was going. I had just cut a noose off of a girl's neck, the previous night's receipts were missing, Lucky Dogs no longer had a day or night manager, and he wanted to know how everything was going. I wasn't sure where to start. I responded, "I have some good news and some bad news."

"Give me the bad news first."

"The day manager has quit and gone to California."

"Christ! What's the good news?"

"He got a free ride with the night manager, and the girl in the kitchen with the noose around her neck is still alive."

The two managers had been talking about going out west, but both had assured Talbot that they would remain until after he returned from his vacation. Apparently, there had been a change of plans.

The missing cash ended up being approximately what the company owed the men in salary. Doug, his wife Judi, and their two small sons, Mark and Kirk, were spending their first day in Florida. It would have been unfair for them to have to repack and head home only hours after reaching their destination. I agreed to run the operation until they returned.

In the previous five years I had accumulated approximately sixty days' experience in managing Lucky Dogs. I had helped on the night shift during the New Year and Mardi Gras celebrations and had filled in as relief manager. I felt that I could handle the business for the week or so until the Talbots returned.

My first task was to assemble a staff. Admittedly, choices were limited. I began by asking the blond what she was doing in the shop. Sally—so she claimed her name was—informed me that for the last several weeks she had been helping the day manager prepare the supplies for the vendors. Though not totally coherent, she seemed capable of filling mustard containers, putting napkins in holders, washing chili pots, and performing other nonstressful tasks. She became my first recruit.

As we began our work in the kitchen, I suddenly heard the sound of splashing water coming from the adjoining room. When I investigated, I found a young shaggy-haired boy about fourteen years old leaning over the large galvanized sink busily scrubbing the hot dog carts' stainless-steel steamer pans. The day manager, I discovered, had been paying Tom six dollars a day to clean the cookers. I offered to double his salary, but first he had to prove that he had parental permission to work. I had enough problems without having to worry about angry parents or the labor board. His mom, who was the barmaid at the Pair-of-Dice, readily gave her blessing. The job had been keeping her son off the streets, out of trouble, and out of her purse. With Tom joining the staff, my management team was complete. Granted, interviews had been brief, qualifications relaxed, and résumés dispensed with. Nevertheless, we were a team.

The first vendor strolled in to set up his cart at 10 A.M. His destination was Jackson Square, a five-and-a-half-block push. The Square was one of the company's premier locations. Tourists often frequented the Cabildo (where the Louisiana Purchase was signed), the famous St. Louis Cathedral, and the Presbytere Museum. All three bordered the west end of the Square. Generally, the vendor positioned his cart near the Cabildo and seldom had any problems. Constant police patrols kept the drunks and street hustlers out of the area. Cleanliness, attitude, seniority, and sales ability determined who received this preferred assignment. Cliff Huline, a quick-witted young black vendor, was presently working the corner.

By 3 P.M. the night shift started drifting in to prepare their carts. The twelve-man crew consisted of ex-carnival workers, seamen between ships, Vietnam veterans unable to resume a normal daily routine, and others who were simply looking for an alternate life style. This rough, distrusting group drank hard, cursed profusely, and scorned authority—especially when that authority was at least ten years younger than they were and was only filling in temporarily.

Using the previous night's records, I issued supplies and reassigned everyone to the same location that they had worked the day before. By 5:30 P.M. the last crew member was heading for his corner. After checking Cliff in, I figured that I had enough time to go to my apartment, take a shower, and eat before making the 8:00 P.M. money-pickup and supply run.

Tom had finished his last chore and left. Sally was now fairly coherent and almost helpful. As I was about to leave, I asked if she had a telephone number where I could contact her in case she overslept and failed to report for work in the morning. "You don't need a number," she responded. "All you have to do is come upstairs. I live in the storeroom above the office." I was beginning to feel the next five days were going to be long ones.

Upon my return I prepared for my first run. I realized that the vendors were going to test me like a class of students tests a substitute teacher. I had seen them in action against Sammy, Bill, Jim, and Eddie. I knew that I had to maintain control. I wanted to be friendly but firm.

My first stop, the cart at the corner of Canal and Bourbon, the uptown gateway to the French Quarter, involved no problems. The next vendor up the street, at the corner of Iberville and Bourbon, had to be told that his girlfriend could not sit on the cart. Following this adjustment, he made his money drop and I issued supplies. It wasn't until I reached the corner of Bienville and Bourbon that I ran into a bit of trouble. The old codger working the cart insisted that he had no money to turn in but requested supplies. Logic tells you that if a vendor needs supplies, then he must have sold something. If he sold something, then he must have money. I glanced at the empty bun wrappers in his cart's garbage basket and calmly asked once again how much money he was going to turn in.

"I don't have any money," he grumbled.

I looked him in the eyes and responded, "If you don't have any money, then I have no alternative but to press charges against you for nonpayment of a food bill." As I slowly walked toward the police officer across the street, the vendor laughed and called me back. He dug into his pocket and pulled out a wad of cash. He had had his fun and was now ready to conduct business.

My next stop was outside the Famous Door Jazz Club at the corner of Conti and Bourbon. Kelly, a tall, rugged merchant seaman in his mid-fifties, was hawking Lucky Dogs at this location. He knew that vendors weren't suppose to drink while working, but he wanted to see if I had enough guts to enforce the rule. As I walked toward his cart, I could see a fifth of Jack Daniels sitting out in the open next to his mustard containers. I ignored it until after I had finished collecting the money. Then I asked, "You're not drinking on the job, are you?"

"Not me."

Then with a smirk on his face and bourbon on his breath, he proclaimed that the bottle had been left there by a drunken tourist. That declaration put him exactly where I wanted him. I picked up the fifth, slowly unscrewed the black cap, and started emptying its contents into the gutter by the cart. As the bourbon splashed on the pavement I remarked, "God only knows what kind of disease the owner of this bottle might have had. We certainly wouldn't want to be responsible for spreading it." Kelly couldn't object. Only seconds before he had insisted that the whiskey wasn't his. After the last drop had fallen to the ground, I tossed the empty bottle into the public trash can nearby.

Kelly stood silent for a moment sadly gazing at the wet asphalt. I knew that he'd buy another fifth. I wasn't that naïve. But I also knew that next time he would be more discreet about his drinking. Word of my pouring out the whiskey spread like wildfire. I found no alcohol on Bill McCarty's cart, my next stop, or for that matter on any other wagon.

The remainder of the night ran smoothly until check-in. As the first vendor approached the counter to return his unsold product, Kelly broke into a tirade. From the front of the shop I could hear him shouting that some raggedy-ass piss-ant had emptied his fifth of Jack Daniels and now some f——ing bastard had stolen his new pair of Levi's. He had bought the jeans earlier in the day and had hidden them in the shop where he thought they would be safe. Someone had discovered the pants and taken them. First his Jack Daniels emptied, now his Levi's stolen: Kelly was furious. He ranted and raved. If he found the "thieving son of a bitch" that had taken his jeans he was "gonna break his f——ing neck."

Awakened by the loud outbursts, Sally stumbled from her storeroom apartment to see what was causing all the commotion. As she started down the stairs, Kelly noticed her out of the corner of his eye.

"There's the f——ing thief. The bitch is wearin' my jeans."

He started towards her. I intersected his path, and with the help of two other vendors we physically restrained him. As we tried to get him under control, I shouted to Sally to go back into her room and change. She didn't move. Instead, she just stood there on the stairs crying and proclaiming that she didn't have any other clothes.

"You have to have the clothes you were wearing before you put on Kelly's jeans."

"I don't know where they are," she sobbed.

Kelly, having calmed down, promised no violence. He helped me search her room. There was no sign of any other clothes. We checked in the kitchen, the bathrooms, the garbage cans, and even in the alley out back; but we never found any sign of her pants. God only knows where she left them. I persuaded Kelly to let her keep the jeans. In return, I assured him that I would personally see to it that the company bought him, not one, but two pairs of new Levi's the next day.

By the time the last vendor was checked in, it was 6 A.M. I was home asleep by 7 A.M. I had scheduled Tom to arrive at 8 A.M. to begin cleaning the carts. Sally was to let him in, then begin cleaning and filling the mustard containers, wiping off and refilling the napkin holders, filling the chili pots, and issuing Cliff his supplies so that he could push to the Square. Once that was done, she was to start sweeping the shop. I was to return at 11 A.M. The plan worked well for two days.

On the third day Sally strayed from her routine. She didn't wake until Tom rang the delivery buzzer. As he started his chores, she began her shower. Located behind the shop was a common patio that the adjacent buildings had long since stopped using. Oddly enough, in the vacant building next door there was a complete shower, accessible only from the patio. Though the building was unoccupied, the water had never been turned off.

As Tom busily scrubbed the cookers in the sink, Sally apparently felt a sudden urge to use the bathroom. She left the shower and strolled totally nude past the stunned fourteen-year-old. With a pounding heart and dilated pupils, Tom ran down the block and told the guys hanging out at the Pair-of-Dice about his incredible luck. Unfortunately for Tom, his mother also heard him describing his experience.

When I arrived I found a clean but incomprehensible Sally, and no Tom. She explained that she had spent the night on the roof: that just as she was about to fall asleep, fighter planes burst through the clouds, guns blasting. Bullets hit all around her. Shingles flew. The patio was engulfed in flames and she had barely escaped being killed. A bomb, she believed, had hit the Marriott Hotel nearby. She wasn't sure what she was supposed to do, never having been in combat before. I politely showed her the front door and told her that when she returned to normal, whatever normal was, that I would gladly pay her for the days she had worked.

I then went to the Pair-of-Dice looking for Tom. His mom explained about the incident involving a naked Sally. She felt that perhaps Tom needed to take a sabbatical. I understood, but her kid was no suburban innocent. In the mid-1970s the two hundred block of Decatur where we were located was the haunt of sleazy prostitutes, low-class pimps, strippers, and small-time drug dealers. Tom had not been running the streets of Disneyland when I hired him.

My management team was in shambles; I was the sole survivor. Carts had to be cleaned, propane tanks in each unit changed, chili cooked, mustard containers filled, supplies issued, and deposits made. Vendors also had to be sent out and checked in. To work both the day and night shifts for any length of time was physically impossible. But, as Talbot was due back in a few days, I figured that I could survive the grueling hours until his return. Besides, the following day I planned to assemble a new management team. This time, however, I was going to be a little more selective.

That night as I prepared to make my midnight supply run, the front buzzer rang. It was Sally. I assumed that she had managed to elude the Red Baron and was now coming to collect her pay, but I was wrong. When I opened the door, she stumbled in followed immediately by Frenchy. Both had been drinking, but for the moment they seemed a happy couple. Frenchy needed to use the restroom. Sally wasn't sure what she needed.

Once her escort stepped into the men's room, she placed her arms around my neck and started whispering in my ear that we had wasted two nights and that we shouldn't waste this one. I reminded her that I was happily married and that she had a date. As I tried to pry her arms from around my neck, Frenchy stepped out of the restroom. My life flashed before me.

By the grace of God, he was sober enough to realize that it was Sally and not me who was initiating the contact. He called for her to join him and continue partying. She shouted back, "Let's get blitzed and have an orgy."

The idea lit up Frenchy's face. It combined his two greatest interests in life, booze and sex. But he insisted that, if his girl was going to take part in an orgy, then it was only fair that my wife should also participate. Not wanting to offend the ex-boxer, but desperately wanting to free myself from this mess, I quickly assured them that the idea sounded fantastic to me, but that Jane, Protestant prude that she was, would never agree to such a fun evening. She was the old-fashioned, church-going, sing-in-the-choir, PTA type. Since Jane wouldn't participate, I certainly couldn't expect him to share Sally with me. As a gesture of friendship I gave him ten dollars and suggested that he and his girl have a few beers on me. They left happy and I breathed a sigh of relief. I listed the ten dollars on the nightly balance sheet as an entertainment expense. The remainder of the evening passed calmly, but anything would seem calm compared to the company of Frenchy and Sally.

The following day I instituted a new policy. The daily two-dollar cart-rental fee was temporarily waived; subsequently, each vendor was made responsible for cleaning his own cart. This arrangement saved the vendor a little money and allowed me to concentrate on organizing the kitchen and issuing supplies. I also hired one of the crew to sweep the shop and sidewalk, to clean the bathrooms, and to assist new vendors in setting up their carts.

Seven days after I started, Talbot had returned from Florida and we were conducting a desperate search for two new managers. Lucky Dogs was a seven-day-a-week, twenty-four-hour-a-day operation. Managers had to be able to cope with long hours and a diverse work force. They also had to be reliable enough to deliver supplies and collect money from our vendors on Bourbon Street, while resisting the temptation of friendly bars and even friendlier women. It was a difficult job to fill.

We asked Leo Wilkins, a Vietnam veteran in his mid-thirties, if he would take my place. He had worked as a Lucky Dog vendor not long after his discharge from the army and for a short time had even served as relief manager. He knew the operation but had already once rejected an offer to become the full-time night manager. In fact, he had started driving one of Talbot's Mister Tastee ice-cream trucks in the suburbs to escape the Quarter. But with summer ending and kids reentering school, ice-cream sales had plummeted, along with his commissions. Leo now decided to accept a Lucky Dog managerial position.

He was the logical choice. Furthermore, he had a friend, Curly, who was interested in becoming the day manager. I wasn't certain that Leo and Curly would work out, but I was certain of the most important fact: they were my replacements. When Talbot confirmed that they had accepted the positions, the first thing to enter my mind was Martin Luther King, Jr.'s famous proclamation: "Free at last, free at last, thank God Almighty I'm free at last."

2

Never Say Never

August days in the Quarter are brutally hot. My last day on the job that summer of 1976 was no exception. The Pair-of-Dice's porter, white shirt partially unbuttoned and hanging out, stood in front of the corner bar hosing the previous night's discarded beer cups and assorted litter off the sidewalk. The city's street sweeper with its large swirling brushes would suck them up as it made its morning pass down the block. On Decatur, traffic was starting to build. Nine-to-fivers were driving past the bar, past the Greek joints, and past Lucky Dogs as they headed to their offices in the central business district.

As I stood there on the sidewalk in front of the shop watching the city come alive, my shirt was drenched with sweat and my jeans clung to my legs. I had spent the last three hours in the sweltering warehouse checking in vendors and putting away their unused condiments and supplies. However, for the first time since I had started, I didn't notice the heat. I was completing my final grueling shift as manager. I was through with the Quarter, the panhandlers, prostitutes, con artists, and drunken tourists. No longer would I be the target of hecklers as I pushed the old, beat-up green supply cart down Bourbon. No more working until dawn. No more refereeing a crew of misfits who acted like children but who could become violent without warning. No more Kelly, Sally, or Frenchy. As of that moment they were Leo's headache.

Before me lay the challenge of Tulane University's doctoral program in history, the next hurdle in my academic career. A strange turn of events had led to my enrollment at this hundred-year-old private institution. It had never been one of my primary choices. I had wanted a new challenge in a totally new environment. Earlier in the year, I believed that I had found it.

Alfred D. Chandler, professor of history at both Harvard and Brandeis universities, had contacted me in February and recommended that I apply to both of those Ivy League institutions. Stephen Ambrose, who had directed my master's studies at the University of New Orleans, had apparently made his friend Chandler aware of the research that I had done on Andrew Jackson Higgins. Higgins was the outspoken, rough-cut designer and production genius of World War II's landing craft and PT boats. Supreme Allied commander Dwight Eisenhower once referred to him as "the man who won the war for us." Adolf Hitler during the war had called him the "new Noah." Higgins was a man whose enormous accomplishments had thus far been ignored by historians.

The invitation from Chandler to apply was an extraordinary opportunity. Immediately, I forwarded the admissions applications to both universities, hopeful that I would be studying somewhere under Chandler in the fall. I knew that Harvard was a long shot since my Graduate Record Exam scores were only slightly above average and since I had listed financial aid as a determining factor. But Brandeis, I felt, might be tempted by my 3.9 graduate-level grade point average to act on Ambrose's and Chandler's recommendations and award me a scholarship.

In April, when universities notify applicants concerning their acceptance or rejection for the fall semester, I received the collegiate version of the "dear John" letter from Harvard. But from Brandeis I received nothing. Puzzled, I tried contacting Chandler, but he was traveling in Europe. Next, I called Brandeis' admissions department. The secretary nonchalantly informed me that no action had been taken on my application because it had been submitted incomplete. Instead of receiving the three required letters of recommendation from my undergraduate professors, the monotone voice on the other end of the line insisted, the university had received only one.

I was stunned. I had watched the secretary in UNO's history department place all three letters in the same envelope. I had then hand-delivered the envelope to the clerk at the campus post office. If the envelope arrived at Brandeis still sealed, then the university had to have received all three.

Two days later the mystery was solved. Indeed, all three letters had arrived at Brandeis. The same monotone voice explained, however, that a clerical error had accidentally led to two of the letters being misfiled. Thus, my folder was incomplete and as such had been disqualified. Regrettably, all scholarships for the upcoming year had already been awarded. The voice recommended that I apply again the following fall. Thank you. Good-bye. A clerk's simple mistake had destroyed what I considered the opportunity of a lifetime.

After Harvard's rejection and Brandeis' error, I wasn't sure what my future held. Ambrose, aware of the mishap, contacted an associate at Tulane University. Because of their recommendation and effort on my behalf, Tulane awarded me a full fellowship. I received a complete tuition waiver, plus a monthly stipend to help cover living expenses. It was a tremendously generous gesture.

Enthusiastically, I entered college in September. All went well until one cool November morning. As I browsed through the library, an article in a historical journal caught my attention. It predicted that in 1980 (the year in which I intended to receive my doctorate) 940 doctoral candidates in American history or related fields would graduate. In contrast, only 40 university-level teaching positions were projected to be open. I shouldn't have been surprised. Historians for some unexplainable reason tend to live forever. In any case, the employment prospects looked grim for those soon to be emerging on the market with doctor-ates in American history.

Even worse, I had found little challenging about my coursework at Tulane. In colonial American history I sat in an undergraduate class dully taking notes with a room full of pink-cheeked freshmen. It wasn't at all what I had expected. My historical reading course was just as dis-appointing. I was instructed to read from the left side of the professor's bookcase to the right. There didn't appear to be any rhyme or reason to the assignment. I read a book on Christopher Columbus, another about the history of the English banking system, a biography of Robert Ful-ton, two books on America's westward expansion, a book on Henry Ford, and one on the stock market crash of 1929. By mid-November I had become discouraged. I was going through the motions, but I was no longer focused. I had trouble recalling facts from books that I had just finished. I was starting to question why I had ever entered the doctoral program. Perhaps the professor at LSU had been right. History might not be for me.

Past frustrations combined with present discouragement and the lack of future employment opportunities brought me to a decision that I had never remotely anticipated: to withdraw from Tulane. During the gut-wrenching days that followed, I spoke with Dr. Ben Wall about my disillusionment. He was sympathetic, explaining that he likewise had become discouraged during his doctoral studies and had left before re-ceiving his Ph.D. He had turned to writing speeches for political can-didates in North Carolina. Later, he became even more troubled after politicians whom he had successfully supported turned out to be no better than those that he had helped to throw out of office. He had re-turned to Chapel Hill and completed his doctoral requirements. Wall insisted that someday I, too, would return. But he suggested that I not wait too long. He anticipated retiring within four or five years and spending his afternoons deep-sea fishing in the Gulf of Mexico. As long as he was at the university, he assured me, the door would remain open.

By mid-November I was out of school. The hardest decision of my life was past. I felt guilty about letting Ambrose and Wall down. Never-theless, while reluctant to quit, I sensed that I had lost the inner drive necessary to succeed at the graduate level. I found employment teaching at a local middle school for six weeks while they searched for a permanent math teacher. As Christmas approached, I telephoned Doug Talbot to wish him a happy holiday. We talked of my leaving Tulane, my teaching experience, and also of Leo's recent departure from Lucky Dogs.

The pressures of running a twenty-four-hour-a-day, seven-day-a-week business had taken its toll. Leo had changed. He had become impatient with and verbally abusive toward vendors; on more than one occasion he had even used his fists to settle disagreements in the shop. He had proved totally ineffective as a manager. His hot temper and vengeful nature were causing the company to lose vendors and, in turn, sales. Talbot tried to discuss the situation with Leo, but the veteran refused to admit that there was a problem. His response was, "Screw it. If you don't like the way I run things, then I'll quit."

Leo was one of thousands of soldiers who had returned home from Vietnam and never found inner peace. Nightmares haunted him. He wanted a new life but couldn't escape the past, especially at Lucky Dogs. Other veterans came in daily and applied for a job. They, too, couldn't fit into corporate America. They wanted limited responsibility, limited stress, and only enough money to cover their room and board. They weren't opposed to hard work, but they were opposed to having a boss constantly looking over their shoulder. They had had their fill of orders and authorities. Street vending was an ideal alternative. It offered them daily cash commissions and, within reason, the ability to set their own schedules. Leo, like the others, had been drawn to Lucky Dogs because of its loose work environment. He later experienced the same freedom while working on the ice-cream truck. After he became manager of the vending operation, however, he again encountered responsibility and stress. By quitting Lucky Dogs he freed himself.

Doug, out of immediate necessity, chose John Provenzano as his new night manager. John was a scrawny, twenty-five-year-old sandy-haired vendor who had worked for the company approximately six weeks. He was conscientious enough, but Doug was concerned about his lack of experience. He was also worried about someone so new handling the large amounts of cash that New Year's and later Mardi Gras would generate.

Somehow, during the course of our phone conversation, the idea arose that I might temporarily return to Lucky Dogs. We discussed the possibility of my serving as general manager and training John—at least through Mardi Gras. Both Doug and I agreed that the position would be only temporary. I intended to teach history at a high school in the fall; from his standpoint, the business could not afford a general manager on a long-term basis.

As I hung up the phone, I was shocked at my own thoughts. I was actually looking forward to returning to a world that only months before I had so desperately wanted to leave. Life without Frenchy, Kelly, Sally, and the rest of the crew had actually been rather dull. Besides, the Quarter was probably safer than the ghetto middle-school that I had just left.

My first day back at Lucky Dogs I discovered some personnel changes. Kelly had shipped out on a rust bucket of a freighter to South America. Curly had become an undependable drunk and been replaced as day manager by Billie. And Sally, gone but not forgotten, had left for the bright lights of New York City. The vendors thought of her often, especially on Monday mornings as they stood in line at the state health clinic waiting for their shots of penicillin.

Another surprise greeting me on my return was a lanky brunette named Karen sprawled across a full-size mattress in the middle of the office floor. She informed me that first Leo and now John had given her "permission to crash there." Karen wasn't the only one who had set up housekeeping in the shop. In the storeroom above the office, where Sally had once lived, John and his girlfriend Liz had taken up residence. Over the peeling grayish white louver door to their furnished storeroom residence, someone had tacked a cardboard sign that read "211$^{1}/_{2}$ Decatur."

Above the restrooms in the left rear of Lucky Dogs' rectangular building was a five-by-ten-foot cubbyhole. There a short, skinny, and grungy male hippie had set up camp. The shop's old wooden stepladder served as his stairs. In the eight-by-twelve toolroom next to the office, two more vendors had spread out their brown goose-down sleeping bags and declared squatter's rights.

Leo had turned Lucky Dogs into a full-fledged flophouse, complete with a clothesline running from above the men's restroom to the walk-in cooler. The shop resembled what a New York alley must have looked like during the Great Depression. As you entered the dimly lit building, you could see clothes hanging everywhere, full garbage cans sitting against the wall, people milling about aimlessly, and litter scattered on the floor.

The shop was in poor condition, but the carts looked even more deplorable. Twenty-five years of constant abuse by a transient labor force had taken their toll on the once shiny fleet of hot dog–shaped vending stands. Their unsightly condition resulted in poor sales; and poor sales, in turn, meant that the company lacked the capital necessary to refurbish the pathetic-looking wagons. It was a self-perpetuating downward spiral.

Additionally, Takee Outee, a new local Chinese fast-food chain, had opened small carryout restaurants in almost every block of Bourbon Street. Their cheap prices and varied menu were capturing a large part of our clientele. Lucky Dogs' revenues began to decline. To counter the loss, Doug had become involved in commercial real-estate sales. More and more he trusted Leo to handle the day-to-day operation of the street-vending business. He visited the shop less frequently than he had in the past. After six years of dealing with unstable vendors and managers, he had begun to lose his enthusiasm for the business.

Since Leo lived relatively close to Talbot, he was delivering all of the company's daily paperwork and mail to his employer's home. This service saved Talbot the fifteen-mile drive into town every morning; from Leo's perspective, it kept his boss out of the shop. When Talbot did visit the warehouse, it was generally in the afternoon. By then the boarders had hidden their mattresses and put away the clothesline. Everything appeared as it should.

My return to the shop meant that the underground community could no longer remain hidden. It also meant that if a vendor had a problem with the day or night manager, he had someone from whom he could seek redress. Vendors were willing to open up to me because I was there repairing the carts, sweeping the floor, unloading the meat truck: doing physical labor just as they were used to doing. I was general manager in title but not necessarily in my actions. Never would they have called Talbot, nor would they have entered my office to voice their complaints. However, during the daily bull sessions in the shop, their problems often surfaced. My apparent neutrality also became a great advantage: I could make policy but blame it on Doug, protesting, "Hey, I don't make the rules. I just enforce them." Doug, as owner, did not have that liberty.

My first objective as general manager was to regain control of the shop. I began by moving Karen out of the office. She wasn't thrilled with my decision, but she understood. The morning following her relocation, a well-spoken, middle-aged-sounding gentleman telephoned her. Discovering that she was not in, he asked if I would relay a message. He wanted Karen to know that the Polaroids from their initial shoot were so stunning that he would like to arrange a second session. I didn't ask for details; I simply agreed to pass on the information. I just hoped that a Lucky Dog cart had not somehow been used as a prop.

That afternoon when Karen wandered in, I pulled her aside and gave her the message. She blushed, then blurted out, "Well, he's an awfully nice gentleman and a helluva tipper." At that point, I thought it best that we talk privately in the office. Karen was in her mid-twenties, a bit unkempt but apparently quite attractive to middle-aged men with Polaroid cameras. She had been doing exceptionally well selling hot dogs at Kelly's old spot: the corner of Conti and Bourbon outside the Famous Door. I just wanted to make certain that hot dogs were all that she continued to hawk.

After Karen, the next to move out of the shop was the tenant living above the bathroom. No one knew much about him. I came to the conclusion that he had just drifted into the warehouse one day, discovered a warm dry place to sleep, and joined the commune. The vendors all figured that for a couple of bucks a week and a little clean-up work each night, Leo had allowed the hippie to call the cubbyhole home.

Finally, the two vendors homesteading in the toolroom grudgingly packed and moved to the Hummingbird Hotel on St. Charles Avenue. That left only John and Liz, and they were in the process of looking for a reasonably priced furnished apartment.

Billie, the lesbian day manager, was overjoyed with the housecleaning. She and Leo had never gotten along. On several occasions they had had marathon shouting matches in the shop, each calling the other a slew of profanities, but the arguments had never gotten physical. Leo wasn't that crazy. Billie was built like an NFL linebacker and had the aggressive nature of a pit bull. If they had come to blows, the smart money would have been on her.

Leo's temperament had caused many a new vendor to quit after his first night. The novices weren't inclined to stand out in the cold, heat, or rain for hours only to have the boss harass them when they reported back to the shop for check-in. Commission and tips weren't that good. Old regulars, on the other hand, just ignored him. Vendors such as Bill McCarty, James (Red) Lott, Daigle, Howard Lewis, Scott Adler, Burt Richards, and Brian Kidd had all been through this scenario before. They knew that Leo, like numerous managers before him, would soon burn out and resign. All they had to do was be patient.

Of the regular crew, Richards, Kidd, and Lewis were the leading salesmen with Adler coming in a close fourth. Lewis had switched from the Square to St. Peter and Bourbon on the night shift. St. Pete (the vendors tend to shorten the street names) is a fabulous late-night location. Though a rougher spot than the Square, its potential for sales is far greater because large numbers of tourists constantly pass the cart either going to or coming from world-famous Pat O'Brien's bar. Common wisdom has it that a visit to the Quarter isn't official until you've drunk at least a couple of Pat O's Hurricanes and then staggered down St. Pete to Bourbon for a Lucky Dog smothered in chili and onions. Lewis had opted for the late-night drinking crowd because he knew that they tipped far more generously than the Square's sober daytime lunch clientele.

Down the block from Lewis, Kidd worked the corner of Toulouse and Bourbon, traditionally a favorite hangout of the biker crowd. Sales were good, but it took a special type of person to deal with the leather-jacket gang members who frequented the nearby bars. Richards worked two blocks up Bourbon from Kidd outside the Royal Sonesta Hotel. His customers were the more upscale tourists. Adler set up by the Old Absinthe House at the corner of Bienville and Bourbon, a favorite bar of visitors and locals alike.

Lewis, Kidd, Richards, and Adler took pride in their work and aggressively hawked their product. Before passers-by caught sight of their carts, they heard, "A piece of bread, a hunk of meat, and all the mustard you can eat"; "Don't be a meanie, buy a wienie"; or simply the age-old "Getcha Lucky Dog." All four dressed neatly, smiled often, and had been blessed with the gift of gab. They didn't simply sell hot dogs; they sold themselves, and the city as well. They were New Orleans' unofficial street-corner chamber of commerce.

However, because of their friendship and cutthroat natures, they took both personal and professional interest in seeing who would have bragging rights as the company's top salesman each night over drinks at the Pair-of-Dice. Each tried to arrive first on his corner in the daytime and last in the shop at night. Their competition was fierce. I know of one instance where Richards switched a full propane tank in Kidd's cart with an almost empty one so that his friend would run out of gas during the peak selling time and have to shut down. The prank gave Richards a good hour's edge in sales. On another occasion, Adler paid a street character a couple of bucks to spy on Lewis. Once Lewis left his cart to go to the bathroom, the spy was instructed to push the cart down St. Pete and hide it in Pirates Alley. He was to remain with the cart so that nothing would be stolen. While Lewis searched for his missing wagon, the rest of his buddies were selling dogs. All pranks aside, the competition increased take-home pay for the vendors and profits for the company.

Of the four vendors, Richards was the best. He was on a first-name basis with the club owners, taxi drivers, street hustlers, hookers, policemen, and bartenders. People often stopped by his stand just to chat or to try and stump him with sports trivia. He was fanatical about basketball and especially about the Boston Celtics. Posted on his cart were pictures of himself with Celtic greats John Havlicek and Dave Cowens.

Also on the cart was a small portable TV, which allowed him to catch sporting events. Power came from an extension cord that was plugged in somewhere up on the Royal Sonesta's balcony overlooking Conti and Bourbon. Burt kept his corner cleared of street riffraff. In appreciation, the hotel's management was happy to accommodate his electrical needs. Also unique to Richards' cart was the wide assortment of postcards taped to the inside of his unit's sneeze guard. Tourists befriended by him often mailed him cards from other exotic locations that they later visited in hopes that their pictures would hang on his plexiglass wall of fame.

Burt was the ultimate vendor. He chatted with his regular clientele who stopped by the cart, but he also kept an eye out for potential new customers. To those passing that he didn't know, he barked out several corny lines to draw their attention. He might say, "I've got a table for two down in the main dining room. You gonna walk her all night, or you gonna feed her?" Another winner was the political line he used during the last several months of Nixon's presidency. "Ya want a Watergate dog? There's a bug in every bun." Some laughed; others were too drunk to make the connection. When all else failed, he simply relied on, "Getcha Lucky Dogs right here. Step right up. Who's next?"

When I became the company's general manager, Richards had worked there for almost eight years. Prior to that, he had been a salesman at Labiche's department store on Canal Street, but he considered the sales job too confining. It interfered with his late-night partying in the Quarter. To eliminate this conflict he quit, but he didn't remain unemployed for long. On many an evening he had stood on corners in the Quarter and shot the breeze with Lucky Dog vendors. It only seemed logical then that he become one of them. Sales was his strong point; he loved the Quarter; he was a night person. Working a cart, he could capitalize on all three traits at the same time, while making a living doing what he liked best: meeting people. He was immediately successful.

The only problem that Burt had was that he didn't like being on the street during the hot, humid New Orleans summers. He solved it by working for Lucky Dogs from Labor Day to Memorial Day. Then, through a contact that he had made while working his cart, he acquired a job at a Cape Cod country club from Memorial Day to Labor Day. Winters in the Vieux Carré and summers on old Cape Cod: few could be so lucky. Eventually, however, even Burt's luck would run out.

With Leo gone, John had taken over the night shift. Billie remained as day manager, and I oversaw the entire operation as general manager. In this way we made it through New Year's. Billie had held her temper, and she and I had developed a good working relationship. She accepted me for what I was: a conservative, straight southern male who didn't agree with her life style. But she also knew that as long as she did her job and kept her private life to herself, I didn't care what she did with whom. When she announced that she and her roommate Bonnie were planning on getting married, I even congratulated her. In 1976 I thought my response was pretty liberal for a conservative redneck born in Sullivan's Hollow, Mississippi.

Bonnie often stopped by the shop to bring her lover lunch. During those daily visits I got to know her. She was short and quiet with graying hair, the antithesis of Billie. Usually accompanying Bonnie was Miss Coolie. Coolie was a black transvestite living with the two lovers whom the couple had chosen to be their maid of honor. Coolie was tall, broad shouldered, skinny as a rail, and wore a long curly black wig. I imagined he resembled what Jimmie Hendrix would have looked like in drag. Once in a while Coolie appeared in heels, though even then, the words *graceful* and *elegant* would never apply to him/her. The most naïve midwestern farm boy could see without difficulty that Coolie was a man. His five-o'clock shadow was a dead giveaway. I couldn't help but laugh when I pictured him strutting down the aisle in a bridesmaid dress.

James Lott, another vendor, was to perform the marriage ceremony. A few years earlier Lott had sent a twenty-five-dollar money order to a California post office box in exchange for an official-looking document stating that he was a minister in good standing in some off-the-wall religion. He had even registered as a minister with New Orleans' city hall.

The couple set the date. Then Billie asked if I would give the bride away and if Doug would stand in as best man. I was honored, but this was 1976. In most places across America, gays were still hiding in the closet. I thought that I had behaved extremely well by offering my congratulations. Doug had even consented to let them use the shop for the wedding and a Lucky Dog cart for the reception. We were trying to be understanding. But I'd be damned if I was going to walk down the aisle in a suit to give a fifty-seven-year-old lesbian to a thirty-six-year-old lesbian in a marriage conducted by a hot dog vendor ordained via the mail for a twenty-five-dollar fee. I had to draw the line somewhere, and giving the bride away seemed as good a place as any. When I mentioned to Doug that Billie had requested that he serve as their best man, he gave me one of those "have you lost your mind?" looks. He, too, was a conservative, straight southern male born in Mississippi. He, too, drew the line.

In late January, a few weeks before the blessed event, Billie called off the wedding. Having earlier refused to give the bride away, I didn't feel that I had a right to ask what had gone wrong. Curious as I was, I knew that her predicament was none of my business. Billie was distraught over the end of the relationship. Down and lonely, she no longer kidded around in the shop. It would take time before she again became the feisty butch that we all knew and liked.

While Billie was singing the blues, Donovan, our vendor on Iberville and Bourbon, was in a state of bliss. Three months earlier he had met Sheila, his true love. It didn't matter to him that she was a hooker or that his first date with her had cost him by the hour. He felt that they had a special chemistry and that fate had drawn them together. She swore that for him she would give up her profession. She was a wiry, stringy blond with a mild case of acne. But to Donovan she was a goddess. She helped him set up his cart, brought him supper, and often met him at the shop when he pushed in at the end of the night. She was the woman of his dreams. He was so in love that he had purchased an engagement ring and was trying to build up enough courage to propose. Then his world came crashing down.

Sheila announced that she was breaking off their relationship and moving in with Billie. Donovan was devastated. His girl had left him for "a bitch with a flattop." As Ignatius might have noted, "Fortuna had dealt him a cruel blow." Donovan walked out of the warehouse as if in a trance. Within minutes he began a record-breaking binge that lasted for days. Finally, he wandered back into the shop at the week's end, filthy, unshaven, reeking of booze. He had spent the previous ninety-six hours roaming from bar to bar and sleeping in alleys. By the time his money ran out, he was so rancid that no one would buy him a drink. He was sobering up when he stumbled into my office, just to let me know that he was leaving town. He felt too ashamed to stay and face his friends. Even worse, he couldn't stand seeing Sheila walking down Bourbon Street with another woman's arm around her. It was more than his masculine ego could endure.

Billie now had eyes only for Sheila. But hers weren't the only eyes casting a lustful glance in Sheila's direction. John, the night manager, was extremely curious as to why both Donovan and Billie were so infatuated with the raunchy-looking hooker. The thought that her talents had to be considerable started to drive him mad. Coincidentally, Liz, John's girlfriend, for whatever reason, had been advised by her doctor to abstain from sex for several weeks. I was aware of this advice because during a heated argument with John in the shop, she had screamed it loudly for everyone to hear. In any case, no such restrictions had been placed on John. To his way of thinking, he simply needed a new partner. Who better to pursue than Sheila?

At the same time, Sheila had decided that she would do everything in her power to capture John's affection. Unfortunately, Liz caught them both in bed in the upstairs storeroom apartment. The result was an all-day knock-down drag-out argument between Liz, John, Billie, and Sheila. Occasionally, I would put a halt to the screaming. In the midst of this chaos I was trying to run a business. But as soon as I had walked back into the kitchen, tempers would flare again. When the day shift ended at 6 P.M. the arguing and name calling persisted. Then Liz, in drastic retaliation against John's infidelity, went home with Billie.

John couldn't believe that his woman would do such a thing. Sheila couldn't believe that Billie would stoop so low as to cheat on her— never mind that she herself was having an affair with John. The following morning, a truce was called and all partners returned to their original beds. The shop slowly started returning to normal. At least as normal as could be expected.

Billie decided that if Sheila was kept busy, perhaps she wouldn't be so prone to roam. And there was no better place to keep her busy than on a Lucky Dog cart. Working the cart she would be invisibly chained to a specific corner. Billie would know where her woman was at all times. The two lovers took over the corner of Iberville and Bourbon. Sheila set up the cart in the afternoon and Billie pushed it out for her. Billie would then return to the shop and finish her shift. The plan seemed successful, at least until Sheila's ex-husband from Texas showed up.

The ex discovered Sheila working the cart and made arrangements one night to meet her after her shift. Sheila pushed in at about 4:30 A.M. sixty dollars short of being able to pay her bill. John simply noted the problem on the sheet and let her leave. At 6:00 A.M. Billie showed up, frantic because her lover hadn't come home. When John told her about Sheila's shortage, she blew up, stomping out of the building in search of "the bitch." By 7:30 A.M., having had no luck in finding her, Billie returned and settled into cleaning the carts. All was going smoothly. Then at approximately 9:30 A.M. Red Lott arrived. He stopped by to tell Billie that he had just seen Sheila down by the French Market making out with some tall black-haired guy wearing cowboy boots. The scene, he contended, rated at least double-X, potentially triple-X if someone didn't quickly throw a bucket of water on them.

I headed out the door to my Chevette hoping that I could find Sheila and the money owed before she and her friend drank it up or were arrested. By the time I got the key in the ignition Billie had thrown Red out of the warehouse, yanked open the car door, and flung herself into the passenger seat. As I drove down Decatur, she kept promising that she would stay in the car and let me handle everything.

It was a quiet, cool Sunday morning. Churchgoers were having coffee and donuts at Café du Monde and Morning Call before going to mass at St. Louis Cathedral. Early-rising tourists were strolling through the Quarter. Artists were beginning to set up their easels along the black wrought-iron fence surrounding Jackson Square. A block down

Decatur at the French Market, men were unloading produce from their trucks. A few early shoppers there were browsing through the different vendor stalls. Everything was calm and peaceful.

A few hundred feet from the produce stalls, at the top of the steps leading over the protective Mississippi River flood wall, lay Sheila and her Texan. He was stretched out on his back, boots dangling over the platform; she was rubbing one of his inner thighs and kissing him on the lips. Before I could come to a complete stop, Billie had bolted from the car and started screaming, "You no-good slut. That's your ass."

As Billie charged up the metal steps, Sheila jumped up and dashed down the other side, two steps at a time. She headed out onto the railroad tracks; Billie followed in relentless pursuit. The tracks run between the levee and the river, servicing New Orleans' busy wharves. As Sheila and Billie followed the rails eastward toward Atlanta, I stopped to talk to the cowboy. He was still lying on his back as if nothing had happened. His only comment as he rose and staggered down the stairs towards the market was, "If she wants the bitch that bad she can have her." Faintly in the background we could hear Billie screaming, "You no-good two-timing whore, you can't run forever."

I sat on the steps on the river side of the flood wall where I would be out of sight of everyone at the French Market. From there I could survey the railroad tracks below. After about twenty minutes of unsuccessfully chasing Sheila in, out, and around parked freight cars, Billie came up the steps huffing and puffing. I ordered her to wait in the car. In her exhausted condition she readily agreed.

A few minutes later Sheila's head poked out from behind an Illinois Central boxcar a couple of hundred yards down the track. She motioned with her hand for me to approach her. She was still worried that Billie might come storming over the levee at any time like an angry marine.

Just like in the old spy thrillers we rendezvoused in the middle of the tracks. I began by assuring Sheila that I didn't give a damn about her personal life but that I did want the sixty dollars that she owed the company. She swore to me that the missing money was in the hot dog cart under the propane tank. It had been hidden there earlier in the night as a safety precaution in case she was robbed. She maintained that at check-in she was too drunk to remember what she had done with it. Now, as the effects of the booze wore off, it was all coming back to her. Her story wasn't believable, but I knew that I couldn't bring both Billie and her back to the shop in my small car. Sheila wouldn't have survived the trip. I left her standing in the middle of the tracks and returned to the warehouse.

There was, of course, no money under the tank. When Billie saw that it wasn't there, she blurted out, "Lying no-good slut. Cheated on me and stole the company's money. Let's get the bitch."

I had no intentions of rounding up a posse and tracking down the villain. Billie would have turned the group into a lynch mob. But within minutes the phone rang. It was Sheila admitting that she had lied. The money had been used to bankroll her early morning binge with her ex. I gave her a week to come up with the cash. After that, I explained, I would have to file charges with the police for nonpayment of a food bill. It wasn't something that I wanted to do, but I couldn't allow a vendor to take the company's money without repercussions. If I did, theft would spread like an epidemic. Sixty dollars here, ninety dollars there: before long there wouldn't be any funds to deposit. I had seen it happen when I had worked at Lucky Dogs before. One night one vendor comes up short and gets away with it. The following night four or five try it.

Sheila insisted that she would be at the shop in two hours to clear her bill. She knew of a seamen's bar off St. Charles Avenue where she could turn a few quick tricks. I responded that I didn't want her doing anything illegal to obtain the money. She reluctantly agreed, but then declared that honest money would take a while to acquire. I extended the deadline to two weeks. She accepted.

Fourteen days later I had not received a single dollar. Fifteen days, sixteen days, seventeen days, and still no money. Billie proclaimed that besides being a slut, a thief, and a bitch, Sheila couldn't be trusted to keep her word. It was the type of statement that didn't deserve a response. Instead, I took action. I immediately visited the First District police station and filled out the necessary papers to have Sheila arrested. Two days later I got a call from Central Lockup. "Asshole, why the hell did you have me locked up?"

"You gave me no choice," I replied. "You made no effort at repaying the money, and then you went up and down Bourbon Street bragging that there was nothing that Lucky Dogs could do to you. I couldn't allow that to continue." When I finished, she suggested I should do something that was anatomically impossible and slammed down the phone.

Sheila was scheduled to go before the judge the following afternoon. At worst, she would be sentenced to thirty days. More than likely, she would simply be given a warning and then released with time served. As I sat in court waiting to testify, an elderly gentleman reached over and tapped me on my left shoulder. This was followed by a hand motion indicating that we should go outside. As I stepped into the hall, he handed me three twenty-dollar bills to fully pay off Sheila's shortage.

I reentered the courtroom just in time to hear the clerk call my name. I approached the bench and explained to the judge that I had just been repaid the full amount that was stolen and therefore wanted to drop all charges. The judge slightly lowered his head and looked at me over the top of his wire-rimmed glasses. He sat quietly for a moment then warned me that if I ever dared to use his courtroom as a collection agency again, he would throw me in jail. Personally, I thought the system had worked extremely well. The company had recovered its funds, Sheila had spent time in jail for a minor crime, and the court had to pay for only an overnight stay instead of thirty days' worth of care.

Word on the street had it that the man who had handed me the money was Billie's landlord. Billie had been going crazy during the previous thirty-six hours. She couldn't bear the thought of her "woman" being locked behind bars with hundreds of horny, desperate women. That prospect was apparently worse than having her out roaming the streets with her ex. Therefore, Billie had persuaded her landlord to approach me. She wanted it kept a secret that it was she who had reimbursed the company. Isn't love wonderful?

Before things could return to normal, three new misfortunes occurred. The first one involved Burt Richards. A few years earlier he had had the bad luck to walk through the doors of a bar where a shooting was taking place. Early one morning as the clubs were closing, Richards was selling his last Lucky Dog. He habitually stayed out late to get the last few stragglers as they were forced out of the closing bars. The tactic was generally good for a few additional sales. The extra money was often just enough to push his gross slightly over Kidd's, Adler's, or Lewis'. Thus, he would have bragging rights as the evening's top vendor. On this particular night, just after selling his last dog, he decided to have one beer for the road. It was a critical mistake. As he walked through the barroom door, a shot rang out. Burt recognized both the triggerman and the man lying dead on the floor. The gunman reputedly had mob ties. The police questioned Burt, but he testified that he had seen nothing.

A few nights later two men in dark suits stopped by Richards' cart and strongly recommended that he consider permanently relocating. After the heart-to-heart talk, Richards pushed his cart in. He looked rather pale. As he walked out the door, he mentioned that he had to leave town for a few days, never elaborating as to why. I could tell that something was troubling him. Normally, he bragged about beating Kidd, Adler, or Lewis. That night he wasn't even curious about their sales.

Shortly after Richards' departure, the second unfortunate event occurred. Richard Daigle, a longtime Lucky Dog vendor, died. Daigle was a quiet, meek little guy in his early sixties who always wore a faded green corduroy jacket, even during the summer. It was his security blanket. He had begun working as a Lucky Dog vendor long before Doug purchased the company. He worked six, sometimes seven days a week. Selling hot dogs was his life, but it could never have been his livelihood. He seldom stayed by his cart long enough to make a sale.

He arrived at the shop at approximately 4 P.M. every afternoon. Then until almost six o'clock he would piddle around. Sometimes he talked to himself; other times he just stood by his cart twiddling his thumbs. Once in a while something that he considered humorous would flash through his thoughts and he'd chuckle to himself. He was a little eccentric but totally harmless, and he loved being a Lucky Dog vendor.

Once his cart was completely set up, he carefully went over it as a pilot might inspect a plane. Chili hot, dogs cooking, buns steaming, garbage basket in place, napkin dispenser filled, mustard containers filled, tongs and ladle handy, tire pressure OK: let's roll. Firmly gripping the cart's handle, he would push the wagon through the open doorway, head left up Decatur, then left on Bienville, and then roll towards Bourbon. But he never rolled far and he never rolled fast. It took him forever to reach his corner, which was only five blocks away.

Frequently, he stopped to dine at Arnaud's, Galatoire's, Brennan's, or one of the other fine restaurants in the Quarter. While his cart sat on the sidewalk, steam bellowing out of the cooker, Daigle, wearing his green corduroy jacket, sat at a window table eating supper and keeping a watchful eye on it. By the time he finished his meal, had coffee and dessert, and got to his corner it was after 8 P.M., but he still wasn't ready to open for business. He would take another ten or fifteen minutes to say hello to all the street people that he knew. Other vendors had been selling for over three hours, but that didn't bother Daigle. He didn't need the money. His parents had been quite wealthy and had left him a trust fund. For many years he had been receiving a monthly check, which covered his basic expenses. The Lucky Dog cart simply gave him a purpose. When he died, all of his friends from the street contributed and bought flowers. Doug and I, along with many of Daigle's other Quarter companions, attended his funeral.

The third unfortunate and disturbing event occurred on a Saturday night in early February. Business had been relatively good. John and Liz had just finished their ten o'clock supply run when I arrived at the shop. I rang the buzzer, but no one came to unbolt the door. I rang again. Still there was no answer. I peeped through the crack between the shop's two big double doors and could see John counting money at the kitchen counter. I rang once more; finally he started heading towards the front.

When he opened the door and saw me, he stammered for a second then started describing his recent mishap. He said that he had stuffed the money from the last run into a brown paper bag. He claimed that he had set the bag in his supply cart thinking that it would be safe. However, when he had arrived back at the shop, the bag containing over six hundred dollars was gone.

I knew that I had just seen him counting several stacks of money at the kitchen counter. I asked, "Are you certain that you lost it?"

"Positive," he replied. "All I have is the forty dollars that the last vendor turned in." Then he pulled three twenties, not two, from his pocket. He quickly covered by saying that the third bill was his. The entire discussion seemed unreal. I wasn't sure what was going on, so I determined not to mention what I had seen until I knew more.

John kept apologizing for his carelessness and offering to repay the money out of his next several checks. Then he offered to retrace his steps and see if he could find the missing bag lying on the street. Perhaps, he theorized, it had fallen from the supply wagon and not yet been noticed. Before setting off on his search, he insisted on putting out the garbage.

Our trash room was located just to the right of the front door of the shop. Only a few steps separated it from the curb. I countered that I would put the garbage on the street myself so that he could begin his investigation immediately. I also suggested that he go alone as Liz would only slow him down. In truth, I didn't know then what was going on, but I knew that I didn't want the two of them leaving together—not until I had the money.

John hesitated. Then after quietly speaking to Liz for a few minutes he left. Liz went upstairs to their small storeroom apartment. I began setting out the trash. As I did so I noticed that just before John rounded the corner by the Pair-of-Dice, he looked back twice. What could possibly be so interesting? Then it struck me. He must have hidden the money in one of the bags before he opened the door. That would explain why he had been so keen to take the garbage on his way out. It also explained why he wanted Liz to leave with him. They both would have been on the outside with the money, while I was shut inside without it.

The second plastic bag that I opened contained the missing paper sack. I slipped it under my jacket and calmly walked back into the building. Next, I locked the bag in the office safe. As far as I could tell, John had not seen me and Liz was still upstairs.

About thirty minutes later John returned proclaiming his search to have been unsuccessful. This time he truly looked puzzled. As he and

Liz talked near the front door, I could see him motioning as if to say, "I don't know what happened. It's not there." In the office they sat in front of me, and we both played out our parts. I told them that since John had lost the money, I agreed that he should pay it back. John sat there looking bewildered. He kept repeating, "I don't know what happened to the money." At this point he was telling the truth.

After we came to the agreement that John would repay the missing money over the next several weeks, I volunteered to make the final run of the evening at 2 A.M. This plan served two purposes. First, by making the run I would deprive John of the opportunity to steal again. Second, it would give him and Liz enough time to gather their essential belongings and leave before I returned. We could then avoid a late-night confrontation. If I had revealed that I had found the money stuffed in the garbage, then I would have divulged that I knew he was lying, that I had caught him in the act of committing a felony. A desperate human, like a cornered animal, often strikes out in fear. I wasn't certain if John was armed, but I didn't want to find out. By the time I returned from my run, a few of the vendors had already pushed in and were waiting outside the padlocked shop. John and Liz were gone. They had taken advantage of the opportunity afforded them. I had the money and saw no need to call the police. All we needed was a new lock and a new night manager.

Mardi Gras was near, but the loss of John wasn't a major problem. Curly had just arrived back in town and was eagerly looking for work. The night shift would be his as long as he could stay sober. All in all, things could have been worse. By the end of the week they were. Karen, Adler, and five other vendors began complaining that they wanted a larger percentage of the gross, shorter working hours, better working conditions, three days off a week, and a say in the making of company policy. Some of the requests could be fulfilled, others were simply impossible. Dissatisfied, Karen led an effort to unionize.

It was a disorganized and motley crew that burst into my office and made their demands late one Friday afternoon. Unlike the horde of protesters that Ignatius led at Levy Pants, none of our workers carried banners or bore crosses. There were no marching songs, no chants in the background. Instead of Ignatius I had Karen, queen of the Polaroids, standing in front of my desk vehemently pressing the group's demands. She felt invincible. With her fellow vendors firmly behind her, she figured that she could paralyze the company and bring management to its knees. She figured wrong.

If all had gone according to her plans, she might have hurt the company financially for a few days. However, even that didn't happen. As she stood reciting her grievances, a group of ten men walked past the open office door heading toward the kitchen. I couldn't believe what I had just seen. I ignored Karen's speech, leaned out the doorway, and looked toward the rear of the shop in amazement. Sure enough. There was a herd of potential strikebearers standing at the counter. This time Fortuna had smiled on me. "Billie," I yelled, "hire seven of the gentlemen. They can start immediately."

Karen was stunned. She stepped from the office and glanced toward the rough-looking crowd of men filling out applications. She immediately declared that I had no right to hire "a bunch of freckin' scabs." I reminded her that she and her co-workers had just given me an ultimatum. If I didn't see things their way, they were "gonna walk a picket line in front of the shop" until their demands were met.

I admitted that I had no right to ask her or her followers to work for less than they considered themselves to be worth. That would be unconscionable. In addition, I explained, I couldn't bear to be responsible for holding them back from other, more promising career opportunities. They were correct. They deserved to make more money. They deserved three days off each a week. They deserved shorter hours and better working conditions. Unfortunately, I couldn't accommodate them. Therefore, even though it greatly pained me, I had no alternative but reluctantly to accept their resignations. I wished them well and hoped that they found what they were looking for. I then excused myself and went to help Billie teach the new crew how to operate their Lucky Dog carts.

The unionization effort died a rapid death. Finger pointing and dissension were rampant before the group ever got out of the office. I knew that before long the strikers would start returning. I, like a parent, was prepared to welcome them back into the family, but only under the company's conditions. I also knew that my seven new vendors were all seamen who were only looking for a few dollars to hold them over until their ship sailed. They had blown their money in a card game and still had three days left in port. I needed Karen and her followers, but I certainly couldn't let them know that. If I did, the entire process would start all over.

The following day, as expected, the protesting employees began drifting back in. Each blamed someone else for the strike. Karen claimed that Adler had put her up to it. Howard swore that Karen had instigated the entire plan. Then Adler arrived. He nonchalantly walked into my office and asked for a private conference. Quickly he closed and locked the door. As I watched him, I thought to myself, "Show time." I knew that he was about to honor me with a stellar performance.

As Adler neared my desk, he fell to his knees and cried, "Jerry, I love this company. I'll do anything to get my corner back."

"Adler, stop the bullshit and stand up." He ignored me.

"Lucky Dogs is my life. I need this job. Without it I'm nothing. Please, please forgive me for what I have done. I meant no harm." His performance was moving, but I couldn't let it continue. It was too embarrassing. As I got up to unlock the door, he leaned toward me, wrapped his arms around my right leg, and cried out, "Just one more chance. That's all I ask. I beg of you."

I couldn't resist such talent. I accepted him back into the fold.

After he walked out of the office, I could hear him telling the other vendors, "I knew that they'd cave in. Jerry got on his knees and begged me to come back, but I just looked down at him and scoffed. I told him what I thought about this cheap, sleazy, two-bit organization. It wasn't until after he promised me a weekly bonus that I finally gave in. Anyway, I hate to see a grown man grovel. I tell you, they can't make it without me. What did you guys get out of 'um?" It was vintage Adler.

Within two days, the seamen were back on their ship and most of the regular crew were back on their corners. Everything was returning to normal. At 7:30 P.M. someone rang the delivery buzzer. Curly opened the door assuming that it was a vendor needing more supplies.

Instead of a vendor it was Frenchy. The intoxicated boxer had come on a sympathy mission. Someone at the Pair-of-Dice had told him that Karen had been fired because she had tried to unionize Lucky Dogs. Now Frenchy wanted to have a few words with the "no-good son-of-a-bitchin asshole who had shit-canned such a nice broad." Curly, faster than lightning, pointed toward me.

I tried to explain to Frenchy that, as we spoke, Karen was selling Lucky Dogs on her corner. He didn't comprehend what I said. Once again he mumbled his view concerning Karen's job loss, and then he shouted that he "wasn't gonna stand for that kind of crap. Piss on it." He was "gonna beat the f—— out of Jerry right now."

He was so drunk that he still thought he was talking to Curly. As he turned and started toward the kitchen looking for me, he tripped over our mop bucket, plummeting face first onto the hardwood floor. The boxer was down for the count. Curly rolled our old steel-wheeled railroad cart over near Frenchy's limp body. Normally, we used the flatbed to carry our meat deliveries from the delivery truck to the walk-in cooler. That night we used it to haul Frenchy out. Curly grabbed him by his arms, I grabbed his legs, and together we flung him onto the wagon and pushed it out of the shop onto the sidewalk.

Using a bicycle chain and padlock we managed to fasten the cart to a pipe connected to the exterior of the building. This way the street people couldn't steal it once Frenchy had gotten off. For hours the ex-boxer lay there resting under the full moon and stars, oblivious to the world: stretched out, face down, arms dangling over either side of the cart, feet hanging over the end. Shakespeare in *Cymbeline* wrote a line befitting the scene. "He that drinks well, sleeps well, and he that sleeps well thinks no harme." I was especially fond of the part about thinking "no harme."

3

Shoes in the Steamer

Mardi Gras's endless parades, all-night street partying, and massive crowds had come and gone. So had John Provenzano, the man I had been hired to train as Lucky Dogs' new night manager. By mid-April, 1977, Billie had also left the company. She had become depressed after Sheila left her for a young Greek taxi driver. Now Billie, like Donovan, who previously had been jilted by the unfaithful hooker, fled the Quarter in search of a new life. Street talk had it that she had headed for California, where the beaches were overflowing with shapely young coeds. In reality, she had moved to a run-down apartment in the suburbs and begun a new career as a night cashier at a twenty-four-hour convenience store. But if she wanted her friends to believe that she was chasing beach bunnies up and down the Pacific shoreline, then so be it. The truth would remain our secret.

Tom Nathan had taken over Billie's position. Tom wasn't the ideal choice. In fact, he wasn't even a good choice. He was a forty-four-year-old diehard alcoholic who could best be described as a smartass. I dreaded having to promote him from vendor to day manager, but at that moment I saw no alternative. No one else wanted the job.

Tom knew that his history of excessive drinking concerned me. He tried to combat my fears by insisting that he could lay off the booze. All he needed, he claimed, was a chance. Against my better judgment I reluctantly consented to a week's trial period. He didn't make it to the fourth day. The first day he showed up promptly and actually did better than I had expected. The second day he came in thirty minutes late. The third morning he failed to show up at all. For over two hours I did his work. The more carts I washed, the madder I got. Finally, I put down the sponge, picked up my truck keys, and went after him.

Tom lived in a one-room second-floor apartment on the corner of Julia and Camp Streets. In the mid- to late 1970s the skid-row area was the mecca of New Orleans' booming wino population. Back then we didn't think of the winos as "victims," or "the less fortunate," or the "homeless." They were no-account drunks and drifters, bums who didn't have steady work and didn't want it. They hung out in packs. They leaned against lamp posts, street signs, sides of buildings. They lay on steps and in alleys, or simply stood in clusters on the sidewalks passing the bottle and shooting the breeze with no particular place to go. When the wine ran out, they moseyed on down the block seeking a few swigs from someone else's bottle.

As a whole, the street people of the seventies weren't driven by drugs and, therefore, were not as desperate and unpredictable as the street people of today. When the winos needed money, they panhandled or collected refundable bottles. On occasion they threw advertising circulars door-to-door, unloaded produce trucks at the French Market, and even worked Lucky Dog carts. Most still possessed a faint trace of a work ethic. They just didn't want to exercise it unless it was positively the last resort.

Tom's apartment overlooked the city's premier wine-tasting corner. Also located within the view from his window were several dollar-a-night flophouses. These offered cheap, bare-essential accommodations. The walls needed painting and the floors weren't clean, but the buildings did offer shelter from the elements. Also, for no additional charge, the boarder had access to a shower and restroom.

The flophouses were large gutted buildings usually containing cots placed in rows against the walls and down the middle of the room. They reminded me of old run-down military barracks. But what could you expect for a buck? You paid your dollar and you got use of a cot for eight hours. Each bed served three shifts a day. If you wanted to sleep longer, you paid another dollar.

There were also a few unwritten rules that new boarders needed to master quickly. First, before going to sleep, you needed to put your shoes under the head of your bed between the mattress and the springs. If you didn't, more than likely when you awoke your shoes would be on someone else's feet. Number two: in winter, if you are lucky enough to have a jacket, use it as your pillow. If someone then tries to steal it, you'll probably feel the thief's tug. The flophouses weren't the Hilton, but they filled a much-needed niche.

Tom's one-room efficiency apartment at Julia and Camp was a small step up from the flops. The walls were dirty and dingy. The only light in the room was a naked bulb dangling from the ceiling by an electrical cord. The kitchen facilities consisted of a hot plate and coffeepot sitting on the dresser. One bathroom serviced the entire floor. Tom's room, however, offered one great advantage over the flophouses: privacy. The six-paneled wooden door had a sliding bolt mounted on the inside for security. On the outside there was a hasp so that he could padlock the room when he left.

The building itself was a nineteenth-century, four-story, red-brick structure with a balcony that ran across the front and the left side of the second floor. The six-foot-high windows opening onto the balcony generally were raised to allow air to circulate throughout the un-air-conditioned rooms. The rental agreement was simple. You paid a week's rent in advance on Sunday or you were out on the street by noon Monday. You knew and accepted the terms before you moved in. No excuses, no exceptions, no checks.

Several old geezers sharing a bottle of Mad Dog 20/20 were standing on the corner of Camp and Julia when I arrived. They were trading tall tales about the unfortunate set of circumstances that had led to their financial demise and thus resulted in their being on this corner this very morning. I wasn't interested in their tragic past. I had problems of my own in the present, the most immediate of which was finding Tom.

I discovered that the task was more difficult than I had expected. His building's main entrance was locked from the inside. I banged on the door; there was no response. One of the windows to his room was open, so I shouted his name. When I still received no answer, I began tossing rocks against the windowpanes. This tactic didn't attract him, but it did rouse the interest of the downtrodden on the corner. As they moved in toward me, I could hear them arguing over whether I was a narcotics agent, a bill collector, or a bounty hunter. A few staggered up and offered pitching instructions, while others just cheered or jeered depending on the accuracy of my throw.

Getting nowhere, I decided to switch to a more aggressive tactic. I pulled the company's old white supercab Ford pickup truck up on the sidewalk, climbed on top of its roof, then hoisted myself up onto the balcony. On the sidewalk below me an increasing crowd of intoxicated cheerleaders waved their bottles over their heads and chanted, "Go, go!" Rush-hour traffic on Camp Street almost came to a halt as drivers slowed down to catch a glimpse of what was creating such a commotion.

Once on the balcony I could see through Tom's open window. Stretched out face down across the sheetless bed was Tom, fully dressed and snoring loudly. I yelled his name several times. He didn't budge. The more he snored, the angrier I got. I crawled through the window, walked to his bed, leaned over, and shouted, "Wake up!" He rolled over, looked up through glazed, bloodshot eyes, then tried to talk. His brain was sending messages to his lips, but only garbled sounds were exiting his mouth. It didn't matter: he was alive. If he was alive, he could work. If he could work, he was coming with me.

Once I got him to his feet, I went down the stairs and out to the truck. I was met with rousing applause, a strange-sounding chorus of off-key "hip hoorays," and a few slaps on the back by the locals. One or two asked if I had busted the guy. A couple offered swigs from their bottle in honor of a job well done. And one highly inebriated, scraggly character informed me that until that day he had never really believed in Batman. But only moments before he had personally seen the caped crusader leap from the roof of a truck onto a balcony and then gracefully disappear right before his very eyes. His interpretation of what had just transpired brought some humor to a rather dismal morning.

Tom made it through the day, but both he and I knew that he couldn't handle the job on a steady basis. He was too tied to the bottle. The following day I reassigned him to his corner. At least there, if he showed up late for work, it didn't affect anyone but himself. To take his place I hired Daniel. Daniel had wandered in off the street hoping to find employment as a vendor. Instead, he suddenly discovered that he was being hired as a manager. He was clean and neat, in his late thirties, and he seemed capable of handling the job. As when Sally had been hired, there was time neither for a background search nor for extensive interviews. Daniel's training began immediately. I figured that a more detailed investigation into his past could be pursued later in the week if he lasted that long.

The new recruit caught on amazingly fast. By the end of the first week he was performing excellently. By the end of the second week he had advanced enough that I spoke with Doug (the formality of "Mr. Talbot" had long since been dropped) about giving him a raise. Finally, I thought, I have found someone capable who was willing to handle the day shift. The future was starting to look bright.

Unfortunately, during Dan's fifth week of employment he quit. I was stunned. There was absolutely no reason from management's point of view that he should leave. I asked for an explanation.

"It's the money," he said.

I reminded him that at New Year's and Mardi Gras he would receive a generous bonus. "That's not it," he explained. "I'm making too much money."

"You're quitting because you're making too much money?" I was confused. The idea that I was overpaying him had never entered my mind. Daniel had been staying at the mission. His only possessions were those that he could safely stuff under his mattress. The weekly paycheck allowed him to move from the rescue mission into a one-room efficiency apartment. In addition to the small transistor radio that he had depended on for entertainment, he now owned a black-and-white television. He also had purchased a toaster, a few pots and pans, an electric clock radio, towels, sheets, and a bedspread. His apartment was becoming home. He was settling down.

However, suddenly having roots and responsibility frightened him. His solution was to quit. He stuffed what belongings he could into an old army duffel bag, sold the rest, and went back out on the road. Every so often he would drift back into town, work a cart for a couple of days, then disappear again for months. I haven't seen him since the early 1980s. I hope he finally settled down, or else changed his migratory route. I worry sometimes that in our increasingly violent world he may have ended up an urban murder statistic. His life style made him an extremely vulnerable target.

To take Daniel's place I hired Jim Sloan. Sloan originally worked for the company as a night vendor on Bourbon Street, but more recently he had taken over the spot in the Square. I had tried to persuade him to accept the manager's position before I hired Daniel, but he had declined. With the position once again open he changed his mind. Pushing a cart to the Square and working out in the elements day after day had become a little too much for this man in his late fifties.

Sloan was reliable, well spoken, and a good organizer. Physically he could do the job. His drawbacks were that he was high-strung, temperamental, and impulsive in his reactions. However, he assured me that he could keep his emotions under control.

As he settled into his new position, there was an atmosphere of stability in the shop. Four vendors in our crew of fourteen had been with us for over a year, and one as long as five. The others were basically transients, but that wasn't a problem. Lucky Dogs had a large pool of vendors that regularly wandered in and out of town depending upon the season. The largest influx occurred shortly after the first heavy snowfall up north. The greatest exodus occurred in late spring as sweltering heat and increasing humidity blanketed the Quarter. New faces also regularly joined our ever-increasing herd of migratory laborers.

Summer was the toughest time for us to maintain a full crew. We lost our professional carnies in early spring as their road shows broke winter quarters. They wouldn't return again until the fall. Other vendors also headed north or west where prearranged summer jobs were waiting. Their departures left us with a large vendor void during June, July, and August. Four or five corners were always open. It was a problem, but eventually a few of the old regulars would drift into town broke and needing work. Until they arrived, I tried to overcome the shortage by running help-wanted ads in the paper. I visited the missions trying to recruit workers, canvassed the streets, and offered a five-dollar reward to our present vendors for anyone that they brought in who worked a full night. On more than one occasion I even picked up a hitchhiker who looked like potential vendor material. I hated the summers. The temperature was always too hot and the vendors too few.

Another problem surfaced shortly after Sloan came into the shop. Vendors on Bourbon began being harassed as they tried to work their corners. Normally, obnoxious drunks caused such hassles. My response was then to ask the police to run the troublemaker down the block. This time that recourse wouldn't work. Our problem was the police. The great majority of officers in the Quarter were professionals who did a marvelous job, but two cops in particular loved making the vendors' lives miserable.

Police officer A (I refuse to give him any notoriety) would walk up to one of our carts and inform the vendor that he could no longer remain where he was presently parked. It didn't matter that we had had a cart at that same exact spot for over thirty years. The vendor was ordered to move his cart across the street immediately or he'd be hauled to jail. Naturally, the vendor moved. Officer B would then appear demanding that the vendor push back to where he belonged. The vendor would try to explain that he had been forced to move to this spot by another officer. Officer B would get in his face, as a marine drill sergeant might do to a raw recruit, and shout, "Do you see any other police officer? No. So move your ass back across the street or I'll haul it to jail."

Predictably, the vendor pushed his cart back across the street to its original location. Suddenly, Officer A would reappear, hostile because the vendor had failed to follow his orders. After filling a few minutes with threats, Officer A would change his approach and announce that he'd give the vendor a break. Instead of running him in, the officer would let him go. However, the vendor had to close down, push his cart back to the shop, and stay out of the Quarter for the remainder of the night. Naturally, the vendor accepted these terms.

This scenario generally played on Friday and Saturday nights. We lost sales and the vendors lost their weekend commissions and tips. This power drama made it difficult for both the company and the vendor to survive financially. The clean-cut, conscientious vendors who had never had a problem with the law became frightened and quit. Of course, the street-hardened guys weren't bothered in the least. They had been in tougher joints than New Orleans' Central Lock-Up. A few even suggested that we call the cops' bluff by refusing to move. They volunteered to get arrested so that our company attorney could argue the case before a judge. Doug and I considered the offer, but our fear was that the officers might book the vendor on a more serious, trumped-up charge. That twist had happened once before.

Not long after I started working full-time for Lucky Dogs, two police officers came to the shop wanting to see Doug. I made arrangements for them to meet with him that afternoon. The officers were furious because during a sting operation, one of our vendors had stung them. They had purchased from the vendor a small plastic bag containing what they believed to be marijuana. The police lab's analysis concluded that the bag's contents were simply leaves from ordinary house plants. As a result, the officers had taken considerable ribbing from others in their precinct. In spite of the embarrassment, they claimed that all they wanted was for the vendor to return the money. No charges would be pressed.

Unfortunately, the vendor had left town. We assured the officers that if he returned, they would be notified. In less than three weeks the vendor in question, Vince, was back in the shop looking for work.

I asked him about the incident. He remembered the two men immediately and claimed that they had badgered him about buying marijuana. He tried to convince them that the only goods he sold off his cart were Lucky Dogs, but they persisted. So he figured, what the hell, he would teach the "doinks" a lesson. He filled a plastic bag with dead leaves from his neighbor's garden, and that night when the two men returned he sold it to them. He hadn't realized then that he was selling the bogus drugs to undercover policemen.

As a result of his actions, a warrant was issued for his arrest, but the officers had assured us that the problem could be resolved, especially since Vince was willing to return the money. A meeting between all parties took place in my office. Vince refunded the money and the officers reiterated that all charges would be dropped. However, it would be necessary for Vince to accompany them to the station to clear up the remaining paperwork. Within an hour, they surmised, he should be back at the shop ready for work.

Vince didn't return that afternoon. Nor did he return the following morning. The third day he called in a panic. He was in Central Lockup being held for possession of cocaine with the intent to distribute. The officers had exacted their revenge.

The situation could have been disastrous. Fortunately, Doug knew the judge that was to hear Vince's case. After speaking with Doug, Vince, and the officers involved, the judge dismissed all charges. Vince had come extremely close to spending several years in the state penitentiary on a trumped-up charge.

With that past experience imbedded in our memories, we decided not to let any of the vendors risk being arrested. If necessary, we would find another way to bring our difficulties with Officers A and B before the courts. To begin with, we followed the proper chain of command. I reported our problems to the sergeant in command of the Bourbon Street detail. Though he assured me that he would look into the matter, nothing changed. I next spoke with the captain of the First District. He honestly tried to help, but he had bigger problems demanding his attention than the bullying of a few Lucky Dog vendors. As a last resort, I went out on the street to try and reason with the two officers. It was a waste of time. I was informed that if our vendors were not wearing their red-and-white striped Lucky Dog shirts and the company's paper overseas-style caps, they would be run in. It didn't matter that our vendors were violating no law: the two cops made their own rules, and those rules were not subject to debate.

When I left the street that night, I was frustrated. I went home and typed a three-page, single-spaced report describing in detail exactly what had happened. The next morning Doug read it. Afterwards, he telephoned Joel Loeffelholz, the attorney who had represented the city in its Supreme Court case concerning street vending and who presently was the city attorney assigned to the police department. Loeffelholz assessed the problem and concluded that it was simply two officers wanting their palms greased. He advised Doug to turn my report over to the NOPD's Internal Affairs division.

Not long after taking Loeffelholz' recommended course of action, I was notified by the city's permit department that I had to attend a meeting at city hall.

Doug decided that we should have legal representation at the meeting. Therefore, he hired Loeffelholz, the most knowledgeable attorney in town in matters concerning street vending. Loeffelholz had just resigned from the city attorney's office and gone into private practice. Also to be present at the gathering were a representative from the finance department, Officer A, and the owner of a restaurant who had complained to the city that we were illegally operating outside of his establishment.

It's true: our vendor had occasionally parked on the street near the gentleman's establishment, but only after Officer A had forced him to move there. Even so, according to the law, we were within our legal rights to set up at that location, but we didn't want to be there. We wanted to be across the street where we normally parked. That was the point of greatest foot traffic: the greater the foot traffic, the greater the sales. But the troublesome cops looked after the jazz club on that corner during their nightly rounds, and they worked there as private detail officers on their days off. They had decided that they didn't want a Lucky Dog cart outside of "their club."

In fact, all of our problem locations were spots outside of clubs where Officers A and B occasionally worked as private detail officers. It didn't matter that Lucky Dogs had worked those corners since 1947. It didn't matter that we were legal. What did matter to the officers was the old Chicago-style mob tactic: pay a protection premium or be forced out of business. Filled with self-importance, Officer A intended to use the meeting at city hall to showcase his power. The representative of the finance department was completely unaware of the underlying coercion. All she had seen was the information supplied by the officer and the complaint from the restaurateur, who was a friend of the officer's.

I was the first to arrive for the meeting. The finance department's representative walked in next, followed a few minutes later by the officer and then the restaurateur. The officer and businessman sat side by side. I was seated directly across from them at the large wooden conference table. The duo chatted, joked, and were apparently quite certain that once and for all they were going to have the hot dog carts kicked off the corners in question. Their faces radiated confidence.

With all parties appearing to her to be present, the finance department's representative requested that the meeting begin. I asked that we wait. My legal counsel had not yet arrived, I explained, and it was still ten minutes until the meeting was officially scheduled to begin. The officer appeared surprised. He had not anticipated that an attorney would represent us.

When Joel walked through the door the patrolman's face lit up. He assumed that he himself would receive Joel's legal representation. He greeted our attorney, shook hands, and offered him a chair. When Joel walked around the table and sat beside me, the cop turned pale. Joel, seeing the reaction, explained that he was now in private practice and was here on behalf of Lucky Dogs.

The officer knew that he didn't have a prayer. Suddenly, he changed his strategy and blamed the restaurant owner for making too big a deal out of a vendor accidentally parking on the wrong side of the street.

Naturally, the restaurateur was stunned. His compatriot had suddenly turned on him and was attempting to make him the sacrificial lamb. Immediately, he shot back that the whole problem had been created because the patrolman intentionally forced the hot dog vendor to move his cart from his normal location.

Joel, taking the offensive, informed the officer and those assembled that he had requested and received a ruling from the city attorney's office explaining in detail where Lucky Dog carts could and could not legally operate. From this point on, he warned, he never wanted to hear about the illegal shifting of carts from one side of the street to the other. As a result of the meeting, our problems with Officers A and B disappeared.

However, three other challenges beset us during the fall of 1977. The first involved a heavyset, sixty-five-year-old vendor named David Overstreet. Overstreet, earlier in life, had been a motion picture actor. He had never reached star status, but he had managed to eke out a living. Because of his involvement in the movies, he considered himself an authority on the art of film-making. This conviction came to create problems for one modern-day producer.

Late one afternoon, a rather distraught gentleman walked into my office. His movie crew was attempting to shoot a street scene down the block, but unfortunately, for the last half-hour one of our vendors had kept wandering onto his set shouting commands. Cameramen were being told how to position their equipment. Actors were being coached on how to deliver their lines. Lights were shifted and props were being rearranged. As fast as the police escorted him off one side of the set, he would reappear from another direction. Not only was it irritating, it was causing delays; and in the movie industry, time is money. The producer had thus far resisted having the vendor arrested but warned that, if I could not control the man, then he would have to call for police assistance.

I accompanied the film-maker to the site. There amid the cameras and actors was Overstreet barking out commands. He was moving at lightning speed. His eyes shone, his voice had new life in it: he looked twenty years younger. He was doing what he loved.

It hurt, but I had to destroy his dream—either that or watch him go to jail. Reluctantly, I called him over and explained that I expected him to proceed immediately to the shop, set up his cart, and push to his corner. If he didn't then he was fired. I hoped that the ultimatum would work and that he would accompany me back to Lucky Dogs. It did. Ostentatiously, Overstreet sauntered over to the producer and announced that the shoot would have to continue without his expertise. His talents, at this very moment, were in great demand elsewhere. At that point he gallantly motioned farewell to the actors and strolled off the set. It was a grand performance and justifiably drew an ovation from the cast.

Six weeks later I had to contend with another incident involving Overstreet. This time the results were not quite so pleasant. Doug and I had kept him working even though we both knew that it was detrimental to the company's image. We knew that if we released him, he had nowhere else to go. It was a humanitarian act, but a lousy business decision. We had even moved him off Bourbon and put him on Decatur Street near the shop. There it wouldn't matter that his clothes needed washing or that he fell asleep while sitting on his stool. The only people who would see him were the pimps, prostitutes, and seamen. He might even fit in. It worked well for a while, but then his mind started to deteriorate at a rapid rate.

One evening as I was about to enter the shop, I glanced down the block where Overstreet parked his cart. I noticed that he was barefoot. So I walked to the corner and inquired as to the whereabouts of his shoes and socks.

"My feet got cold," he replied.

I was puzzled. "But if you were wearing your shoes and socks, your feet would be warmer."

"My shoes were cold, too."

"Where are your shoes now?"

He reached forward and opened his hot dog steamer. Sitting on the stainless steel tray next to the hot dog buns were two old funky size-ten brown leather shoes and a pair of filthy crew socks. He was getting them nice and toasty before putting them back on his feet. At that mo-

David Overstreet and his soon-to-be-steamed shoes
Courtesy Judy Cooper

ment I knew that the end had come. I pushed his cart in and instructed him to report to the shop the following afternoon. Doug arranged for him to meet with a representative from the city's social services department. We knew that he couldn't continue working a cart, but at the same time we wanted to make certain that he had some place to go. Obviously, he had reached a point where he needed special attention.

Not long after Overstreet left the company, Adler became the victim of an unfortunate attack. The flower vendor who parked his cart beside Adler's hot dog stand mistakenly thought that Adler had stolen something off of his wagon. Witnesses later identified the character that actually had committed the crime, but by then it was too late. Sammy, the flower vendor, had already struck Adler across the face twice with a heavy piece of chain. A couple of the street people wrestled the flower vendor to the ground and halted the attack.

Adler's right eye was almost swollen shut and his face was severely bruised. Doctors advised him not to work for at least a week. The police were never called. Adler had been thrown into a cab and rushed to Charity Hospital. One of the locals pushed his cart to the shop. The flower vendor within minutes had fled the scene. There was no one left to make a police report.

A few hours after the incident, the attacker, frightened that Adler's friends were going to seek revenge, contacted me by phone. I agreed to mediate between him and our vendors, but for the present I suggested that he stay out of sight.

Adler showed up the next morning looking like he had gone the distance with Frenchy. His face was contorted and his right eye looked awful. Besides his physical suffering he now had a financial problem. His rent was due and he had no savings and no potential income. Plus, he had to eat. To him the lack of funds was the key issue. I knew that I could handle that problem. My main concern was to stave off a vending war between the two companies. With the kind of crews that we both had, retaliatory strikes were entirely possible.

That afternoon I came up with a creative solution. I set up an immediate meeting with Sammy and Adler at a neutral public site, the Pair-of-Dice. After some heated discussions, both sides reluctantly agreed to the rendezvous. Adler and I arrived first and sat at the back corner table. A few minutes later Sammy cautiously walked in. The atmosphere was tense. The slightest mistake in the negotiations and I knew that I would have a brawl on my hands.

I first reviewed with Adler the fact that because of his injury, he was going to lose a week's income. Not to mention that he was made to deal with considerable pain and suffering. Then I pointed out to Sammy that one of two things could potentially happen to him. On the one hand, he could be arrested for assault with intent to do bodily harm. He would be tried and then sent to jail. On the other hand, one dark night he might meet an unfriendly group of Adler's allies, and I wouldn't want to speculate on what might happen. Bearing the troubles of both men in mind, I was ready to offer a solution. First, Adler had to agree not to press charges. Second, he had to assure me that there would never be any kind of revenge exacted against Sammy. In return for these assurances, Sammy had to compensate Adler $30 per day for the six days that he couldn't work. He didn't have to pay him for his normally scheduled day off. In addition, a sum of $50 had to be given Adler in reparation for pain and suffering. A total of $230: a small fee for Sammy to pay to stay out of prison and to remain physically unharmed.

Adler scoffed at what he considered to be such a puny settlement. Sammy thought that having to pay anything was absurd. I explained that it was the fairest solution that I could conceive. If it wasn't satisfactory, then they would have to let the police and the courts handle it. Of course, if Sammy went to jail, then Adler would receive nothing. And certainly it would cost Sammy much more than $230 to hire a defense attorney. They both sat in silence. Both knew the unspoken option was that Sammy could just split town.

As I started to rise from my chair, Adler mumbled that he would accept the settlement. Seconds later Sammy agreed to the deal. I sat back down and formally scribbled the terms on a bar napkin. Both signed it and I served as the witness. Case closed. I gave the full cash settlement to Adler that afternoon and Sammy repaid the company in several weekly installments. The following week they were once again the best of friends working side by side on the corner of Bienville and Bourbon as if nothing had happened.

The next crisis involved Dan Myers, the vendor who worked the corner of Toulouse and Bourbon. Dan was a very likable guy in his late twenties. He was of medium height, physically fit, clean cut, and well educated. Like many vendors during the seventies he had a drinking problem. It didn't often surface, but when it did it was obvious. Dan was one of those happy drunks. There were nights when he would suddenly go on a binge, and by the time he pushed in to the shop he was sixty dollars short. He would have stopped off at one of his favorite spots and used the company's money to buy all of his buddies a couple of drinks. When that happened, we would mark the shortage on his check-in sheet and then send him home in a cab. The next afternoon he always showed up asking how much he owed. He would promptly pay his bill and religiously profess that that was the last time he would ever pull such a stupid stunt.

One evening Myers came to the kitchen counter so blitzed that he failed to bring his unsold hot dogs with him. When he walked out into the shop to retrieve them, he started screaming, "Some bastard stole my wienie wagon." But no one had seen anyone push a cart out the door. In fact, no one had seen Dan push his cart in the door. It suddenly dawned on us that the cart had never been brought to the shop; he had forgotten it on his corner. One of his fellow vendors went and retrieved it. By now Dan had slithered to the floor and was sound asleep with his back against the walk-in cooler. Miraculously, on this occasion he had enough money to pay his bill.

There was another time, however, when Fortuna spun his life totally out of control. At 2:30 A.M. on a cold November morning I was sound asleep in my bed when the phone rang. A voice on the other end of the line kept repeating, "Don't hang up, I'm in jail and this is my last call."

I recognized the voice. It was Dan. I responded, "What did you do?"

"Nothing. I was just sleeping in bed when the police came in and arrested me. I didn't do anything. I was just sleeping."

"Dan, cut the crap and tell me what they arrested you for."

"Well, for discharging a firearm in the city limits."

"You shot a gun while you were sleeping?"

"No, it wasn't me. While I was asleep my roommate and some of his friends came back to the apartment and took his .38 pistol and went out on the balcony and shot it into the air. I didn't even hear the gun go off. Someone on the street saw them and called the cops."

I assured Dan that if his story was true, then he would probably be released in the morning. All he had to do was explain to the judge what had happened and have his friends verify it.

"There is one other slight problem," he said.

"What's that?" I asked, growing wary.

"When the police came into the apartment they found a bag of weed sitting on top of my dresser. So they also booked me with possession of marijuana."

"Damn. Firearms and drugs. I really don't see how I can help you, other than to recommend an attorney." Then he admitted that he faced one other slight complication: his roommate's friends were minors. Guns, drugs, and minors. At that point I lit into him. I didn't care how much he screwed up his own life, but to involve kids was lower than I had ever dreamed he would stoop. I yelled that if he was even partially responsible for the minors' corruption, then I hoped he was found guilty and rotted in jail.

He kept pleading, "Wait. Wait. Don't hang up. I swear I had no idea that my roommate was bringing anyone underage home." Then he switched gears. "Please, I need a favor. I have a P.O. box. In a few days a brown envelope will arrive there. A man owes me some money for some photography work that I've done for him. I need you to bring the cash in the envelope to me. Just tell the postal worker that you're me and that you forgot your key. I'll tell you my address, social security number, driver's license number, etc. He should give it to you."

"Are you crazy?" I exclaimed. "That's a federal offense. Besides, brown envelopes filled with cash mailed to P.O. boxes tend to frighten me."

"OK, then would you at least go to my apartment and get a black briefcase out of my closet and hold it for me. It has some photographs in it that I would prefer the authorities didn't find."

I reiterated that I didn't want to get involved. I knew that he had been a professional photographer and that he still did some picture taking on the side. He had always claimed that he was shooting weddings and receptions. No one would mind the police seeing such photographs. I now suspected pornography, perhaps even involving minors. I felt that the chips should fall where they may. Again I declined to help in anything that I considered possibly illegal.

I recommended that he call his mother. On two occasions, she had called the shop looking for him, and I had spoken with her. From our conversations I gathered that she was a widow and financially well off. She seemed to be a charming woman who had spent much of her life bailing her only child out of bad marriages and county jails. He admitted that he had already called her. This time she had advised him that he was on his own. Then she politely told him good night. I recommended that he contact a good lawyer and a very understanding priest.

Two days later I received a letter at home. There was nothing unusual about the envelope other than it provided no return address. Inside I found two five-hundred-dollar money orders made out to Dan. Enclosed was a note simply stating, "Please see that Dan gets this." It bore no name, just a P.O. box number from a small town in central Louisiana. I made photocopies of the money orders, the envelope, and the note. Next, I wrote a letter of my own fully explaining the circumstances surrounding my receipt of the money orders and included a photocopy of the envelope that they had arrived in. Only then, with these documents, did I mail Dan his money orders. I wanted to make certain that whoever screened his mail would learn up front what had happened. I didn't know what Dan had been involved in, but good or bad I didn't want to be implicated in any part of it. I then sent a note to the mysterious P.O. box stating that in the future I would appreciate it if Dan's mail was sent directly to him, care of New Orleans' Central Lockup. At the bottom of the note I included his cell number and address. I figured that the money orders had come from either his mother or the owner of the brown envelope. If his mother was responsible, I didn't mind passing them on to him. But I wanted no part of anything from the mysterious money man.

By the end of the week Dan was out of jail. All charges against him had been dropped. His roommate was charged with discharging a firearm within the city limits and contributing to the delinquency of minors. Neither had been charged with possession of marijuana. The bag was never mentioned in court, and they certainly weren't going to ask the cops what happened to it.

A few days after his release Dan moved out of his apartment and put his belongings in storage. He then headed home to mend his relationship with his mother. Several months later he stopped by the shop. He was in town retrieving his belongings. He wanted me to know that he was trying to turn his life around. He was permanently moving back to his hometown. I applauded his decision.

After he left, I found an envelope addressed to me on my desk. Enclosed was a thank-you card and seventy-five dollars in cash. Dan wanted me to take my wife out to eat at his expense. It was a gesture of appreciation for all of the times that I had put up with him coming in blitzed, that I had loaned him money to pay his rent, that he had called my house in the middle of the night. His idea was thoughtful; but instead of taking Jane out, I decided to order pizza for the entire crew. After all, they were the ones who had pushed his cart in when he got drunk, held him up while he staggered toward the shop, and waited an hour while he fumbled around at the check-in counter.

In the fall of 1977 Dan wasn't the only employee to leave Lucky Dogs. Jim Sloan, our day manager, also departed but under rather suspicious circumstances. At about 1:30 on a busy Saturday afternoon, Sloan decided to go out to lunch after having dispatched the night vendors who had shown up early for work. The Tulane Green Wave were playing at home, the LSU Tigers were playing in Baton Rouge, and the Saints had a game in the Superdome on Sunday. The Quarter already had a heavy influx of partying football fans. Sloan said that he would be back within a half-hour, but by 6:00 P.M. he hadn't returned. His glasses were still lying on the check-in counter. The basket of personal clothes that he had brought to the shop to wash was still sitting in a corner in the kitchen where he had left it.

When Sloan didn't show up the following morning, I checked his apartment. He wasn't there. None of his neighbors had seen him. He didn't drink, so I knew that he wasn't on a binge. I talked to his artist friends in Jackson Square, checked the restaurants that he frequented, called the hospitals, called Central Lockup to see if he had been arrested, and even checked the city morgue. There was no trace of him. Even his police friends in the Square were worried about him. After forty-eight hours the officers put out a missing-persons bulletin on him. Sloan had simply vanished without a trace. More and more it appeared that he had been the victim of foul play.

I put his glasses in the safe. I washed his clothes and packed them in a box. Days turned into weeks, and fall turned into winter. Thanksgiving came and went and the number of shopping days remaining before Christmas was dwindling.

On a cold, damp morning I was alone in the shop when I had the distinct feeling that someone was watching me. I turned around, and standing at the check-in counter was Sloan. For a split second I didn't

Jim Sloan on a quiet day in Jackson Square
Courtesy Gene J. Hymel

think that he was real, but there he stood wearing a heavy jacket and wool gloves. I was elated that he was alive. Then I was furious that he hadn't called to let us know he was OK.

As if he had never been gone, Sloan asked, "Do you know where my glasses are? I left them lying here on the counter." The more the reality set in that he was alive, the angrier I grew. I hauled him into the office, threw him into a chair, and lectured to him as a father would do to a son.

"Do you know the trouble that you've caused? The grief? The time wasted looking for you? Do you have any idea how many people were upset when you disappeared?" I ranted for a few minutes, then calmed down. I was twenty-six; he was in his late fifties. He sat quietly and just stared down at the floor until I finished.

He then explained his disappearance. With Thanksgiving drawing close, he began to feel lonely. His only living relative was a niece in St. Louis. As he started walking to Mena's for lunch that final Saturday afternoon, he suddenly felt a tremendous urge to visit her. He simply walked past the restaurant to the Greyhound bus station, purchased a ticket, and within minutes was aboard a bus heading north. He hadn't planned the trip. It just happened. Several times, he confessed, he had thought about calling, but at the last minute he always decided against it, choosing instead to wait and explain in person what had happened.

I would have strangled him then and there, but death would have been too kind. Instead, I wanted him to have to squirm and sweat as his police officer friends in the Square grilled him about his whereabouts for the last several months. They were not going to be so forgiving. After all, they had put out a missing-persons bulletin on a transient who had simply gone on an extended lunch break. That kind of action is tough to live down back at district headquarters.

4
The Board of Health and the Mafia

Standing in the entrance to the shop was the shadowy figure of a man, arms folded, sun shining brightly behind him. He was hesitant about entering. When I approached him, I saw that his was an unfamiliar face.

"Is there something I can do for you?" I inquired.

"I don't think so. I need a job, but I don't need no trouble."

"What makes you think that you would have trouble?"

"I heard about your vendors getting hassled by the cops."

"Where did you hear that?"

"In Atlanta."

"Atlanta!"

"Yeah. A guy came into the mission where I was staying yesterday. Used to work for y'all. Told us all about the cops messing with him."

I was amazed that the news had traveled so far so fast. I mention this incident because it shows how the underground communication system in this nation works. Wealthy travelers stay at four-star accommodations. Businessmen frequent nationally known hotel and motel chains. Transients hit the road and spend the night at relief missions and flophouses, where they find cheap clean beds and free meals. Information travels with these drifters at the speed of a Greyhound bus or as fast as their thumbs can carry them. As they hang around the missions waiting to register for the night, they hear stories about the best places to make a few bucks as well as the towns to avoid. They learn about local sheriffs who do and don't like drifters. They discover where others have been or where they're going, mention wardens they've known and women they'd like to forget.

The transients' communication system is not technologically advanced, but it is highly efficient. On several occasions people passing through New Orleans have dropped by the shop to say, "So-and-so asked me to tell you that he'll be back in about six weeks, so save him a good corner." Other times it was I who needed to pass on information, to ex-vendors, for example, who had left our employ. I would simply ask the next vendor heading out of town to spread my message wherever he traveled. Usually within a couple of weeks I'd get a call: "I heard you wanted to talk to me." The success rate of this system was incredible. Tapping into the network, the drifter from Atlanta knew that we had had problems, but also jobs. Once assured that our troubles were over, he filled out an application and joined our ranks.

During this latter part of 1977 Sloan had returned and was once again assigned to work the Square. Red Lott was serving as night manager, Darryl Haggerty was day manager, and part-time vendor David Borell was being trained as relief manager. On the street were regulars: Bill McCarty, William Gillette, Howard Lewis, Scott Adler, Jim Campbell, Dixie Doonan, and Andrew Walsh. Five or six other corners were filled by less permanent personnel.

As was normal, the managers' positions were in constant flux. The night manager would get tired of working the late shift and transfer to days. The day manager would temporarily take over nights. Sometimes a manager would choose to get out of the shop altogether and return to selling on the street. A vendor would then come in and take over the vacant manager's position. I always had managers. I just never knew from day to day who they were going to be.

On the morning of December 30, 1977, while Darryl Haggerty was on the day shift, a vendor unscrewed the control valve on a propane tank too far. As a result, the mechanism's stem was broken at its base, and the release valve was thus locked in the open position. As long as the cylinder remained connected to the Lucky Dog cart's burner, the *off-on* knob of the stove could control the gas. Petrolane Gas Service recommended that the tank remain in the cart until all of the gas was consumed. Once emptied, the cylinder could be disconnected from the regulator and brought in for repair. It seemed so simple.

Three days later, on the morning of the 1978 Sugar Bowl game, the shop was swarming with activity. Vendors were loading their carts with hot dogs, buns, and condiments prior to pushing to the Superdome in hopes of catching hungry football fans outside the stadium. Darryl was checking each cart to make certain that it had enough gas to last until the next morning, and I was issuing supplies. When Darryl came to the broken tank, he lifted it to check its weight. It felt extremely light. He then tried to light the cart's stove, but the burner would not sustain a flame. He concluded that the tank was empty; and after I, too, had checked the cylinder, I agreed with him. At that point, we judged that it would be safe to remove the tank from the cart.

As a precautionary measure, I pushed the cart out of the shop and into the common patio that adjoined the rear of our building—the same patio where Sally had been attacked by the dive-bombing fighter planes. Darryl carefully loosened the gas regulator's brass fitting. No distinctive odor of propane was noticeable, nor did we hear the hissing sound of escaping gas. Carefully, Darryl removed the tank from the cart. Because of his training as a fuel specialist in the air force, I felt confident that he had everything under control.

The morning was cold, with temperatures in the twenties. Darryl was wearing a jacket. I had on a heavy sweater. All went smoothly until

Darryl unknowingly set the cylinder down on a piece of brick instead of on the flat, concrete patio floor. As he released the tank, it tumbled over. A massive cloud of gas erupted from the bottle and engulfed us. Suddenly, it ignited—no one really knows why—and the result was a flash fire that lasted but a split second.

During that second, my sweater melted, my jeans were scorched, my hair was singed, and my eyebrows were burned off. Instinctively, I had raised my hands, palms out, to cover my eyes. Both hands were severely burned. Scorched flesh dangled from them as if it had been peeled. The blaze had only flashed, but I sustained second-degree burns of the face and deep second-degree and third-degree burns on both hands. I also had burn areas on the abdomen, back, left elbow, and right leg. Had it not been for the sweater and denim jeans, my injuries would have been much worse. Darryl's lightweight trousers disintegrated, leaving him with a greater degree of damage around his calves and thighs.

When the gas ignited, I dived through an opening in the patio wall that had once been a window, belly-landing in the shell parking lot next door. After rolling over several times to smother the fire on my jeans and sweater, I jumped up and ran around the block to the Pair-of-Dice in search of ice. There wasn't time to ask the bartender for permission. I simply leaped over the bar, flung open the door of the stainless steel ice bin, and began grabbing giant handfuls of ice cubes and pressing them against my hands and face. The bartender was momentarily stunned. Once over the shock yet failing to recognize me because of my condition, he demanded rather emphatically that I "get the f—— out from behind [his] counter."

I thought, "Screw him. There's nothing that he can possibly do to hurt me any worse than I am hurting now." At first the ice soothed the pain. But the relief didn't last long. Without going into lengthy details, I recovered without any noticeable scarring, thanks to a doctor who knew and applied the latest burn treatments. For six weeks, though, I lost the use of my hands. I was also advised to stay out of the sun for a year in order to give my skin ample time to recover. As a precaution, I wore broad-rimmed hats. The pimps on Decatur all thought I was trying to copy their stylish ways. On several occasions I heard "right on" as I passed them on the sidewalk.

Someone had called the fire department in response to the ignited gas, but the building sustained no physical damage. Had Darryl and I not been burned, there would have been no evidence that the fire had occurred. However, a local television station monitoring police and fire frequencies picked up the emergency transmission and sent a young reporter to the scene.

The newsman was shocked at what he discovered. Carts were parked haphazardly throughout the building. Vendors who had stayed out past dawn to catch the Sugar Bowl fans in their last feeding frenzy of the night were still waiting to be checked in. Day vendors were just preparing to go out. Admittedly, the premises looked a wreck, especially since no one was in control. Darryl and I had been taken to the hospital, Doug had not yet arrived, and Red was home sleeping after completing the night shift.

Certainly, to the reporter or anyone else not familiar with the company's changing of shifts during Mardi Gras or New Year's, the shop would appear to be a mass of confusion. However, on these occasions, within less than three hours, all of the carts are cleaned, the supplies are reissued, the floors are mopped, and everything once again appears calm. During the entire period, the meat is kept either in the walk-in cooler or in the carts' cookers. Both maintain the required temperatures for safe food handling.

On the day of the fire, everyone was milling about waiting for someone to take charge. Finally, one of the vendors ran four blocks to the Toulouse Hotel to wake up Red. A tired and dragging Lott returned to the shop, and with the help of the vendors everything soon started looking organized. The following morning David Borel took over as day manager, and Robert Cooper, an ex-carny, was promoted to the relief slot. Cooper on a good day was an average vendor. He was in his mid-thirties, had the capability to handle the job, and as best as we knew was honest. His biggest drawback was that he easily fell in love and then, when he got jilted, would always go on a drunk. But he was only filling in one night a week. Besides, how often could he possibly fall in love?

Everything appeared to be running smoothly: that is, until the morning I called the shop and no one answered the phone. Borel should have been there. About the sixth time I phoned, Robert Cooper answered. He described the scene for me since I was still unable to report to work. The trash had not been emptied, the floor had not been swept, and the carts had not been cleaned. A shipment of frozen meat had just been delivered and was sitting on the dolly in front of the walk-in cooler. Borel's keys were lying on the kitchen counter. When the urge to quit hit him, he just walked out and left the front door wide open.

Luckily, Cooper had wandered in. I instructed him first to check the temperature of the meat. Once I established that it was still frozen, I had him put it in the cooler and then start on cleaning the shop and carts. As Cooper prepared to start his tasks, the same young reporter who had walked into the warehouse the day of the fire walked back in to hear how Darryl and I were doing. He was hoping for a follow-up story. Once again he found the commissary in an awful condition. With the Super Bowl coming soon to New Orleans, he felt obliged to contact the board of health and levy a complaint against the company. Only persons associated with the board of health knew that a surprise inspection of Lucky Dogs' warehouse was to take place. This imminent inspection set off a strange series of events.

For months prior to the fire, whenever I assigned a vendor to the corner of Iberville and Royal, on the following day the health department came to inspect us. We perceived the pattern soon enough. Under normal circumstances we would be inspected perhaps twice a year. Now we were being visited as often as three times a week by the same inspector. He cited such violations as "no soap in the kitchen's soap dish." In reading his report one would assume that there was no soap present, when in reality the soap had only fallen from the dish into the sink. He had seen it but had chosen to ignore it. Another violation once listed was "no towels in hand towel dispenser." Someone had placed the pack of brown single-fold towels on top of the dispenser instead of unlocking the front and placing them inside. The violations were petty and questionable. I came to believe that the inspector was trying to convey some other message.

Specifically, a fast-food restaurant near Iberville and Royal hadn't been doing well. It blamed its lack of success on our cart parked on the corner. The owner of the establishment had openly stated that he would do whatever it took to get rid of us. I believed that he was responsible for initiating our frequent health inspections. However, I had no concrete proof, so I couldn't go over the inspector's head and appeal to his superiors.

As time passed without our relinquishing the corner, the restaurateur tried a more direct approach. On two occasions, his cook came to our cart with a baseball bat in hand and threatened to crush our vendor's knees if he didn't wheel his buggy down the street. I hadn't been thrilled when the restaurant opened, but I didn't go into the establishment and threaten his waitresses. After all, he had a legal right to operate, just as we did. Under those circumstances, we could never forfeit the corner, even if it wasn't very profitable. A retreat here would result in most of our locations coming under siege. The present club and restaurant owners didn't care that our carts had been on the corners years before they had purchased their businesses. They simply did not want anything near their doors that could take a potential customer's money before they did: no newspaper stands, no taxis, no horse and carriages, nothing.

I had to find someone who could work our Iberville and Royal location and not succumb to the pressure to leave. The company couldn't possibly maintain its presence without a stalwart vendor. All seemed dark and hopeless for days. Then Fortuna blessed us. A rugged, scar-faced hulk of a man walked into the shop seeking employment. This brutal-looking character had potential, and I knew immediately where it could best be put to use. I explained our problem. When I got to the part about the baseball bat–wielding cook, he just grinned. At that point I felt confident that he could handle the situation.

The Quarter's version of brinkmanship began. The question was, who would blink? We didn't have long to wait. The fast-food cook must have taken one look at our new vendor and decided to stay in his kitchen. Unfortunately, all of our potential customers took one look and also shied away. We were going to have to polish up our brute's appearance; otherwise, he would never sell enough to survive.

The cook may have retreated, but the restaurateur had yet to resign from his cause. Predictably, the afternoon following the brute's emergence on the scene, the health inspector arrived. This led to a frank closed-door discussion in my office. I showed him a graph of the days that we had worked the problem corner and then a graph of the days that he had inspected us. I suggested that if I were a suspicious person, I would see a definite correlation between the two. He stood there silently looking at both sheets of paper. "Admittedly," he said, "it looks bad." But he adamantly proclaimed his innocence. Nevertheless, his petty bureaucratic harassment stopped.

Our new recruit had halted the cook's physical threats; the line graphs had stopped the frequent health inspections. Then the fire had occurred, prompting the young reporter to contact the health department. It scheduled a surprise inspection for the morning of January 18. But this time we were not in for a routine inspection. Because a television reporter had levied the complaint, we were going to be honored by a visit from some of the department's top brass. Understandably, they were feeling the heat.

What followed made our worst possible fears a reality. I had assigned Robert Cooper to fill in as night manager so Red could have a day off. Cooper was finishing his shift when two men walked into the shop. They asked to use the restroom. Both apparently were neat and clean, and since a few vendors were still hanging around, Cooper gave them permission. In appreciation for his kindness they gave him and each of the three remaining vendors a Budweiser from their six-pack.

Everyone had been checked in and the money was in the safe. Cooper figured there could be no harm in having just one can of beer before cleaning the shop. Unfortunately, after he downed the first one, they offered him a second. When that six-pack ran out, one of the men walked to the corner and bought a couple more. Six-packs continuously appeared.

The next morning when Red stopped by the shop, he discovered a wreck. Nothing had been cleaned. Cooper was passed out in the messy kitchen. The three drunken vendors were asleep by the carts. A few minutes after Red arrived, the board of health showed up for the surprise inspection.

The report by Gus Rosemann, Regional Sanitarian Supervisor, and William Barlow, Assistant Chief Sanitarian, was not favorable. There was no way that it could have been. We didn't exactly put our best foot forward. The violations cited, however, dealt mainly with the physical appearance of the building: walls needed painting, restroom doors needed self-closing springs, plaster walls required smoothing, an old free-standing heater in the cart storage area needed to be removed, and the buckling wooden floors needed to be repaired. Other violations included the haphazard storage of hot dog carts, signs of personnel sleeping in the building (signs? hell, there were four bodies on the floor), large quantities of garbage near the building entrance, an open vat of mustard in the kitchen's three-compartment sink, improper storage of a chlorine sanitizer, and failure to clean kitchen equipment from the previous night. Some, but certainly not all, of these charges would have been corrected had Cooper not gotten drunk.

Then the forces of mass communication intervened. The young reporter announced on the evening news that the city's board of health was scheduling a meeting with Lucky Dogs to discuss possibly revoking the company's license. My hands were still wrapped with gauze and I was weeks away from going back to work, but I attended the meeting with Doug and Joel Loeffelholz, who was now Lucky Dogs' legal representative. At no time during the discussions was a threat to revoke our license mentioned. The inspectors went over the two-and-a-half-page report item by item, wanting to know how long it would take us to rectify each of the cited violations. My interpretation of the meeting was that the board's backs were to the wall and they wanted this situation to clear up as much as we did.

Although they never suggested that we cease operating, sales were devastatingly slow due to the cold January weather, so Doug decided to close during the middle of the week. For three days I oversaw the restoration effort. We repainted the walls, floors, and ceiling. One by one every item cited was corrected. Some violations were easily remedied, such as setting the fifty-pound sacks of raw onions on a pallet instead of on the kitchen floor. Repainting the warehouse floor and repairing the sagging false ceiling in the kitchen took a little longer.

This episode represents the low point in the company's history. Because we chose to close and correct all of the violations at once, people automatically assumed that the health department had shut us down. The rumors were wild and rampant. They were easily started but damn near impossible to kill. We had one advantage, however: the tourist and convention business in the city generally turns over every three days. By the weekend none of the newly arriving out-of-town visitors were aware of what had happened and sales were back to normal. Years would pass, however, before the rumors died out locally.

To this day I firmly believe that the two gentlemen providing the endless supply of beer on the eve of the great inspection were sent by the antagonistic restaurant owner. His contact in the health department probably informed him that his competition from Lucky Dogs might not be a problem much longer. I suspect that the restaurateur, wanting to ensure our demise, then hired the two men to sabotage our staff.

Nevertheless, many of the problems that the inspectors cited as violations had existed for years. An old building needs constant attention. Neither the landlord nor the company had put forth enough effort or money to maintain the building at modern health-code standards. Because the board of health had a television station looking over its shoulder, it had to enforce the code in its strictest form. Three days after the surprise visit, the board of health reinspected. No violations were cited.

When we reopened, Cooper was once again relegated to being a vendor. As a manager he had made two critical errors in judgment. First, he knew that he was to never let anyone in the shop at night other than vendors checking in. Second, he knew that under no circumstances was he permitted to drink while on the job. With Cooper reassigned to the street, I needed a new manager and so hired Mike Giles. Giles had been on a cart for several months and performed relatively well. He was in his mid-thirties, blond and paunchy, and he had a mild personality.

Originally, he had come to New Orleans in hopes of finding a job in the oil fields, but thus far he had been unsuccessful. When he couldn't pay his rent and his landlady threatened him with eviction, he decided to sell hot dogs.

Giles worked well for the first few months. He stayed sober, completed his paperwork more than adequately, and developed a good rapport with the vendors. It wasn't until he started trying to shed his excess pounds that his troubles began.

Doug and I had taken a day off to go speckled-trout fishing in the Gulf of Mexico. It was a chance to relax away from the mania of the Quarter. On this peaceful day, the gulf had been glassy and full ice chests reflected our success. After returning to the dock at dusk I telephoned the shop to confirm that all was well there. It wasn't.

This happened to be the day of the Rolling Stones' first concert appearance in New Orleans. Doug and I had expected sales to be good, perhaps on a par with sales surrounding a major Saints game, so I had prepared accordingly. We never dreamed that business would actually surpass that of a Super Bowl. When I called the shop, Giles was hysterical. He couldn't handle the pressure. Vendors outside the Dome needed supplies, carts in the Quarter needed supplies, and part of the crew was still waiting to be sent out. As I tried to calm him down via long distance, he suddenly screamed, "My f——ing nerves are shot. I can't take this anymore. I quit." Then he slammed down the receiver.

Doug and I were ninety miles away when the night manager went wacko on what ended up being one of the biggest days in the company's history. I had heard other voices in the background while I was talking to Mike. I called back to find out who else was in the shop. George Stafford, the vendor from St. Peter, answered the phone. He had come in to pick up supplies while his helper worked his corner. Not only did Giles refuse to return to the phone, but as Stafford and I spoke he stormed out of the building. My only hope was to persuade George to take over the night shift until I arrived back in town. I had done him several favors over the years, and he readily agreed now to reciprocate.

By the time I arrived at the shop, Stafford had the vendors in the Quarter resupplied. Then using my truck we resupplied the carts outside the Dome and made another supply run down Bourbon. Stafford volunteered to finish off the night and to continue working in the shop until a permanent replacement could be found. Thus relieved I went home, showered, and went to bed.

At 2:30 A.M. the phone rang. It was Giles babbling that he knew that Doug and I were mafia and that a very reliable source had informed him of our plans to have him killed because he had run out on us. Giles also warned me that he had just called his hometown sheriff in Pennsylvania and warned him that if he was found dead, Doug and I were responsible.

Wearily, I responded, "Mike, that's absurd. Doug's not the Godfather and I'm not his henchman. Nothing is going to happen to you. In fact, if you come by the shop tomorrow, you can pick up your check. But right now all I want to do is go back to sleep. Good-night."

Mike never showed. The next week I saw him walking down Decatur Street toward Jackson Square. I called to him. He looked back, then took off running in the opposite direction. It wasn't until almost three weeks later that I discovered what had been fueling Mike's distress. He enjoyed having a few beers now and then, and he was also trying to lose weight. The alcohol and prescription pills were incompatible. The combination was affecting his mental stability.

To complicate matters, Andrew Walsh, a seemingly gentle sixty-year-old vendor who worked Bienville and Bourbon, was seeking revenge against Mike. Walsh was positive that the ex-manager had once cheated him out of thirty dollars, and he had sworn one day to get even. His opportunity struck on the night that Mike quit. When Mike stopped by his cart half-looped, Walsh convinced Mike that Lucky Dogs was a mafia-owned business designed to launder drug money. He also convinced Mike that Doug and I could never allow his disloyalty to "the Family" to go unpunished. In fact, he told Mike that he had heard from a very reliable inside source that the plan was to wrap him in chains and drop him off the Toulouse Street wharf into the Mississippi River. Walsh suggested that Mike needed to find some way to take the offensive. Thus, Mike came up with the idea of calling his hometown sheriff.

Not until after Mike had disappeared from town did I learn what disastrous advice Walsh had been feeding him. Walsh had gotten far more than his thirty dollars' worth of revenge. Portraying himself as a caring friend, he invited Mike to stop by his cart each evening to learn what he had overheard in the shop that day. Nightly, Walsh told horror stories to Giles. He explained that since Giles had notified the sheriff, we had changed our plans. We were instead going to make his murder look like a robbery attempt gone sour. Professional mafia hit men were being brought in from Chicago to brutally work him over. His mangled body would be dumped in a gutter somewhere on the fringes of the Quarter.

Mike became paranoid and went into seclusion. When he did resurface, Walsh told him that the "big boys" had decided that his case should be handled in a more respectable manner. Instead of employing physical violence, his source had informed him, "the Family" had decided to use finesse. The mob had obtained his payroll records from his previous employer. These records would be used to prove that he had intentionally committed income-tax evasion by failing to claim the tips that he had made as a waiter. Walsh's lie hit a nerve. The following Monday, a highly intoxicated Mike Giles walked into the Hale Boggs Federal Building on Poydras Street in New Orleans and confessed to an IRS agent that he had indeed falsified his previous year's return.

The entire incident seemed out of character for Walsh. He appeared to be such a harmless man: clean shaven, well spoken, gentle in nature. He dressed neatly in black pants, white shirt, and black bow tie. He didn't look vicious. I had no idea that he even had a mischievous streak in him.

During Walsh's first day at Lucky Dogs, he mentioned that he had been a career postal worker who had led a normal suburban life: that is, until six weeks prior to his scheduled retirement. It was then that his wife of twenty-seven years walked into their house and informed him that she didn't love him, had never loved him, and that now that their last child was grown she was leaving him. As he sat in my office telling this story, he admitted, sure, they had had problems now and then, but every couple has disagreements.

Walsh thought that, up until his wife's confession, he had had a successful marriage and an almost picture-perfect life. His family had a nice home in the suburbs and a cabin in the mountains. They attended church regularly and often talked of traveling once he retired. But then his wife revealed her feelings to him, and his world collapsed around him. He reacted by walking away from his job, his house, and his past life.

In the Quarter, Walsh had been trying to start a new life. Then the thirty-dollar incident involving Giles occurred. This time, Walsh was determined not to run; this time, he would force the other party to flee. And so he did. When Walsh later sat in my office, apologizing for his influence on Giles, he assured me that in the future he would bring his company-related problems directly to me. I hoped that would be the case. I couldn't afford to have him repeatedly running off managers.

With Giles gone, Lucky Dogs needed someone to take over the night shift. Fate happened to bring Eddie Vinterella back. Eddie had decided that New York's winters were too harsh and that he wanted to spend the colder months down south. I welcomed him back into the fold and immediately reinstated him in his old position. I thought that perhaps now we could achieve some stability, but I should have known better.

The second week after Eddie returned, I got a call at 3:30 A.M. from a panicked Adler. "Jerry! You gotta get down here fast. Cops are everywhere. They have Eddie handcuffed and they're planning to take him to jail. He beat the hell out of a guy in the shop."

I asked Adler to calm down and let me speak to the officer in charge. The sergeant explained that indeed Eddie had been in a fight. A merchant seaman walking down Decatur with his girl had become enraged when someone shouted out a vulgar statement about what they would like to do to the woman. The man assumed that the remark came from inside our shop where Eddie was sweeping. The doors were wide open, and Vinterella was only a few feet from the entrance. According to the sergeant, the seaman made two mistakes. First, he picked up a bar stool that was sitting just inside of our doorway. Second, he swung it at Eddie and missed. At that point, Eddie's instincts took over. He beat the seaman with his fists from the front of the shop to the building's rear wall, a distance of ninety feet. There he picked up the old piece of pool cue that he had once used on Frenchy and beat the sailor with it all the way back to the front door. The seaman's girl had been standing on the sidewalk screaming. Someone hearing her pleas called the police.

After the officer completed his story, I inquired. "You did say that the seaman entered our building, picked up a bar stool, and assaulted our night manager?"

The officer was doubtful. "I know where you're going with this. You might stretch self-defense to the back wall, but it ended once your man picked up the pool cue."

I insisted that I wanted charges pressed against the seaman for trespassing, attempted robbery, and assault with intent to do bodily harm. Whether the charges would stick or not would be for the courts to decide. The officer paused and asked to phone back. When he did so, he informed me that both parties involved had agreed not to file charges, case closed. I thought this outcome was fair. On the one hand, it kept Eddie out of jail and stopped a potential lawsuit against us because of Eddie's excessive force. On the other hand, it allowed the seaman to stay out of jail and to get on with his life; he had, after all, greatly overreacted to a childish remark that should have been ignored. While the seaman could have killed Eddie had he hit him in the head with the stool, Eddie, in turn, certainly more than defended himself. Now with the matter settled, Eddie went back to work and the officers took the seaman to Charity Hospital to see just how many bones were broken.

I had managed to keep Eddie out of jail, but a few days later I had to put one of our vendors in Central Lockup. David Garcia was an extremely likable young man. He was friendly and presented an excellent company image, dressed typically in clean black slacks and white shirt. His downfall was that he loved to drink and to pick up handsome young college guys.

Garcia generally never created problems. However, his lover had left him, and he was currently looking for a new companion. He began using the cash from his hot dog sales to entertain young new acquaintances that he befriended on the street. He would get one of the street characters to watch the cart while he spent the company's money buying his potential lover drinks in a nearby bar. The first night that David came up short, I gave him a warning. When on the second night he was again short in the thirty-dollar range, I informed him that he was suspended from work until he cleared his sixty-five dollars in unpaid bills. He responded, "If I can't work, then I can't pay the money back. I promise that it won't happen again." His pleas persuaded me to give him one more chance. However, I promised that if he came up short again, I was going to press charges for nonpayment of a food bill. Convictions generally carried a fifteen-day sentence in the parish prison. David agreed to the terms.

The very next night he came up seventy-five dollars short. According to him, he had spent the money "buying cute guys drinks." I called the police and pressed charges. As David left the shop in handcuffs, he shouted, "I can't believe that you are doing this. How in the hell can you do this to me?"

David spent four days in jail and then was released for time served. He came straight to the shop. He swore that if I would just give him another chance, he would repay the company everything that he owed and that he would never drink again. In fact, to prove that he had no hard feelings about my having put him in the slammer, if I would lend him ten dollars he'd buy us both a couple of rounds at the Pair-of-Dice. I wasn't foolish enough to lend him the money or to believe that he would never drink again. I was foolish enough to put him back out on a cart. David, when he stayed sober, was one of the best salesmen that we ever had. Moreover, potential vendors weren't exactly knocking Lucky Dogs' doors down. We had as usual to make do with who was on hand.

Sending David to jail had the secondary effect of stopping other vendors from coming up short—with one exception. An idealistic young female social worker contacted me about a nineteen-year-old who deeply needed our help. Misfortune had forced him into a life of crime. She was determined to help him break out of the destructive cycle. Recently, he had been caught stealing a ten-speed bicycle off the front porch of a house in the garden district area of New Orleans. According to the social worker, he had been driven to this act of desperation by the basic human need for food. If he had an honest way to make a living, she was certain, he could turn from his life of crime. Unfortunately, no one wanted to give him a chance. Our help-wanted ad in the newspaper had caught her attention, and she hoped that we might at least be willing to talk with him.

His record was extensive, but none of the incidents involved violence or drugs. They were mostly penny ante crimes: shoplifting, trespassing, and possession of stolen goods. The social worker brought the young man to Lucky Dogs' office, where I explained what I expected of him. His manner and speech showed that he had no desire to work for us or anyone else. However, he was smart enough to realize that this social worker was probably solely responsible for keeping him out of prison. So he took the job we offered.

We set him up with a cart, explained how to operate it, issued him a minimal amount of supplies, and then assigned him to a corner. I asked one of our seasoned vendors to work with him for the first hour. I just didn't feel comfortable about hiring him. The social worker beamed as her soon-to-be-reformed protégé pushed his wagon down the street toward his assigned location.

The following morning she stopped by the shop to find out how he had done. I explained that, as best as we could figure, when he left he had approximately seventy dollars on him. She was ecstatic. Never had she dreamed that he could earn so much his first night. He must be a natural salesman; he must have found his niche.

"He didn't exactly earn all of it," I responded. The figure included fifty-five dollars of company money that he stole. He had abandoned the cart on the corner, taken the cash, and fled before the 10 P.M. supply run and money pickup.

Suddenly, before my eyes she was transformed from a caring and kind idealist into a vicious and vengeful terminator. His offense had become personal. She growled, "I promise you he will serve time in the state penitentiary for this."

"Whoa!" I cautioned. "What happened to helping the misguided young man who simply needed a break in life? Let's keep things in perspective. We knew his past history, but we put him in a position where he had limited supervision, available cash, and the temptations of alcohol and friendly prostitutes. Certainly, he's guilty of theft and should be punished, but the state pen might be a little much."

In the long run, the fifty-five dollars that we lost was probably the best contribution the company ever made to the state. For less than it would have cost to send the young utopian social worker to some weekend seminar on reversions of the criminal mind, she learned firsthand that not every criminal wishes to be reformed. The next time she dealt with a con artist, she at least would have the advantage of experience on her side. I don't know where her future took her, but I do know that she never sent us another recruit.

5

Bourbon Street Bride

I ain't got no money!"

"Don't lie, bitch! Hand it over."

I could hear them arguing all the way from the rear of the shop. Then came the sound of a body crashing against the closed front doors. Whatever was going on outside had just gotten violent. Venturing to the entrance I looked through the peephole. There, near the curb, was a pimp and one of his associates in the midst of a heated business conference. He was slapping her up-side the head with his open hand, and she was retaliating by attempting to gouge his eyes out with her daggerlike fingernails.

I opened the door and shouted, "Time out! Do we get involved in your business? No. Do we make a scene where you conduct your transactions? No. Then why the hell are you brawling in front of our shop? Return the courtesy and take your argument down the block."

For a moment there was a hostile silence as the flashily dressed young black man stared at me. A few tense seconds passed, then he approvingly nodded his head. Gently, he gripped his associate by the arm and escorted her half a block to the corner of Iberville and Decatur, where they immediately resumed discussing company policy. Respect: I couldn't ask for more.

It was scary, but after two years as manager I was beginning to fit into the Quarter. My vocabulary had already appreciably degenerated. A few choice four-letter words with the proper inflection, and I could communicate effectively what I needed to say. I also started to understand the street mentality and adjusted my managerial style accordingly. When guys couldn't pay their bills at the end of the night because they had spent the company's money on booze, I didn't call the police. I handled their problems in-house. Offenders owing less than twenty dollars were assigned the task of cutting onions, washing carts, or cleaning the shop until their labor covered their shortage. Those owing twenty dollars or more were required to work plus put up collateral. Collateral was generally a watch or a wallet.

One particular incident concerning this new policy comes to mind. On a cold February night in 1978, a vendor pushed into the shop sixty-five dollars short. According to his story, he had lent the money to a friend who was three weeks behind in rent and about to be evicted. It didn't bother the vendor that he was generously lending company money. To help him understand the severity of the offense, I demanded that he empty his pockets. He produced nothing but his room key and a couple of pennies. I made him take off his shoes and socks. No bills hidden in them. I returned his left shoe and sock, but placed his right ones under the kitchen counter. When he asked, "What the hell are you doing?" I calmly explained, "each time your bare foot hits the freezing pavement outside, you are going to think: 'Damn, I shouldn't have come up short.'" The following afternoon he returned, cleared his bill, and walked out of the building on two warmly clad feet.

My position with Lucky Dogs was originally meant to be temporary, but almost two years later I was still serving as the company's general manager. Jane and I had had our first child, Christopher, in August, 1977. The job at Lucky Dogs had filled my need for security, and in turn, I filled the company's need for managerial stability. In fact, Doug adhered to this philosophy: hire someone that you believe can do the job, and as long as he is performing to your satisfaction, leave him alone. He had faith that I would manage the company to the best of my ability. After all, by 1978 I had been employed by him off and on for ten years. He knew my strengths and my weaknesses.

Doug no longer had to worry when vendors did not show up or when managers walked out. I handled the day-to-day operations. He paid the bills and took care of all financial matters. Each morning we would sit at his kitchen table and go over the previous night's sales sheet and discuss any pertinent matters concerning the business. For months at a time he never visited the shop. Instead, he reviewed the daily records and frequently spoke with vendors over the phone. Such an arrangement led one of our crew to refer to Doug as "God" and me as "Jesus." He contended that Doug, as the all-powerful one, had sent me to the Quarter to walk amongst the street people in his place. Another vendor claimed that working for Doug was like working for Charlie of the television series "Charlie's Angels." Doug, like Charlie, was that mysterious voice of authority who gave instructions over the phone.

My handling of the daily operations allowed Doug the freedom to pursue other interests as much as he liked. I, in turn, enjoyed the freedom of managing without a boss constantly looking over my shoulder. Business was on the increase, and we were beginning to build what very well may have been the best overall crew in the company's history. Howard Lewis was still working the street along with Adler, Walsh, McCarty, Stafford, Sloan, and Gillette. Joining the ranks during the fall of 1978 and the spring of 1979 were Joey Bronson, Ben Bullard, Kevin Russo, Julie Bennett, Dixie Doonan, and Joe Mayfield. Jim Campbell also had returned late in 1978 when the carnivals went into winter quarters.

It was from Campbell that I discovered why several months earlier David Borel had left the warehouse unlocked and the boxes of meat in the middle of the kitchen floor. Borel and Campbell had been talking together about joining up with a road show. By chance they had learned from one of their street buddies that a carnival was setting up in Port

Sulphur, Louisiana. Without so much as a good-bye they took off. They bolted from the shop in the morning, and by that evening they were pounding tent stakes as members of the show's grounds crew, positions that they held for the duration of the carnival circuit. Campbell figured that since several months had passed I might have forgotten about his disappearing act. He figured wrong, but I still took him back. Jim has a certain quality that just makes people like him. Besides, we were still desperate for vendors.

One of our new recruits at that time was Joey Bronson. He was a long-haired, six-foot-tall, grizzly-looking, marijuana-smoking Vietnam veteran. His appearance made me uneasy, but he turned out to be a relatively good vendor. He kept his personal life and his vices away from his cart. Admittedly, at times he got highly intoxicated and stumbled into the shop. On one such occasion he passed out in the middle of the warehouse. We tried to awaken him by shaking him. It didn't work. Next, someone came up with the idea of putting frozen gel packs (the ones that the vendors used to keep their hot dogs cold) under his shirt. They didn't faze him. So I decided to run the shop's garden hose up the right leg of his jeans and turn the cold water on full force. With the ground temperature outside below freezing, Bronson shot up like a Polaris missile.

Ben Bullard was another vendor whose appearance was extremely deceiving. Bullard was in his early forties. His graying hair was pulled back in a short ponytail. Prior to coming to Lucky Dogs he had been a bartender on the West Coast at one of the Hell's Angels' favorite hangouts. Before that, rumor has it, he had been climbing the corporate ladder in a West-Coast company. He decided to abandon the climb for a freer life style.

Bullard was huge, with massive shoulders and arms. He is the only guy that I ever knew whose size overshadowed his Harley's. As Campbell recalled, "Ben was a big m—— f——, but he had a heart of gold. He'd never hurt anyone. He never got physical. He was so big that he didn't have to. He was a very very gentle soul." His size did, however, help to increase his income. When a customer bought a dog from him, Ben would look the person in the eyes and say, "That's two dollars without the tip." He never said that the tip was mandatory. He didn't have to. His fellow vendors often remarked that Ben had the best-tipping clientele on the street.

Bullard proved to be the perfect vendor for Toulouse and Bourbon, the bikers' favorite corner. He talked their talk and walked their walk. His motorcycle cohorts bought from him in droves; and they, like the average tourist, felt that such fine service deserved to be amply rewarded.

Shortly after Ben arrived, Kevin Russo and Julie Bennett stepped off a Greyhound bus on Tulane Avenue and headed toward the Quarter. They had met at the bus station in Houma, Louisiana. Julie was twenty years old. The year after she graduated from high school she had gotten pregnant. Once the baby was born, she left it with her mother and went to search for work in a nearby town. Months passed before she returned home, jobless and once again pregnant. To her surprise she discovered that her mother had turned her young child over to the state welfare department claiming that her daughter had abandoned it. Julie insists that she had frequently spoken with her mother via the phone, and that her mother was well aware that she was planning on returning for her son once she was settled. But now, the state had custody of her child. Julie had little money and no lawyer. She wasn't sure what to do. Suddenly she decided just to board a bus and leave the small town and her past behind.

Kevin was a fun-loving redneck from the piney woods of central Louisiana. Much of his youth had been spent in and out of reform schools as a result of his continually running away from home. During his early twenties he had even spent a stretch in the state pen for car theft.

The day that Kevin met Julie, he was passing through the Houma bus station on the way to his job on an offshore oil rig. She was broke, three months pregnant, and had no place to stay. He felt sorry for her, so he offered to put her up for the night. That evening she slept in his motel bed, and he slept on the hard floor. The next morning he decided to change his plans. He really didn't want to go back offshore. He was lonely. She was lonely. Perhaps they would be good for each other. He convinced her to accompany him to New Orleans.

Within the hour after they stepped off the bus, they were filling out applications at Lucky Dogs. Kevin had hustled dogs for the company a few years before, and he was confident that he could once again earn a living pushing a cart.

It wasn't long after Ben, Kevin, and Julie joined our crew that Eddie Vinterella disappeared. Eddie had done an excellent job since returning, not just as a manager, but also as a repairer of the carts. He was an accomplished body-and-fender man, and he had converted our tool room into a mini–body shop. One cart at a time he was restoring our fleet to near-perfect condition. Granted, he often put in more hours than he should have, but that was his choice.

Then one evening something clicked in his head. He made the 8:00 P.M., 10:00 P.M., and midnight runs. I spoke with him over the telephone after his eight o'clock pickup, and I didn't detect anything abnormal in his voice. But when his vendors arrived at the shop at 3:30 A.M. to check in, the big silver American padlock was on the front door and there was no sign of Eddie. McCarty called me at home.

The first thought that always enters my mind when the phone rings in the middle of the night is that something tragic has happened to the night manager or to a vendor. When I arrived at the warehouse and unlocked the door, a few of the vendors entered the building with me. At this point we were not certain if Eddie had become the victim of foul play.

We found no sign of him inside. I checked the safe. The money was gone. Lying on the floor in the tool room were a couple dozen Dixie beer cans. One of the regular prostitutes on Decatur said that she had noticed two rough-looking characters entering the building with Eddie when he came back from his last run. About an hour later she saw the two men leave.

Eddie apparently continued working on the cart. As he sanded the body in preparation for painting, he must have downed a few more Dixies. At some point, for whatever reason, he had decided, "To hell with this. I'm outta here." He took a little over a thousand dollars of company money and disappeared. Another of the Decatur Street hookers saw him lock the door and stumble off by himself shortly after 2 A.M.

The great thing about Decatur was that there were always ladies of the evening working the one and two hundred blocks. Nothing went on outside of our shop that one of them didn't see. The first couple of weeks after I went to work at the Decatur Street warehouse, I got propositioned eight to ten times a night. If I just opened the door and stepped out on the sidewalk, two or three girls would ask if I wanted "to have a good time." By the end of the second week the regular streetwalkers were telling the new girls, "Don't bother with him. He's just the wienie man." The solicitations stopped, but the hookers continued to wave or greet me with a friendly hello when I walked past.

The night that New York Eddie disappeared, I filled out a police report; but he was never apprehended. To replace Eddie I chose Ben Bullard. True, Ben was a biker; and I admit that early in my Lucky Dog career, I had had a negative experience with a member of a motorcycle gang. But this time things were different. Ben wasn't just any old biker: Ben was my biker. He was on my side. He was part of my management team, and it felt damn good. Besides, he was extremely likable and highly intelligent. Another major plus was that the vendors respected him, even trusted him. And they really didn't want to piss him off.

Bullard's co-worker in the shop was Hippie Mike. Mike was a short-bodied, long-haired hippie with a bushy brown beard. I had promoted him from cart washer to day manager when Red Lott suddenly quit. Having worked in the shop, Mike already knew the routine; but he wanted to make changes. The biggest proposal was to eliminate pushing the supply cart down the street: it was "like totally uncool." Uncool or not, vendors had to be resupplied. After only a week Mike requested that he be allowed to return to the less demanding position of washing carts. I couldn't possibly refuse. He had the distinction of being the only manager in the company's history who had ever given notice that he intended to leave his position. I was impressed.

Joe Mayfield took over Mike's position. Mayfield had joined us as a vendor in September, 1977. Previously, he had been a lab technician in

Pittsburgh, but he ended up quitting because of a salary dispute. When Mayfield's immediate supervisor at the lab had resigned, the company's president asked Joe to take over the departed chemist's duties. He agreed, but asked that his salary be increased to compensate for his additional responsibilities. His employer replied, "But you don't have a college degree, and without a degree we can't possibly pay you more than you're making now." Mayfield couldn't accept the fact that they were willing to trust him to do the work without a degree, but couldn't compensate him accordingly because he didn't have one. He recommended that they split the difference between the two salaries. He would receive a raise and the company would still be paying him twenty-five percent less than the previous supervisor had received. His boss rejected the idea. Joe walked out.

Not long before, Mayfield had divorced. Now he was unemployed. He was starting life over. Since his youth he had longed to visit the South, and this seemed to be the perfect time. His travels brought him to Morgan City, Louisiana, where he worked on tugboats and shrimp-boats. Later, he was hired to pilot a small utility boat. The craft wasn't Coast Guard approved, so it wasn't necessary for him to be a certified captain. The following year when the company's business declined, he found himself again without a job. He headed for New Orleans in search of work, where someone recommended Lucky Dogs.

Mayfield started out selling dogs on the corner of St. Louis and Bourbon outside of the Al Hirt Club. From there he worked his way into the shop. At first he performed little chores, like taking the railroad dolly to pick up the fifty-pound sacks of yellow onions from Guercio's Produce Company around the corner on South Peters Street. Later, he started helping the cart washer. Gradually, he worked his way into the position of relief manager and then, during the spring of 1979 when Hippie Mike went back on the street, he took over as day manager.

Mayfield, as manager on the day shift, only collected money from the cart at Jackson Square. He seldom handled more than fifty to sixty dollars—that is, until May, 1979. The week prior to Mother's Day, Ben accidentally left the safe unlocked. Mayfield saw the handle in the unlocked position; he walked over, pushed the bar down, and spun the dial. The safe was secure. Then, the Saturday morning before Mother's Day, Ben once again accidentally left the safe unlocked.

I had gone out of town for the weekend. Doug was planning on picking up the night's receipts and making the deposit, but his pregnant Treeing Walker coonhound, Patty, started giving birth to puppies. He called Mayfield and informed him that he would be delayed in coming in to the shop. As Mayfield filled mustard containers, cleaned chili pots, and cut onions, he was only a few feet from the safe. He kept glancing at its unlocked door. Curiosity finally got the best of him. Later he recalled thinking, "Aw, this is too much." He pulled open the safe's iron door, and there on the wooden top shelf was $877 and change. He stuffed the money in his pocket, locked the safe, locked the warehouse door, and headed for the Trailways bus station.

By the time Patty finished having her fourteenth puppy, Mayfield was cruising down the highway. When Doug arrived he found the building locked. There was no sign of a struggle or forced entry. The only certainty was that Ben, Doug, and I alone knew the combination to the old black iron safe. Doug found the safe still locked, but the previous night's gross receipts were missing.

Coincidentally, Scott Adler and Dixie Doonan had also left town that morning. Dixie was a flaming homosexual who claimed to have once been crowned the "Queen of San Francisco." The duo's disappearance raised the question of whether or not they might have been involved in the theft.

No one knew what happened to Mayfield. Did he steal the money? If so, how did he get into the safe? If not, then where was he? There were a lot of questions, but no answers. A police report was filed, but we figured that we had no chance of ever recovering the stolen cash.

Ben, as the last person to handle the money, accepted responsibility for its loss and agreed to repay it over a period of time. Respect for his character meant everything to him. What bothered him the most was that whoever committed the crime had caused a cloud of doubt to be cast upon his reputation. In a very calm voice he promised me that if he ever found out the thief's identity, nothing on earth could save that person. I, for one, believed him.

It wasn't until 1988 that I discovered that Mayfield was the culprit. It wasn't until mid-1994 that I finally got a confession out of him. He sat in my office quite ill from emphysema and described the events of that Saturday morning sixteen years before. He admitted to succumbing to the temptation of the unlocked safe. He said that he had stuffed the cash in his pockets and headed for the bus station, where he caught a scenic cruiser for Biloxi, Mississippi. Part of the stolen money was spent on room and board. The rest was invested in sex and booze. Shortly after the money ran out, so did the women. Once that happened, Joe signed on as a deckhand on a big commercial Gulf of Mexico shrimpboat. Then in the summer of 1990 he reappeared at Lucky Dogs.

Back in 1979 after Mayfield disappeared, we tried hiring a day manager via newspaper ads. None of the respondents worked out; they all had significant problems. One had great credentials. He had just retired from the army and was receiving a pension. In the service he had been a counselor for a drug and alcohol rehabilitation program. His problem was that he should have been the client and not the counselor. The first week that this man was working the night shift, McCarty called me at home a little after midnight and suggested that I come haul our new manager out of a Bourbon Street club before all of the company's funds ended up stuffed into strippers' G-strings as tips.

Another gentleman that we hired became overly friendly with the Decatur Street girls. One evening when I went to the shop to check on him, I discovered a prostitute energetically kissing and fondling her john inside our building. Neither of them had heard the deadbolt click as I unlocked the front door, nor did they notice me step inside. Once I saw them, I quickly withdrew back onto the sidewalk. I had no idea how the john would react to being disturbed, and I didn't want to take a chance that he was armed. I knew for a fact that he wasn't wearing a shoulder holster because his shirt was lying on the floor. However, I couldn't be certain whether or not he had a gun stuffed in his pants. A minute or two more and I would have learned the answer to that question, too. But southern etiquette tends to frown on peeping Toms.

I quietly pulled the door shut and went out on the street in search of our manager. When I found him, I fired him on the spot, took his keys, and finished the night shift. The following morning I changed all of the locks. Obviously, the ex-manager was getting either cash or credit for allowing the hooker to use our shop. I still wonder how many more managers may have made similar deals that Doug and I never learned about. It is possible that for a very brief time two street-oriented businesses might have been operating out of the same building: one comprised of street vendors, the other of streetwalkers.

The newspaper ads brought us guys who were worse than those we were trying to replace. On paper some applicants looked great, but the temptations of the Quarter simply overpowered them. I had no choice but to bring Hippie Mike back into the shop temporarily until I could find a permanent replacement.

Actually, Mike named his own replacement when he recommended Jim Campbell. Campbell had been helping him deliver the supplies and make the money runs. Once I discovered that Jim was doing the work, I offered him the job on a permanent basis. Mike wanted out of the shop and Jim was willing to come in. During Campbell's stint as manager, Penny started working a cart for us outside the Famous Door Jazz Club. For some reason, everyone called her "Pepper." I thought a much more suitable nickname would have been Olive Oyl: she bore an uncanny resemblance to that "Popeye" cartoon character. Pepper and Jim became friends. Friendship blossomed into love and love led to marriage in August, 1979.

In the shop Campbell and Ben worked well together. Both were soft-spoken and easygoing. They respected one another, and each one went out of his way to help the other. Of great importance to me, they were both dependable. During Ben's tenure I consistently got a good night's sleep.

While Jim and Ben were in the shop, on the street selling was a regular crew made up of Lewis, Walsh, Russo, Gillette, McCarty, Sloan, and Stafford. The only new notables were Bill Odom, who was a short leprechaun of a man, and Big Al Parrish. Between our Big Ben and Big Al there were big differences. Ben was tall, broad shouldered, basically still in shape. Al also was over six feet tall, but he was badly out of condition. Ben always appeared neat and clean, even in blue jeans. Al

Big Al munching away profits
Courtesy Lee Crum

would have looked slovenly in a tuxedo. As a vendor Ben worked the crowd for sales. He drew people over and enticed them to make a purchase. Al, on the other hand, sat on a stool by his cart and read paperback westerns. Only when people rudely interrupted his concentration did he grudgingly serve them.

Al lacked ability and drive. However, at Lucky Dogs during the

1970s ability and drive weren't prerequisites for employment. We had good corners for good vendors and bad corners for bad vendors. Vendors were paid by commission. If they didn't sell anything, then they only cost us the propane that the cart burned. Al was a body, and there was many a night when we suffered from severe vendor shortages—especially cold rainy nights. Al's greatest strength as a vendor was that, even in the most inclement weather, he showed up. Since he never sold much anyway, he preferred the foul conditions. With fewer customers he had more time to read. The cart gave Al a purpose. And the signs from the clubs on Bourbon Street gave him enough light to peruse his books.

Odom and his wife stand out in my mind as the only two people I know of who ever got married while working a Lucky Dog cart. I mean while *actually* working a cart. They met when he was serving her a chili dog. The steamed frank, warm bun, hot chili, and freshly cut onions were apparently so tasty that Denise became a regular customer. Before long she was helping her favorite vendor dish up chili dogs for others. Several weeks passed, love took hold, and as scores of tourists strolled by the cart and the aroma of freshly chopped Vidalia onions filled the air Odom proposed to his helper. With tears in her eyes, a chili ladle in her hand, and jazz blaring from a nearby club, she joyfully accepted. Then and there they decided that their wedding would take place on the corner of Toulouse and Bourbon next to their Lucky Dog stand.

I was once again asked to give the bride away. I was honored, but I thought that surely there must be someone more appropriate than me to fill those shoes. Had they considered a father, a brother, an uncle, or even a close friend? I wanted to avoid responding to their request. I knew that the couple had called the local television stations about their impending nuptials, and theirs was just the kind of crazy human interest story that draws cameras and reporters. I had no desire to be seen on television and so reinforce my old college mates' opinion that "Strahan has gone off the deep end." The local beat cop ended up giving Denise away.

As I predicted, the ten o'clock news carried the story. I watched a legitimate minister pronounce them vendor and vendorette and thought, "Thank God I'm sitting at home watching the ceremony on television like a normal person." As the crowd on the street cheered and people on nearby balconies applauded, the blissful couple took a bite out of a big juicy quarter-pound Lucky Dog. The short Bill and tall Denise, though apparently looking mismatched on screen, beamed and chewed happily. The crowd passed a hat to take up a collection as a wedding present. After throwing the bouquet, these fortysomething newlyweds spent their honeymoon hawking dogs to those attending the cash reception. Their sales were extraordinary and the tip cup overflowed. The crowd realized the significance of the moment. They might never again have the opportunity to buy a dog off of a cart shaped like a giant wiener from a lady wearing a veil.

While Odom and Denise served the crowd of well-wishers, Stafford was one block up the street depressed because he had not sold a hot dog in over an hour. Only recently had he returned as a vendor, and that night he was sitting on his stool next to his cart wondering if the street had gone bad, or if he had lost his touch, or if it was the wedding on the next block that was killing his sales. In 1977 Stafford had left Lucky Dogs and gone to work in one of the small takeout beer joints on Bourbon Street. Club owners constantly had labor problems similar to ours. To solve their personnel shortages they tried to lure away our best vendors with promises of giant commissions and better working conditions. George left us having been seduced by their promises.

During his stint in the beer joint he fell deeply in love with a stripper. After six months of courtship, the two were married. Darlene was a native New Orleanian. Her father, who held a high-level position with a very respectable shipping company, hadn't been thrilled about the courtship. He abhorred the fact that his daughter was shedding her clothes on stage, but even more he detested the fact that she was going to marry George. Grudgingly, once Darlene and George were married, he appeared to accept the situation and to hope for the best: perhaps she would at least give up stripping. When a few months later Darlene became pregnant, her father's attitude soured again. Every man wants the best for his children, and here his little girl had gone and married a man who could neither read nor write beyond the third-grade level. To make matters worse, the guy made his living selling beer out of an alley. According to George, his father-in-law had hoped that the marriage would fail and that his daughter would leave the Quarter and its riffraff behind and return home. The pregnancy angered him by making the possibility of her return less likely.

A son was born. Stafford left the street and hired on as a cook on a Gulf of Mexico oil rig. With a wife and a child he felt the need for a more stable income. His job kept him away two, sometimes three weeks at a time. Darlene had given up dancing and stayed home with the infant. In time her old problem of excessive drinking began to consume her. Finally, George convinced her to go into the hospital for treatment. He then tried to find someone to temporarily care for his son so that he could continue working on the rigs. George's older sister and brother-in-law in Arkansas offered to help. As they had three children of their own, they assured him, caring for one more infant would be no problem. The child stayed with them for almost four months while his mother went through a detox program.

Once Darlene was released from the hospital, her parents drove her to Little Rock to be reunited with her son. Unbeknownst to George, Darlene's father had persuaded her to file for divorce on the alleged grounds that George had abandoned both her and their child. George decided not to contest the divorce. If she no longer loved him, then he was man enough to accept it. All he wanted was the right to help raise his son. He naïvely trusted in the fairness of the court system.

Darlene was granted full custody of their child, but she didn't retain that custody long. She went straight back to the bottle. Her parents then assumed legal guardianship of their grandson, and George began having serious visitation problems. His former in-laws knew that he had never had a driver's license. George believes that with this fact in mind they sold their house uptown, which was on a bus line, and moved to the outskirts of New Orleans beyond the reach of public transportation. To visit his son George's only option was to take a taxi from the end of the bus route, a trip that was costly in both time and money. On several occasions, after having made arrangements to visit his son, he arrived at the house and discovered they had left. The situation constantly ate at him. Yet as badly as his former in-laws treated him, he still paid his child support. After all, the money was for his son.

Eventually George gave up his job on the oil rig. His inability to read had created too many problems for him. He knew that at least in the Quarter, as long as he could make change, he could find employment. So in 1979, as Campbell began managing the shop, George returned as one of our regular vendors and again worked the corner of St. Peter and Bourbon. However, the size of the crew didn't grow, because at the time that we regained George we lost William "Pops" Gillette.

Pops had started complaining that his legs constantly hurt, and complaining was something that Pops never did. He was always jovial and kind. Then one morning in the shop he pulled up one of his trouser's legs and uncovered several tremendous purplish blotches on his skin. I was concerned that whatever he had might be contagious; it certainly appeared serious. I insisted that he allow me to take him for medical help. On several occasions we had talked about his World War II experiences, so I knew that he was a veteran. With that information in mind I took him to the VA Hospital.

Pops was diagnosed as being in the advanced stages of cirrhosis of the liver. The odds of surviving were not favorable and he knew it. One evening as we sat talking in his hospital room, I asked him if there was anyone whom he would like me to contact. Following a silence he said, "I would like to see my son just one last time. He used to live in Cleveland, but that was twenty years ago. I haven't seen him since then."

I called information in Cleveland, but there was no listing for his son. I next went to the New Orleans public library and searched through the latest copy of the Cleveland telephone directory. I called every Gillette listed, but no one claimed to be related to Pops. Within a week of my search he passed away.

I had still to deal with the matter of Pops's legacy. Gillette had befriended a young couple while he was working the street. I had heard him tell others that they had invited him over to their house for Thanksgiving dinner, and on at least one other occasion they had picked him up to spend a Sunday afternoon with them. They must have seen his death listed in the obituaries because soon after he died, they called the shop requesting a meeting with me. I wasn't sure why they were coming, but I didn't have to wait long to find out. Gillette had given them a note, addressed to me, stating that if anything ever happened to him, I was to turn over to them his coin collection that was locked in the company safe.

I'm not certain what kind of tales Gillette had told the couple, but they envisioned an enormous collection: a collection so valuable that it had to be kept secured in a commercial vault. In reality, Pops had a few silver dollars and a few old quarters sealed in a bank coin envelope. The couple was stunned when I handed them the small package. Then they became irate. They insinuated that I had stolen their inheritance. Certainly, they insisted, Mr. Gillette must have had more than a few coins. I pulled out an itemized account signed and dated by Gillette listing everything that I had been holding for him.

Now it was my turn to become irritated. Pops had left the couple his most precious possessions, and these ingrates felt that they weren't receiving enough. I thought that they had gotten well more than they deserved. Obviously, they had only befriended Pops because they thought that there was something in it for them. They must have seen him as guardian of the mother lode or keeper of the pot of gold at the end of the rainbow. He probably had spun some yarn that led them into believing that he was a Howard Hughes–type character in disguise. I don't know. I do know that I wanted to throw them both bodily out of the shop. But since Gillette had considered them friends, out of respect for him, I held my temper as best I could.

Later, the humor of the situation struck me. Here this couple was trying to take advantage of an old man, and in the end they felt that they had been suckered. Pops was a sharp old codger. It's a shame that they never got to know him for who he was, so distracted were they by what they thought he had. I also felt obliged to continue my search for his son and for his ex-wife. I enlisted the help of the Red Cross and the Veterans Administration, but to no avail. Pops was laid to rest in a military cemetery in Baton Rouge, alongside his fellow soldiers who had fallen before him.

As Gillette was leaving this world, Julie Bennett was preparing to bring another life into it. She had been a little over three months pregnant when she and Kevin Russo met in Houma. Six months later, as she stood selling Lucky Dogs on the corner of Decatur and Iberville, she noticed that the time between her contractions was growing shorter. A United Cab driver happened to be buying a hot dog when Julie decided that her time was near. The cabby gulped down his dog as he rushed her to Charity Hospital. Kevin pushed the cart into the shop, then he, too, headed for Charity.

Because of medical problems, Russo could never have children of his own. He claimed to love kids, but didn't think that he and Julie could properly care for a child given their sort of life style. So he kept telling her during the six months that they had been together. During this period he totally dominated her. She did nothing without his approval. Four months after she and the baby were discharged from Charity, Kevin convinced her that the child should be given up for adoption. He argued that the baby needed to grow up in a proper home, the kind they would never be able to give him.

One sunny afternoon on their day off Kevin and Julie stopped by the shop. The child was not with them. Everyone assumed that they had turned him over to the state. Then a rumor surfaced on the street that the infant had been sold on the black market for five hundred dollars. Julie and Kevin both vehemently dismissed the charges as vicious lies.

Years later, however, I discovered from Julie that Kevin had made all of the arrangements for the child to be adopted. He had not made them through legitimate channels. Instead, he consulted an attorney representing the number-one madam on Decatur Street. She was in her late forties and could never bear children. She also could never meet the state's requirements for adoption, but she desperately wanted a child and was willing to pay cash to get one. Julie remembers going to an attorney's office and signing papers that were purportedly official adoption documents. She tried to read them but couldn't understand the legal terminology. Finally, she just gave up and accepted the lawyer's claims.

Several years later her curiosity impelled her to go to the state bureau of vital statistics and order a birth certificate of her son. Computer records still listed the child under her name. This convinced her that her son was never legally adopted. Old friends on the street have told her that he is now living somewhere in Nebraska with the madam's parents. The madam and her boyfriend several years ago were convicted of selling cocaine and sentenced to lengthy prison terms. Looking back, Julie still believes that she made the right choice, though not with the right people. Yet she never questioned Kevin's powerful influence over her—or his actions. She might not approve when, for example, he brought women to the apartment and banished her for the duration of their play, but she never walked out on him. In her mind she had nowhere else to go. Right or wrong, he was her man and she was his woman.

As the 1970s progressed, Lucky Dogs slowly changed. From 1974 through 1979 the company handled the concessions for the Blue Angels Air Show when the precision flying team performed at the Naval Air Station just outside of New Orleans. Our carts were the perfect means to feed the thousands of people who daily crowded the base's grounds. At the same time, hotels began renting the uniquely shaped carts when they re-created miniature Mardi Gras parties in their grand ballrooms for major conventions. The exposure generated new interest. People eating with us at the air show and in the hotels began to hire us for their private parties. Charities also began requesting that we participate in their fund-raising galas.

The hotel events and parties led to another opportunity. Tulane University's athletic department asked us to take over their concessions operations in the fall of 1979. The previous concessionaire had recently died of a heart attack, and the university was having trouble finding a replacement. Martin MacDiarmid, business director for the athletic department, appealed to us, and we decided to give it a try. We accepted knowing that the possibility of making a profit was slim. We figured that the work would benefit us primarily in terms of public relations.

Thus, Dr. Ben Wall's prophecy had proved true: I did return to Tulane. However, I don't think he imagined that I would come back to handle the hot dog and beer concessions for the university's athletic events.

6

Farewell to Frenchy

In June, 1980, Lucky Dogs was in the midst of its annual summer vendor shortage. The carnies had left to rejoin their road shows. Other crew members, those who had wintered in the South to avoid the cold northern climate, had by now also migrated home to enjoy the more pleasant days of spring and summer. In addition, we lost the services of Ben Bullard, Jim and Pepper Campbell, and Bill McCarty.

Bullard had headed to Ocean Park, California, to have his Harley restored by the man he dubbed "the Michelangelo of body and fender repair." No one but the master could be trusted with her precious frame. Campbell and Pepper had also headed to the Golden State. There they intended to visit Jim's mom. Two years would pass before they returned to Bourbon Street. The last of the group to leave was McCarty. Unlike the others, he departed somewhat mysteriously.

McCarty checked in late one Saturday night. He uttered no complaints, mentioned no crisis. However, Sunday afternoon he failed to report for work. Days passed without any word from him, and rumors concerning his fate began to spread. One had him in jail for public drunkenness. However, Central Lockup had no record of his having been arrested. Another tale had him in Charity Hospital recovering from a brutal mugging. But the admittance desk there had no listing of a McCarty. Then, one of the street people reported that Bill had left for Florida in a fast convertible with a hot blond. No way to follow up that lead.

As if inspired by the last theory, McCarty's fellow vendors contended that if Bill had really taken off with the blond, then it was only appropriate to down a few rounds at the Pair-of-Dice to celebrate his good fortune. Of course, they were merely looking for an excuse to guzzle a few cold brews before starting work. They would have toasted his health, his death, or—perhaps most sincerely—the hot blond in the convertible. As unsociable as it might seem, I declined to participate in their proposed festivities. This was not a sanctioned company function, and I wasn't about to be coerced into picking up the tab for a trumped-up going-away party. Once they realized that the drinks would be Dutch treat, their brotherly spirit and insatiable thirst vanished.

The following day I happened to stop in at the main branch of the New Orleans Public Library. There, sitting in a cushioned chair in the periodicals section, was McCarty, completely engrossed in the latest issue of the *Wall Street Journal*. I had checked the morgue, the hospital, and the parish jail, but it had never dawned on me to search the public library. He explained that plastered tourists, scuzzy hustlers, and constantly begging Quarter bums had all been chipping away at his sanity. As an antidote to the madness, he chose to concentrate for a week or so on more worldly matters, until he felt rejuvenated. By the time he hit the streets again, he theorized, he would be prepared to dazzle his sober customers with an up-to-date analysis of the nation's business climate. As an added bonus, he could even offer his own potentially lucrative investment tips. I left him studying the magazine.

Like McCarty, in the summer of 1980 I, too, became mentally

weary. I even considered changing professions. Summers in the Quarter are depressing: hot dog sales drop and temperatures rise. Tourists, mostly strait-laced families, make up the greatest percentage of visitors. They don't have that "party 'til you drop" mentality of fall football fans or conventioneers on company expense accounts. So our summer sales plummeted. Decreasing sales meant lower commissions, and lower commissions made it more difficult to keep vendors. That summer, as we lost vendors and the company's gross intake lessened, I felt considerable pressure to find new bodies to replace those that had moved on.

To combat our loss of staff we tried recruiting personnel out of the Baptist Mission and from the street corners of the Quarter. We ran ads in the newspaper, and we even offered a cash reward to anyone who brought us a new employee. We tried everything but shanghaiing drunks out of bars. We considered the idea but killed it because they probably wouldn't be able to make correct change.

Frustrated, I began questioning what kind of future I could possibly expect from a street corner wienie-vending operation. I had climbed the company's corporate ladder; admittedly, it was only a stepladder, and I was already standing on its top rung. In the end, I hesitated to take any drastic action. The previous January, Jane had given birth to Jeffrey, our second child. Thus, the need for security compelled me to stick it out through the miserably hot summer.

By late October the cool northern winds brought the return of the snowbird vendors, the college and professional football fans, and the conventioneers. With them came a new feeling of optimism. Sales increased, and as a result, so did our stable of vendors.

One of the first ex-vendors driven south by the cold temperatures was Burt Richards. It had been almost two years since Burt had walked into the barroom on Bourbon Street as the shot went off and a fellow patron fatally fell to the floor. He figured that by this time he could safely return to New Orleans. He figured wrong. Less than an hour after Burt arrived in the Quarter, two men in dark suits approached him and recommended that for health reasons he consider a less humid climate. Valuing his existence, Richards readily accepted their advice.

I was doing paperwork at my desk that afternoon when Burt walked into the office. "Jerry, I need a favor," he said.

I was happy to see him. Hell, I was happy to see anyone who might want to work a cart. But employment wasn't on Burt's mind. He was looking for a safe way out of town. He had already eliminated transportation by bus or plane as being too dangerous. Someone might be waiting at the terminal to follow him: someone contracted to make certain that he would never again peddle puppies in the Big Easy or anywhere else.

Richards asked if I could secretly "give him a lift" beyond the city limits. From there he would hitchhike to parts unknown. Whether the problem was as grave as he perceived, I have no way of knowing. I do know, however, that he considered the threat to be real.

I saw no reason not to help him. He wasn't a fugitive. He wasn't fleeing to avoid testifying. He had never even been subpoenaed. As far as I knew, he was just an ex-employee desperately wanting to leave town in a hurry.

We came up with a plan. Richards sneaked out the back door of the shop and hid on the patio. I nonchalantly walked out the front entrance, got into my Chevette, and drove around the block. When I came to the parking lot on Iberville Street, I pulled in next to the hole in the wall that I had dived through when I was burned. Burt climbed through the opening and slouched down in the passenger seat. Thus far all had gone according to plan.

I pulled out of the lot onto Iberville, took a quick right turn onto Decatur, and damn near ran over one of the local hookers. Without looking she had jumped into the street to strut her stuff before the construction workers on a nearby two-story scaffolding. I slammed on my brakes. A produce truck coming up Decatur came to a screeching halt within inches of my rear bumper. The driver laid on his horn, while the prostitute stood in front of my car making unladylike gestures with her hands and verbally questioning the legitimacy of my birth. Burt and I hadn't made the most professional of getaways, but hey, I wasn't exactly a seasoned wheel man. Plus, a four-cylinder Chevy Chevette is not the ideal vehicle to use for covert operations, even if it is the Rally Sport model with the 1.6-liter engine.

In spite of our less-than-perfect escape attempt, we managed to make it safely to the interstate. Burt, all the while, kept a constant watch out the rear window. He had me exit the highway twice and wind through neighborhoods to reassure himself that we were not being followed. Finally, we headed out I-10 west through the swamps toward Baton Rouge. When I reached the I-10/I-55 split in LaPlace (about twenty-five miles west of New Orleans), he suggested that I pull over and let him out.

His departing here, he said, would be safer for the both of us. The last time I saw him, he was standing on the shoulder of the interstate, thumb out, hoping for a quick ride to anywhere. When the guys at the shop asked what happened to him, I responded: rumor has it that he headed to Florida in a fast convertible with a hot blond. And no, I don't want to go to the Pair-of-Dice to down a few rounds in honor of his good fortune.

Even without Burt's services our crew grew that fall. The same highway that had taken Richards north, a few days later brought Bob McGregor south. McGregor was a clean-shaven fellow a little over six feet tall. His short dark brown hair curled and had a touch of gray at the temples. He looked like a Wall Street banker or perhaps the movie version of an FBI agent. When he first walked through the shop's doors, I zeroed in on his hands. Federal agents on occasion had visited us looking for fugitives that they felt might be hiding in the Quarter. From experience I had learned that government agents generally carry their wallets in their hands. That way they scare the hell out of you when they flash their I.D. It's a G-man tradition. McGregor's hands were empty; he wasn't a fed.

Mac was just a man short of cash and looking for temporary employment. From his appearance, manner, and speech it was obvious that he was several cuts above our average applicant. I had positive evidence of his quality background once when a vendor happened to say "To be or not to be" during the course of spinning some off-the-wall tale, and

McGregor finished Hamlet's soliloquy. I immediately thought, "This man is definitely management material."

Days turned into weeks and weeks into months, and Mac's past remained a mystery to us. Finally, one rainy afternoon as he was waiting for a thunderstorm to stop before he pushed out, we had a chance to sit and talk. He revealed the circumstances that had brought him to New Orleans and thus to Lucky Dogs.

He had grown up in the Northeast. After college he became a successful accountant and married the love of his life, his childhood sweetheart. They bought a house and a few years later were blessed with a daughter. Tragically, the infant died of pneumonia. Her death led to guilt, guilt to arguments, and arguments to alcohol. The marriage collapsed. After a storybook beginning, his life had suddenly turned into a nightmare. Following months of depression, Mac resolved to resume living again.

In starting over, Mac decided against following any type of fairy-tale script. This time he would just drift. He journeyed across the northern tier of the nation and finally ended up homesteading on an island off Alaska. He declared squatter's rights and then moved into an old deserted trapper's cabin. His closest neighbors were a tribe of Indians in a nearby village who initially ignored him. They theorized that, as an ignorant mainlander unknowing about the ways of the woods, he would surely freeze to death before the spring thaw. If they befriended him, when he died they would lose a friend. If they kept their distance, however, when they discovered his frozen remains in the snow they would suffer no great loss.

To the Indians' amazement, Mac survived the winter. Gradually, they began to accept the fact that he might be around for a while. The first local to befriend him was a young boy whose only parent was an alcoholic mother. Curiosity brought the child to Mac's cabin, and a strong friendship was born that lasted for almost two years. Then tragedy struck again. The boy ventured offshore with his grandfather in an old, rickety wooden fishing boat. The boat capsized in the frigid waters and the boy drowned. Mac had lost his natural daughter on the East Coast, and now he lost his unofficially adopted son on the West Coast.

Engulfed by sorrow, he boarded up his cabin and headed back to the mainland, where he spent months drifting aimlessly across the country. Finally, his travels brought him through our doors.

Mac would become a phenomenally good vendor. He never barked out slogans. He didn't have to. His clean-cut appearance and his warm personality attracted customers to his cart. He developed an incredible local trade. Barmaids, hotel workers, streetwalkers, and businessmen would walk past four or five other vendors just to buy from him. The shoeshine boys and tap-dancers in the Quarter all befriended him. He would watch their shine rags and polish when they went to the restroom. In turn, they would keep an eye on his cart when he needed a break. Even the hustlers and hookers respected him enough to keep their scams off his corner. Mac was unique: a gentle person in what was often a not-so-gentle environment.

McGregor more than adequately filled one of our open spots. Not long after his arrival Barbara Huggins joined our ranks to fill another. Huggins was a stout, frizzy-haired woman in her early twenties. Prior to coming to New Orleans she had been a pickle packer in a small north-Mississippi town. She was married and assumed that she and her husband had a solid relationship. Life was good for two years. Then one evening she came home and discovered her husband in the arms of another.

As Barbara recalled, "I walked in after working eighteen hours and there he was naked in our bed with another man. I went into the bathroom and got a warm face rag and wiped my face. I thought I was dreaming. I looked out the bathroom door and around the corner and they were still there. I went into the bedroom and packed some clothes and on the way out the front door said, 'Well boys, y'all have a good night now.'"

She immediately headed south to New Orleans. Her first morning in town she noticed our "vendors wanted" advertisement in the *Times-Picayune.* By late afternoon she was rolling her cart out to her assigned location at the corner of St. Ann and Bourbon. Unbeknownst to her, this area was generally known for its gay trade.

She pushed the ten blocks to the corner and set up for business.

Everything was going smoothly until approximately 9 P.M. "It was weird," she said. "Four guys walked up near the cart. Two of them pulled out their wingdings right there. I just turned the cart off and pushed back in."

The next day I assigned her to work the Moonwalk: a safe, calm, family-oriented area across from the southern entrance to Jackson Square. Certainly, she would not have any problems there. But Barbara later recalled, "I was working my cart when a real nice-looking lady came up and told me that her husband had walked down the block to the bank to cash a check. Would I please fix her two hot dogs while she waited? So I fixed the dogs. It was only three blocks to the bank. It was taking her husband a really long time. I asked her if she had any money. She said no, so I called a policeman over. It ended up the lady didn't even have a husband. She was about twenty-eight. She was really kind of wacko. They took her away.

"Then this nice young guy walks up. He was in a three-piece suit so I guess he was a businessman. He ordered a hot dog with chili. I fixed his stuff. 'You got any potato chips?' he asked. No, I told him. 'How about beer?' 'No. No liquor license. My boss doesn't want to put alcohol on the cart because he knows that the vendors would drink it all.' Finally, he got a hot dog and then he started walking away. When he got halfway down the block, he started trying to pull out all of his hair. I thought, 'Lord, Lord, I hope it's not the hog dog that's making him do that.' He came back and put his face close to mine. He just stared at me. I pushed him away, and he walked on down the street and started trying to pull his hair out again. Boy, you meet some real weirdos in the Quarter."

Barbara did, however, meet one very nice young man during her second day of employment. He, too, had come to New Orleans looking for work and by chance stopped by her cart. She brought him to the shop, but she wasn't interested in the reward for bringing in a new employee. What she was interested in was him. He had that Norman Rockwell all-American look. There wasn't a callus on his hands. His skin was smooth and his brown hair was neatly trimmed; he was dressed in a polo shirt, clean jeans, and penny loafers. Like Mac, he didn't fit our typical vendor profile. Huggins was willing to show him the ropes. Given the chance she would have liked to tie him up in them.

The young man informed me that he wasn't interested in permanent employment. He just wanted something to hold him over until he caught on with a large national corporation. Our new recruit was a recent graduate of Columbia University's School of Marketing. He had come to New Orleans in hopes of finding a job, but thus far he had not received a single suitable offer. He was broke, but too proud to call home for any more money. Huggins insisted that she could convince him to stay. I didn't ask what method she intended to use. Some things are best left unsaid.

I hired him. However, I made one stipulation. He was not to let his mother or father know that he was working as a hot dog vendor, at least not until after he landed that perfect upper-level marketing position that he was so determined to find. I tried to imagine what his mom would have said had she discovered that her recently graduated son was selling wienies on the streets of the French Quarter. Her response probably would been much like that of Ignatius Reilly's mother when she confided to her friend Santa Battaglia, "He's a hot dog vendor."

"Aw, come on," Santa croaked. "A hot dog vendor? You mean out on the streets?"

"Out on the streets, honey, like a bum."

In the end, our new recruit's mom was spared the worry. After only a week he came to several important realizations. First, he discovered that street characters can be tough. They had been bullying him into giving them free hot dogs—hot dogs that he had to pay for at the end of the night. Second, he found out that standing on a street corner selling Lucky Dogs in all types of weather was physically a lot more demanding than he had ever imagined. Third, Huggins' tenacity and sexual aggressiveness was frightening the hell out of him. Those entry-level marketing positions that he had earlier rejected suddenly were not looking so bad. He was ready to reconsider them, especially if they would transfer him out of town and away from Barbara's lustful advances.

His departure left Barbara heartbroken. And it left us short a vendor.

Luckily, we quickly replaced him with Roy Williams, a middle-aged welder. Williams came to work for us because he had been fired for showing up drunk on his previous job. The fact that he had shown up at all I considered a major plus.

This man was no green kid just out of college. He had been around, and his experience showed. One morning about 4 A.M. he pushed in seething. He stormed up to the kitchen counter and set down a brown grocery bag. As he did so, he blurted out, "Two brothers tried to rob me, another brother. I got to the corner of Bienville and Chartres [two blocks from the shop]. These two brothers walked up asking for a light. I stuck my hand in my pocket to get my lighter and the big dude pulls a knife and says he wants my wallet. The other one just stood there like he's gonna hit me. I told him, 'Hey man, I'm your brother.' He just said, 'Gimme your f——ing money, bro'.' I said, 'I keep it inside the cart so nobody will rip it off.' When I reached into the cart, I grabbed this piece of chair leg that I kept there just for this kind of crap. My hand came out swinging. I beat those two punks into the ground."

As he spoke he emptied the contents of the paper bag onto the counter. Cigarettes, keys, a knife, cash, coins, wallets, personal items all fell into a pile. "I rolled their asses. Next time they'll think twice before they try and rob a hot dog man." In this instance, the tables had been turned: the rollers had become the rollees.

Following Williams at the check-in window was David Garcia. Garcia was the vendor that I had once put in jail for failing to fully pay his bill. He had come back, made restitution, and begged for forgiveness. So I had decided to put him back out on a cart. On this particular night he, too, had been involved in an attempted theft. Three men in a red Ford Mustang had stopped at his corner and ordered six jumbo Lucky Dogs. Garcia knew that company policy forbade selling to people in cars. Drive-up orders tended to create traffic problems on the Quarter's narrow streets. But it was late and the streets were deserted. He figured that no one would ever find out, so why not make the extra bucks? Besides, he thought, the guys were cute; maybe the sale would lead to a later rendezvous.

As he handed the blond in the back seat the last two hot dogs, the driver floored the car to avoid payment. Garcia grabbed hold of the blond. The Mustang sped off with him fiercely clinging to the customer. The car swerved back and forth as the driver attempted to force Garcia to let go. On one quick move to the right, the vehicle swerved too far and smashed into a parked pickup truck. David was on the opposite side from the impact and was thrown clear of the collision. He ended up scraped and bruised, but he recovered his dogs. Back at the shop he told McGregor, "One way or another I always get my man."

Later that night another serious incident occurred, this one at the Pair-of-Dice. Frenchy got drunk and hostile. Angered by a remark that the bartender made, he picked up a bar stool and threatened to destroy the establishment. A police car arrived. The two officers wisely called for backups. In the end it took five officers to wrestle the ex-boxer to the floor and cuff him. The last time I saw Frenchy, he was being driven away in the back of a patrol car.

Less than a month after the Pair-of-Dice brawl, a letter arrived at the shop addressed to "Lucky Dogs Manager." It was penned by Sally. She anticipated returning to New Orleans, and she wanted to know if her old friend Frenchy "was still hanging around." If whoever received the letter was unaware of what had happened to him or to the rest of the neat guys that she listed, then perhaps they could ask Jerry. "He's a prude," she wrote, "but he might know where they are." Being labeled "a prude" by Sally helped reassure me that at least thus far, my morals still seemed to be intact.

At the time that Sally was contemplating returning, another former employee was thinking along those same lines. It was a little after 9 P.M. one evening when my home phone rang. I recognized the voice from the past: Mike Giles, our ex-manager who had gotten into trouble mixing diet pills and alcohol. He apologized for having called his hometown sheriff and for accusing Doug and me of putting out a contract on him. The drugs and booze, he proclaimed, had affected his mental stability. His psychiatrist, however, now believed that he was once again ready to become a functioning member of society.

I congratulated him on being wise enough to seek professional help. He responded, "I didn't exactly seek it. One day I was so messed up that

I fell down and smashed my head against the curb. An ambulance hauled me to the VA Hospital. While I was in the waiting room, the television monitor showed a news clip of President Reagan. I never liked the dude. I never even liked his movies. I was pretty out of it. A security guard told the authorities that I said, 'I'm gonna kill that son-of-a-bitch.'

"I was arrested for threatening the life of the president. They put me in an institution for months. When I got out, I came home to live with my parents. I've been seeing a psychiatrist for over a year. He just released me. Now, if you and Doug will let me, I want to come back and work a cart."

I quickly responded that with McGregor, Huggins, McCarty, Williams, Stafford, Garcia, and the rest of the current crew, we really didn't have any choice corners available. I asked him if he was happy. "Yes," he answered. I asked if he liked his psychiatrist. His response was again yes. I suggested that it would be foolish to risk the positive strides that he had made just to come back to the Quarter. The Vieux Carré's environment might affect him in such a way that he'd end up in the same state as before. After a few moments of reflection, he decided that perhaps I was right.

I breathed a sigh of relief. At least for the time being I had dodged a bullet. Ultimately, neither Sally nor Mike returned. I dared not rejoice for long, though, because sooner or later others like them would no doubt drift through our doors.

7

Father Larry

In early 1982 I was asked to testify as a character witness in a court case concerning George Stafford. Stafford was attempting to gain overnight custody of his five-year-old son a few Saturdays a month. It didn't seem like an outrageous request. After all, he was paying child support as well as the youngster's health insurance premiums and kindergarten tuition. George worked six, sometimes seven days a week to meet his financial obligations, often denying his own needs in order to have money for those of his son.

Stafford was far from perfect, but he was trying to do what he believed to be right. At the same time, it seemed as though his former in-laws were trying their hardest to prevent him from having a meaningful relationship with his child. When they denied his overnight request, George saw no alternative but to take the matter to court.

During the hearing I watched the opposing counsel verbally assassinate Stafford until all that was left in the witness stand was a slumped-over, demoralized shell of a man. This litigation was war, and his opposition was merciless. George's attorney just sat there in a daze. The attorney for his former in-laws, however, had lots to say. He made George repeat two or three times that one of the reasons that he sold hot dogs was because he was unable to read. He forced George to admit that he was a slow learner and that he had only finished the equivalent of the third grade. Then he called a childcare expert to the stand. The hired gun had been contracted by the grandparents to investigate whether Stafford's extended visitation request should be granted. To no one's surprise, she testified that such a move would be unwise.

Stafford's attorney sat in silence, never raising an objection. The judge became so perturbed by this lack of action that he asked, "Counsel, are you planning on representing your client?"

"Yes, Your Honor," asserted George's attorney. But he never put forth a concerted effort. He called me as a character witness, but neglected to ask questions that would allow me to give supportive testimony for George. In the end, the judge had no alternative but to rule against Stafford's request. George was devastated. As we walked from the courthouse, he declared, "My lawyer sold me out." Whether that was true or not, I don't know. However, everyone, including the judge, knew that George had suffered greatly from a lack of representation. I felt sorry for him, but there was nothing that I could do.

I had been unable to provide much assistance to George, but a few weeks later I extended critical help to a high-ranking U.S. State Department official. The gentleman had come to New Orleans to lecture at a conference concerning foreign policy. It was to be a quick overnight trip, nothing out of the ordinary.

At the end of the evening, he left the conference for a stroll through the Quarter. To his amazement, on almost every corner of Bourbon Street there was a seven-foot-long hot dog–shaped cart. Each unit was identical to the one that Ignatius had pushed through the streets of New Orleans in the Pulitzer Prize–winning novel *A Confederacy of Dunces.*

To the average tourist, the cart is eye-catching. To the State Department official it was far more than that. His entire office had read Toole's work, and lengthy discussions had ensued about the outrageous Ignatius. Discovering the existence of such carts was for the official tantamount to finding the Holy Grail. He was certain that this news of their existence would astound his co-workers. But instead of expressing astonishment they scoffed at his disclosure. They even went so far as to suggest that he had succumbed to the liquid sins of the Quarter and imagined the carts.

Out of desperation, the official called my office. He was leaving town that afternoon. Could I possibly supply him with a photograph of a cart so that he could prove to his skeptical staff that the wagons were not a figment of an inebriated imagination? To me, the call smacked of a hoax. Surely the State Department, still combating the Evil Empire's attempt at world domination, had more important priorities than proving the existence of Lucky Dogs. Perhaps sensing my doubt, the gentleman pleaded for my assistance. He offered his State Department address and assured me that if I would send a photograph of the cart, I would be reimbursed for my time and expenses.

Certain that this plea was nothing more than a prank, I never followed up on the request. A week later, however, I received a second urgent telephone call. This time the gentleman was supposedly calling from Washington. He claimed that he was being subjected to unmerciful teasing. He had promised the skeptics that evidence would soon arrive that would prove the existence of Paradise Vendors, but thus far he had received no documentation.

I felt guilty, but I still wasn't certain that he wasn't part of a hoax. I agreed to stop what I was doing and try to find at least one piece of irrefutable evidence. If he would give me his telephone number, I would call him back in a few minutes.

I piddled around for five or ten minutes then dialed the number. A pleasant female voice answered, "Office of the Secretary."

"Excuse me, but secretary of what?" I inquired.

"Secretary of State." After a pause, "Sir, are you certain that you have dialed the correct exchange? This is a private line."

"Truthfully, I am not sure," I confessed. "I'm with Lucky Dogs, Incorporated, of New Orleans, and I am trying to reach Mr. X."

"My God!" she exclaimed. "He has been telling the truth. Please hold. I am certain that he will want to speak with you."

Mr. X came to the phone. I explained to him that, just as his co-workers had not believed that we existed, I, in turn, had not believed that he was actually a State Department official. He understood. Apologies aside, I promised to help him restore his credibility.

That very afternoon I sent via Federal Express to the Secretary of State's office a Lucky Dog T-shirt with the company's logo silk-screened across the front, a photograph of a cart, and a letter on official Lucky Dog stationery. In the correspondence I explained that should he ever become disgruntled in his present diplomatic position or should he determine that it lacked potential for further advancement, all he had to do was call. I would personally reserve a cart and assign him to one of our top corners.

A few days later I received his reply. In the upper left corner of the paper was the embossed seal of the State Department. Stamped at the center of the page were the words OFFICE OF THE SECRETARY OF STATE, WASHINGTON. Below that was the official's response:

> The smarmy hordes of East Coast skeptics are scourged, smitten and righteously driven in disarray from their suffocating Temple of Doubt into an eternal diaspora where their cynicism and heresy will justly prosper among the weeds, as Ignatius might have put it.
>
> I am grateful to you for the shirt and the photograph. My reputation (rather mediocre) is restored, thanks to you. Although I recognize I could never replace Ignatius, I take your job offer seriously. I should be able to sell a hot dog or two after all the baloney I've been pushing at the State Department.
>
> Thanks once again.
> Sincerely, Mr. X.

At that moment I realized that Lucky Dogs' labor woes could forever be obliterated. Within our grasp was an entire city of potential vendors.

Instead of running our help-wanted ad in the New Orleans *Times-Picayune*, we should be running it in the Washington *Post*.

As the diplomat wrestled with the decision whether to sell Lucky Dogs in the French Quarter or baloney at the State Department, Stafford wrestled with loneliness. Then suddenly one afternoon, he announced that he was getting married. It didn't matter that he had only known the woman for a week. It didn't matter that she was boisterous, bossy, crude, bleached to the roots, and minus one of her front teeth. Nothing mattered, except marrying her.

I had seen George go through the same scenario almost a year before. Then too, he had been certain he had found the perfect woman. He had even convinced his fellow vendor and roommate, Tommy, of it. He shouldn't have. Soon afterward, George arrived home early one evening and discovered his ideal woman enjoying the comforts of his ideal roommate's bed. Tommy apologized. Stafford forgave him. They blamed the woman for trying to come between them and threw her out. They reasoned that it was easier to find a sex partner than a good drinking buddy.

I tried to persuade George not to make the same mistake again. Quoting Percy Sledge's 1968 rock 'n' roll hit "Take Time to Know Her," I suggested that he "please, please, not rush into this thing." Stafford turned out not to be a Percy Sledge fan. He didn't want to hear Sledge's or my advice. He was determined to get married as soon as possible. Suddenly, the truth dawned on me: this matrimonial drive had nothing to do with love. It didn't even have to do with hormones. What it had to do with was his son. Stafford reasoned that being married would present a more traditional home image. Such an atmosphere might allow him to go back into court and convince the judge to reverse his ruling. He figured that all he needed was a wife and a more aggressive attorney. It was a disastrous plan.

The union was doomed from the start, but problems arose even more quickly than I had anticipated. Two days after the wedding, Tommy came to the shop and said, "Jerry, I need to talk to you in private." Behind closed doors he confessed to having had sex with

George's bride . . . the night after the wedding. So much for the sanctity of marriage. The bridal bouquet hadn't even had time to wilt.

Tommy now felt guilty. He wanted to confess everything to George. "Are you insane?" I asked. "Tell him nothing except that since he is married, you consider it inappropriate to continue sharing the apartment. Then pack your bags and get out."

Tommy followed my advice, but the bride followed him. Over the next year and a half, she leapfrogged back and forth between the two of them. For the life of me, I can't understand why either man wanted her.

As the adulterous bride moved from lover to lover, I was moving from special event to special event. People who saw us at the numerous charity affairs that we supported began requesting that we cater their private parties. Private parties begot more private parties. I generally worked the events because Lucky Dog vendors as a rule don't possess valid driver's licenses. The few that do can't be trusted with the company truck. They might drive right past the party and on beyond the state line.

Most of the events that we catered were interesting, some were unique, and a few I would rather have never done. On one occasion I was working an elaborate private event in the garden district of New Orleans. The house, located in the elite uptown neighborhood, was owned by a little gray-haired lady in her late sixties. She automatically assumed that, since I was working a hot dog cart, I had to be a high-school dropout. I tried to explain that I had two college degrees. She ignored the information. She was confident that if I would just go back to school, then I could go far beyond working a wienie wagon. A whole new world of opportunities would open to me.

Several times during the evening she stopped by the cart to give me encouragement and advice. At midnight, as I prepared to leave, she made one last attempt to convince me of the value of a diploma. I figured, why not make her happy? In the most humble voice that I could muster, I explained that I had been thinking about what she had said, and that because of her I had decided to register for GED classes. She was elated. In fact, she was so thrilled with her accomplishment that she gave me a thirty-dollar tip, which I guess proves that education pays.

The next morning when I returned the cart to the shop, I was greeted by a flood of people leaving the building. McGregor, Stafford, Garcia, and Huggins all rapidly headed out the door proclaiming that they were going to the Pair-of-Dice for a Coke. Damn strange, I thought, especially the part about the Coke. Then, I turned towards the kitchen, and standing before me was a big, rough-looking, muscled guy who appeared to be in his late twenties. In his right hand was a three-foot piece of one-inch-diameter iron pipe. He growled, "You must be Jerry."

I didn't want to be Jerry. I wanted to be anyone but Jerry. I had no idea who this guy was or what he wanted, but I was pretty confident I was about to find out. Before I had a chance to say a word he added, "Fork over the eight bucks that your manager stole from me last night."

Whew! I wasn't the one who had angered him. I could handle this. I checked his bill; it was correct. However, in an act of good faith I offered him eight dollars for his pipe. Taking into consideration the metal cylinder's length and width, and factoring in the size of the arm holding it and the thrust per square inch, eight dollars was a bargain.

Not all new vendors work out. This pipe-wielding one hadn't. But over the next several months I would hire six individuals who would remain with the company off and on for the next fifteen years. The first to arrive was P.J., followed by James Hudson, Alice Knight, Paul Hager, Kenneth Schmitt, and Larry Simmons.

P.J. came to New Orleans in early 1981 from Rossville, Georgia. He had worked as a security guard back home, but after his mom and dad died he got the itch to move to Houston. The big city lights seemed much more exciting than the small street lights of Rossville. After about four hours in Houston, P. J. decided that whatever he was looking for he was not going to find in Texas. He later recalled the decision: "There was something about the place that I just didn't like. I bought a one-way bus ticket to New Orleans. When I came here, I had one bag. In it was a fifth of Jack Daniels and a fifth of Evan Williams. That was all I needed."

His first night in town he hit all the strip joints and bars on Bourbon Street. During his romp from club to club he noticed a help-wanted sign in a shop window. The next day he applied and was hired as a salesman in a sex paraphernalia shop specializing in dildos, vibrators, negligees, blow-up balloon dolls, and an assortment of indescribable battery-operated objects. He managed to hold on to the position until he broke one of the store's more absurd rules. He was caught off duty having coffee at a local café with an ex-employee. If an employee had been terminated, then no other employee was to have anything to do with him.

Unemployed and out of money, P. J. was attracted to Lucky Dogs. For three months he steadily worked a cart, while on his off days he looked for a job that offered a more predictable income. Finally, he was hired by a security company. As a guard he had set hours, set pay, and protection from the elements. He continued to stop by the shop and hang out with the guys on his days off, but it would be almost two years before he returned as a vendor.

Shortly after P. J. arrived, a young kid named James Hudson appeared on the scene. Hudson was a strong, rugged eighteen-year-old from southern Mississippi. I had serious doubts about putting someone so young and so naïve out on the streets as a vendor. The kid had never been around the likes of the people roaming the Quarter. But he was desperate for work, and he was quite persuasive. Certainly, he was physically strong enough to take care of himself. Plus, he had boxed several years in the amateur ranks. I decided to give him a chance.

The first night we put Hudson on what we considered to be an average corner. He had a seasoned veteran working a cart across the street from him. If he had any problems, he could ask the other vendor for help. It ended up that the veteran was the one who needed help. Hudson crushed him in sales. After that first night, the kid's goal was to become the best vendor that ever hawked a Lucky Dog. He succeeded in consistently beating the seasoned vendors. Lucky Dogs became his home, and the vendors his family. As in any relationship, there would be good times and bad. But early on he was content trying to become the best hot dog vendor in the company's history.

Joining our crew in early 1983 was Alice Knight. Alice, like many who come to the Quarter, was trying to leave her past behind. Though only twenty-six, she had been married three times. According to Alice, her first husband had been murdered, her second had been abusive, and her third she had caught in bed with a fifteen-year-old. In her words, "I've had it with husbands. They're not worth the trouble."

As Alice settled into the job of selling hot dogs, Bob McGregor started talking about leaving. I really didn't want to see that happen. Mac was intelligent, clean-cut, and reliable; only twice in the previous year had he come to work drunk. The vendors liked him and I liked him and he seemed to enjoy his job. There was no apparent reason for him to leave. I figured that perhaps if I got him out of the Quarter for a day or two, I might be able to persuade him to change his mind. I was planning to go check on Doug's hunting camp near Natchez, Mississippi, so I decided to invite Mac to accompany me. In the three-and-a-half-hour ride each way, I would have plenty of time to present my argument as to why I thought he should stay.

The trip proved enlightening—too enlightening. I knew that Mac was attending mind-control classes. I also knew that he was taking karate. But other interests that he had taken up I had not been aware of. Unfortunately, they would soon be revealed to me.

We didn't leave Lucky Dogs until 6:00 P.M. It was almost 9:45 P.M. when we pulled into the camp's dirt driveway. The old run-down sharecropper's shack looked deplorable on the outside, but on the inside it had been completely renovated. It had pine-paneled walls, vaulted ceilings, and enough bunks to sleep twelve. All in all, it was quite comfortable.

The fact that the house sat isolated in the midst of a cotton field made it even more appealing to someone looking to escape the hassles of the city. On a clear moonlit night when you stood on the porch and looked out over the land, all you could see were fields, lightning bugs, and the outline of distant trees. It was a desolate area. That night, an overcast sky made it even darker than usual.

As I stepped from the vehicle into the hot evening air, I suddenly felt an incredible chill. I froze for a few seconds. Mac, sitting in the truck, took notice of my shivering, but he made no mention of it until we settled in for the evening. Then he suggested that my chills might not be due to illness. They might be caused by a spiritual presence. He attempted to legitimize this explanation by stating that for the last year and a half, he had been involved in contacting spirits in other dimensions. Initially, he had used a Ouija board, then tarot cards, and finally voodoo. He had discovered that his karate instructor, who was heavily into voodoo, could tutor him in more than the martial arts.

There we were sitting in an old shack with only fields and woods surrounding us. I hadn't come here for a male bonding experience. We didn't have to sing campfire songs, roast marshmallows, or make "s'mores." Nor did we have to try and scare the hell out of each other, which is what I assumed he was trying to do. In this I was wrong. Mac was in utter seriousness sharing his latest investigations with me. He contended that in his apartment in the Quarter he had opened windows to other dimensions—windows that he had not always been able to close.

I really began to regret bringing Mac with me. I knew better than to socialize with vendors, but here I had gone and done it anyway. There was nothing that I could do about it at this hour. I was too tired to drive back to New Orleans, and Mac didn't possess a valid driver's license— at least not in this world. I had no choice but to spend the night there with him. Mac, trying to be comforting, assured me that, should he attract anything from the nether world, he was confident that he could handle the situation. I wasn't worried about the nether world, but I was deeply concerned about this one.

We slept in upper bunks across the room from each other. To bring a little light into the room, I opened the window's wooden safety shutters. The clouds had passed, and a full moon shown brightly down on the cotton fields. I had seen enough old Boris Karloff movies to view this moon with unease. I lay there with one eye open and one eye closed for what seemed like hours. At some point I dozed off.

The next morning I woke to the rising sun and the chirping of birds. I felt relieved. After a quick check of the grounds, we left for New Orleans. Our discussion on the way back centered on Lucky Dogs and Mac's future. He was adamant about going home. I was now encouraging the idea. Privately, I was forming my own resolution: it would be a cold day in hell before I suggested another management/employee camp-out.

The following week Mac packed his belongings and prepared to depart. It was only then that I discovered that he was actually an illegal alien, a Canadian citizen in the United States with an expired green card. When he had filled out his application, he had produced a New York driver's license, a social security card, and a U.S. passport. His confession only occurred because, having to cross the border, he could not take his small .22 caliber derringer, an item that he had only recently purchased. Mac requested that I keep it, along with three boxes of books on the occult. He planned to return in the future, and when he did he hoped to reenter the United States legally.

Because he was so open, I questioned Mac as to how he had obtained the fake documents. "They're not fake," he responded. "They're authentic." It seems that after his daughter's death he had entered the country with a legitimate green card. He first settled in New York City. It was then that he decided that he wanted permanent residence. According to him, he visited a cemetery and found the grave of an infant born close to his own year of birth. He wrote to the state's bureau of records and requested a certified copy of the child's birth certificate. They sent it to him. Next, he made up a social security number and applied for a copy of his card, claiming to have lost his original. To his amazement he received one in the mail. With those two documents in hand he applied for a driver's license. Then he procured a passport.

I don't doubt the accuracy of his tale. I say this because the first time that I listed his social security number on the company's quarterly withholding report, the Social Security Administration called to inquire about his number. As I stood by the phone, Mac explained to the caller that it had been assigned to him by the New York office. "That explains it," the bureaucrat responded. No further explanation was necessary.

After storing his belongings at the shop in Sally's old upstairs storeroom apartment, Mac departed on a Greyhound bus. Six weeks later I received a call from him. He was working full-time in a factory in Saskatchewan. He gave me his home phone number, and on several occasions over the next year we exchanged calls. He always said that he was going to return to the Quarter. If at all possible, he intended to make it back before the world's fair came to the city in the spring of 1984.

For better or for worse, Mac was gone. To replace him we swiftly recruited Paul Hager, or Pauline, as his closest friends refer to him. Hager started working as a helper on George Stafford's cart. He would set the cart up in the morning, push it out to the corner, and work until 6 P.M. at which time George would relieve him. They split the profits.

Prior to coming to Lucky Dogs in June, 1983, Paul (my conservative southern upbringing compels me to call him by his given name) had spent thirteen years as a waiter in various New Orleans restaurants. He started helping Stafford just to vary his daily routine. Working outside on the corner, the crowd constantly drifting by, the sounds of jazz

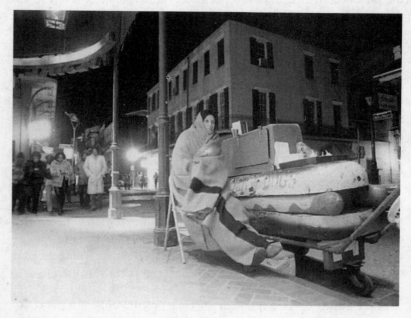

Paul Hager trying to stay warm on a freezing night in December, 1983
Courtesy Times-Picayune/*Chuck Cook*

flowing from Crazy Shirley's, mingling with the shoeshine boys and the street people: all made working the cart exciting. And Hager liked excitement.

He was originally from West Virginia. He had left the hills behind in 1965, headed south for Jacksonville, Florida, then after two years come to New Orleans. The French Quarter was his new love but far from his only one. In 1978 he returned to West Virginia to marry his high-school flame. The union lasted less than six months. She wanted him to remain in West Virginia and work in the coal mines. He wanted to return to New Orleans where he could earn four hundred dollars more a month working as a waiter in a less hazardous environment. He claims that she agreed to move south. Then he headed back to the Quarter to find work and a larger apartment. She was to follow, but she never did.

The broken marriage was the coup de grâce to Hager's heterosexuality. But jump not to the conclusion that the failed union sent him to the other side of the sexual spectrum. His first homosexual relationship had occurred when he was ten years old. A seventeen-year-old boy had convinced him that sexual experimentation was normal. From his youth until his marriage he had remained bisexual.

After helping Stafford for a few days, Hager decided to work his own cart. He quickly established himself as one of our better night vendors, but he preferred the day shift. I transferred him to Jackson Square II, a spot across the park from our regular Square vendor. Hager would never gross there what he had on Bourbon Street, nor would his tips be as great; but he made enough to survive.

Kenneth Schmitt helped fill the void created when Hager left our night crew. Smitty had moved from Cleveland to New Orleans in March, 1976, at the age of twenty-two. He was the product of an affair between a gentleman of means and his housekeeper, neither of whom he ever knew. Much of his youth had been spent in foster homes. Like many others in the Quarter, he was searching for a place where he could belong.

His first job in the Big Easy was at Chuck's, located in the six hundred block of Bourbon. It seemed almost sacrilegious, but the club blared out country-and-western music in the heart of jazzville. For six

Smitty
Courtesy author

years Smitty hustled there as a waiter on the late-night shift. When the club closed its doors for good, he took a job as a cocktail waitress at another Bourbon Street pub. He recalled, "I dressed up in drag just for the hell of it. I didn't get put down by the girls. It was the guys who gave me a hard time. The girls dug the heck out of it. I wore shorts, fishnet stockings, a wig, and a bra." When this club went belly up, Smitty hit the street searching for employment.

Opportunities for guys in heels proved to be limited. Luckily, he ran across us, an equal opportunity employer. We hired him with one stipulation: the heels had to go. I admit that he could walk in them without skittering. But vendors need traction in order to push their carts, and the heels offered little. The fishnet stockings would not pose a problem because company policy required vendors to wear long pants. The wig and bra I left to his discretion.

About being a vendor Smitty says, "I like working the street. Money is part of it, but I like watching the people make fools of themselves. It's never dull. Never dull. There is always something going on out there. It's like a circus. You've got better free entertainment than you could ever get in any of the clubs. People come to the Quarter and let their hair down. They do and say things that they would never admit to back home.

"I put on a simple act out on the street. I get away with a lot of things that people wouldn't let me get away with otherwise. They think that I am kind of on the dumb side. People will think that they're pulling a scam on me, but they're not."

As Smitty settled in, Larry Simmons, the newest member of our semipermanent crew, was also trying to adjust to selling dogs. Simmons had purchased a bus pass in Ohio that said "travel America." He had been to Jacksonville and Miami before he came to New Orleans. He was thirty-five years old, divorced with two kids. He had become a streetwise, seasoned hustler, and this job was more honest and legal than what he was accustomed to.

In Miami he had worked as a dishwasher at the Mayflower Restaurant. The eatery also specialized in making its own doughnuts. Within days Simmons rose from the rank of dishwasher to that of doughnut packer. For six months he packed glazed and jelly delights into small retail boxes. All the while his eyes would focus on the little poem on the front of the carryout cartons. It read, "As you ramble on through life, whatever be your goal, keep your eye upon the doughnut, and not upon the hole . . . Mayflower Donuts." One morning Larry woke in a cold sweat. He simply couldn't face the jingle again. He quit.

Out of work and soon to be out of cash, he needed to find a new source of income. His roommate was running what he considered to be the ultimate scam. He had sent twenty-five dollars to a mail-order company and received documents declaring that he was an ordained minister. He had even started his own church and was now taking in a considerable amount in tithes. Simmons figured that he, too, would become a man of the cloth. He mailed off his twenty-five dollars. Within days he received a certificate declaring that he was an ordained minister. As a member of the clergy, he felt that he should dress the part. He purchased a priestly looking black shirt, black pants, and a clerical collar.

Simmons remembered plenty about his religious work: "You'd be surprised at how easy people will part with their money. They ask you to do all kinds of things. They want you to marry them, bury them, and pray for them. I married one couple. They were twenty-four or twenty-five. I was set up at Lincoln Mall in Miami. I had my little table and I was taking people's blood pressure. I had once taken a course from the Red Cross, so I pretty much knew how to do it. I had a ten-dollar city license and my minister credentials. I wouldn't charge people, but I would ask for a donation. This couple from Brazil came by and got their blood pressure checked. They had already been married in Brazil, but they wanted to be married again in America. I don't know why. They went down and got a license, and they came back and I married them right out on the street corner. They took pictures and I signed their certificate. I even gave them one of the marriage licenses that I had received in my ministerial beginner's package. Their hearts were filled with joy. My wallet was filled with five new crisp twenty-dollar bills. God bless them.

"I never did a funeral. The best thing that I ever did had to do with a woman from Cuba. She was a divorcée with a ten-year-old daughter. The lady was convinced that she was possessed by the devil. She was Catholic, spoke very little English, but her daughter had been born in the U.S. and spoke both English and Spanish fluently. Ever since the mother had been very young, people had told her that she was 'full of the devil.' She wasn't nuts, but she wasn't exactly sane either."

The woman saw Simmons sitting at his table, so she and her daughter walked over. She had been to other priests, but none had thus far been able to help. The daughter told Larry that her mom wanted to know if he could exorcise demons. Father Larry responded, "Well, I probably can."

Father Larry
Courtesy author

He made an appointment for them to meet him at his apartment at three o'clock that afternoon, figuring that they would never show. When they did, Larry at first had no idea what he was going to do. Then it dawned on him. He got out a few candles and a rosary, put his Bible on the table, and then drew some holy tap water, blessed, of course, by him. The entire process of casting out the demons took about two hours because everything had to be translated by the daughter. After just the first session, the woman professed to feel better. Her twenty-five-dollar donation, in turn, lifted Larry's spirits.

However, two days later she showed up again, claiming still to be possessed. Father Larry recommended an extensive program of treatments. After the fifth session, the woman proclaimed in Spanish, "Thank the Lord! The devil is gone." Two hundred fifty dollars had also left her. But according to Larry, "It was such a small price to pay for such a great gift."

"To really succeed in this kind of scam," he warned, "you can't just depend on blood pressure donations. You have to get three or four people who believe that you are doing such a marvelous job that they're willing to bankroll your programs. To get to that level you have to put in twenty-four hours a day, seven days a week. It's hard work. If you don't put in the time and effort, you'll never make it. That's why I decided against trying to build a permanent congregation. Instead, I chose to take my show on the road. That's how I ended up in New Orleans."

Arriving in the Big Easy, Simmons set up his table at the Moonwalk next to the Lucky Dog cart. He was taking blood pressure, passing out religious tracts, and taking donations. He also had flowers, religious pamphlets, and crosses. He didn't sell them, but he did encourage people to give a donation. New Orleanians, however, were used to his kind of scam. They would walk past his table and chide, "Ya ain't no priest, ya phony." Larry would answer, "Yes, you're right. God bless you."

Unfortunately, his daily take was a pittance of what he had projected. He recalled, "The hot dog vendor next to me was making more than I was, especially when winter came. I felt a new calling. God wanted me to be a Lucky Dog man." I was happy to have him on board. An experienced exorcist could come in handy in case McGregor had left behind any of his nether-world buddies.

Larry's first days on the job were filled with problems. Big Al tried to help break him in as a vendor. Al's advice probably did more harm than good. All Al knew how to do was sit on his stool and read westerns as potential customers strolled past. The second hindrance to Larry's success was the friend he hired to help him work the cart. The second day that they worked together, his friend showed up with a pet squirrel. He figured that it would be a great attention getter.

It was. The woman living in the upstairs apartment across from where they worked complained to Larry that his partner had been playing with a huge live rat all day. Larry informed her, "Madam, that was not a rat, but a squirrel." The next day the lady called my office and accused us of having a rodent on the cart. I told her I knew that Larry wasn't the most handsome man in the Big Easy, but I thought her description was a bit brutal. "No, you dimwit," she said, "the vendor had a rodent on the cart." That violation I immediately corrected.

We lost a rodent, but we regained Dan Myers. It was an even swap. Dan had left the Quarter a year or so before, swearing that he was moving home for good so that he could patch up his relationship with his mother. He didn't want her cutting him out of her will. The last I had heard was that he was planning on getting married. He had come a long way since he wanted me to sneak the brown envelope out of his P.O. box and bring the cash to him in jail.

Dan simply could not relax and enjoy the straight life. The Quarter kept drawing him back. In his small town he felt confined. In the Quarter he felt alive and free. Sometimes he felt too free. On one occasion after his return, he got so drunk while working the hot dog stand that the night manager had to lay him across the cart and push him back to the shop.

Then there was the time that Dan was caught sitting on his stool passionately kissing and fondling a young blond gentleman. Lucky Dogs admittedly operates under a pretty liberal set of regulations, but we do have rules. One is that male vendors are not allowed to fondle other males while on the job. A similar rule applies to heterosexuals. I thought that it was a pretty reasonable request, but Myers was having trouble obeying it. The doorman at the 544 Club on the corner was about to douse the couple with a bucket of cold water when one of the beat cops broke up the lovefest and ran the blond down the block.

A few weeks later Myers decided it would be best if he took a leave of absence and ventured west. According to him, he was going in search of the land of the four B's: Beaches, Booze, Bitches, and Boys. Once again he was leaving, but he assured me that he would return before the opening of the New Orleans World Exposition in the spring of 1984. I wasn't certain that that was good news.

8

Nineteen Eighty-Four

As Dan Myers trekked westward, construction equipment rumbled into the Quarter to help upgrade it before the opening of the world's fair. Claw-armed machinery tearing up streets and sidewalks became the norm. Bourbon and Royal streets had to be traversed via temporary plywood walkways. Piles of brick, sand, unearthed gas lines, and construction barricades blocked crosswalks. Bulldozers and dump trucks replaced horse-drawn carriages as the Quarter's most conspicuous vehicles, and jackhammers drowned out the soothing sounds of jazz.

City officials had decided that the Quarter's concrete walkways needed to be replaced with more historical-looking brick and flagstone versions. However, prior to doing the surface work, construction crews were to replace the subsurface drain pipes, gas lines, and telephone lines. The Big Easy's premier historic district took on the appearance of an urban war zone. It had deep trenches and mounds of dirt. All that was missing was barbed wire.

Not surprisingly, tourists were staying away, and retailers were struggling to stay afloat. By the fall of 1983 Lucky Dogs was in desperate financial shape. Adding to our problem, the police department's vice squad started sweeping the Quarter's streets. They wanted to rid the district of hookers prior to the fair's opening. As I entered the shop one evening, I discovered approximately twenty of the Decatur Street darlings standing around in the kitchen. Big Al swore that they were applying for jobs. I knew better. They were playing hide and seek with

A pre-1984 Lucky Dog cart
Courtesy Lucky Dogs, Inc.

the cops, and he had turned our building into a safe house for hookers. I nixed that plan immediately.

After several weeks of this sweeping procedure, the number of prostitutes in the area dwindled dramatically. Unfortunately, so did our sales at Iberville and Decatur. Once the girls were gone, the merchant seamen and the longshoremen also disappeared. The vice squad had all but eliminated our clientele in its drive to morally upgrade the city.

There were other moves to clean up the streets before the hordes of predicted fair-goers arrived. The biggest target after the prostitutes seemed to be the flophouses. One by one they began to shut down. The inhabitants had to move out of the inner city to find a new place to live. As a result, fewer and fewer winos were hanging around on the corners.

The fair was projected to be the catalyst that would forever change New Orleans. It would do that. But of greater importance to Lucky Dogs, it turned out to be a watershed in the company's history. Not even Fortuna could have predicted the metamorphosis that we were poised to undergo.

As work progressed to upgrade the Vieux Carré, the Orleans Parish Health Department began strongly suggesting that we improve the condition of our twenty-six-year-old vending carts. They stopped short of demanding that we do so—probably recalling the earlier Supreme Court ruling concerning the wagons' uniqueness. Times were bleak, but there was hope. Promoters of the fair promised to attract millions of new visitors. All we had to do was find a way to capture a part of this giant new market.

We hoped to be chosen the hot dog concessionaire of the Exposition, but we were realistic about our chances. Therefore, we investigated other ways to increase our gross sales. The most logical move was to add soft drinks to our menu. Sounds simple, but the change would entail board-of-health approval. Modern regulations required all mobile food units to have hot and cold running water, three sinks (wash, rinse, and sanitize), a hand sink, a fresh-water holding tank, and a waste-water holding tank. Heck, I knew people back in Mississippi who didn't have these amenities in their homes. Nevertheless, to receive the department's consent, we had to meet the modern standards.

As we were redesigning our cart, the fair's concessionaire decision arrived: "We regretfully must inform you that the Committee has approved another applicant in this particular category." The rejection didn't upset us, but what did infuriate us was the attempted sabotage that followed.

Famed novelist George Orwell predicted that in the year 1984 "Big Brother" would be watching. From our perspective, Orwell was correct. Big Brother in our case was not the government, as Orwell had theorized, but the power that controlled the Louisiana World Exposition. This entity went beyond simply excluding us from its grounds. It tried to get the city council to pass legislation prohibiting street vending within the "vicinity of the Exposition site." This area, as defined by the proposed ordinance, referred to forty square blocks. Big Brother was no longer just watching, he had opened fire with both barrels.

We never intended to set up at the fair's controversial front gates (adorned with bare-breasted mermaids), but we did want to continue selling along Poydras Street and by the old Rivergate Convention Center. Both sites were approximately a block and a half from the Exposition's main entrance, and we had operated there before the fair's arrival. Someone suggested that we take legal action. Thankfully, the crisis never came to that end. Mayor Ernest "Dutch" Morial had a very capable individual acting as liaison between the city and the fair, Deputy Chief Ray Holman of the NOPD. Holman had me draw a map showing our locations. He then had it approved by the city. Grudgingly, the Exposition accepted it.

While we were fighting to keep our corners, Custom Fabrication, located a few miles west of New Orleans in Kenner, was putting the finishing touches on our new prototype Lucky Dog cart. The modern unit maintained the uniqueness of the original design as recognized by the U.S. Supreme Court. It also fulfilled the health department's requirements, yet lent itself to mass production. Twelve of the new models were produced in less than seven weeks. Another four were delivered a week after the fair opened, and the final six were phased in over the next several months. As each new cart was delivered, a veteran wagon was retired from the fleet.

At 8 A.M. on May 12, 1984, as fair workers completed last-minute preparations for their grand opening, we were unloading the first shipment of new carts off of a flatbed trailer on Decatur Street. They were assigned to vendors and immediately packed with supplies. The production deadline had been met by the narrowest of margins. To ensure success, Stafford, Smitty, and Huggins had Father Larry bless their carts. For a few bucks Father Larry would bless anything you wanted. For a few more he would throw in a confession.

At noon, when the fair's gates opened to the public, our vendors were already serving Lucky Dogs on both sides of Convention Center Boulevard at Poydras, by the Rivergate Convention Center, and at Fulton and Girod near the Exposition's side entrance. Our carts were on sites that had been preapproved by the police department. We anticipated no problems.

The redesigned 1984 Lucky Dog cart
Courtesy Bergeron Photography

The fleet looked gorgeous, showroom perfect. Even the vendors looked presentable in their new red-and-white striped shirts. Watching fair goers purchase hot dogs and drinks from our new state-of-the-art carts, Doug and I felt extremely proud. However, not everyone viewed the wagons with our enthusiasm. There were individuals associated with the Exposition that still wanted us confined to the Quarter.

By late afternoon, trouble was on the horizon. Fair security had stood outside of the main gate all morning and watched Myers on Poydras make sale after sale. Suddenly, at dusk Myers and his cart were abducted and sucked deep into the bowels of the fair. For over two hours Exposition officials stonewalled and denied any knowledge of the incident. Both man and machine had vanished. Then, one of the local winos informed me (for the price of a bottle of Thunderbird) that he had watched the fair's security "bust the wienie man."

Joel Loeffelholz was called in on the case. He contacted the Exposition's legal department demanding an explanation and warning that if the blatant injustice was not immediately corrected, legal action would ensue. Within minutes, the front of the Lucky Dog cart could be seen coming out the fair's main entrance. It slowly headed past the busty mermaids and back down Convention Center Boulevard toward its assigned location.

Fair security, in spite of our special permits, had refused to accept the fact that we were legal. They had seized the cart and shanghaied Myers in one final attempt to stop us from operating. The action undoubtedly had been encouraged by disgruntled fair concessionaires.

Throughout the entire ordeal, Myers had sat in a cushioned chair in security's air-conditioned office. Not sure why he was being held, he decided to make the most of it. The day had been pretty hectic. A break, even an unscheduled one, appealed to him. As he relaxed, he consumed his fill of coffee and Cokes, of course at his captors' expense. By the middle of the second hour, he began demanding a hot meal. After all, as he informed them, he was their hostage, and according to the Geneva Accords they had to feed him. That was the law, and he expected them to comply. To shut him up they bought him dinner. He had just started complaining that they had shorted him dessert when the fair's legal staff insisted rather strongly that security release him posthaste. Well-rested, well-fed, and with an order of bananas foster to go, Myers was escorted back to his corner. Father Larry later reminded him that he had scoffed at the idea of having his cart blessed. If he wanted it blessed now, he declared, the price would be double.

In May, 1984, the company's equipment and vendor attire were both noticeably new and top of the line. Practically everything reflected our move toward a more modern image. The one area that had changed insignificantly was personnel. Myers, Bill McCarty, Barbara Huggins, David Garcia, George Stafford, Big Ben, Big Al, and Smitty were all still regulars. Odom had also returned, but his Bourbon Street bride had not. The fire of love, once removed from the Lucky Dog cart, had smoldered.

Just prior to the fair's opening, Alice Knight had also left our employ. She had fallen for a male stripper and left town with him to work the Illinois carnival circuit. McGregor never made it back to New Orleans, but he did call a couple of times from Canada to tell the old gang hello. Neither he nor I mentioned his opening windows to other worlds. It was a shame. Potential for franchise opportunities in other dimensions would have been unlimited.

James Hudson, the young kid from Mississippi, had also left. His boxer training and quick fists had been getting him into trouble. He was more apt to throw a punch than reason with the unruly street crowd. Before he seriously hurt someone, he took a sabbatical.

Even with these departures, by the fair's opening day all of our carts were manned. In addition, our twenty-two vendors had hired helpers so that their wagons could stay out on the street eighteen to twenty hours a day. We were operating a vendor's version of SAC (Strategic Air Command). Around the clock Lucky Dog carts were stationed throughout the Quarter and near the fairgrounds ready to serve on a moment's notice.

Suddenly, instead of sending out one cart during the day and thirteen at night, we were sending out all twenty-two units, none of which were beat up. We had twelve brand-new carts and the ten best of the original fleet on the street. In fact, we had more vending wagons than we had space to store them. To solve the problem, we rented the fourth floor of our present building. The original fleet's unused carts were moved upstairs and relegated to mothballs. We also leased the ground floor of an unoccupied building around the corner on Iberville as a backup commissary and cart parking garage.

On the morning that the fair opened, Paul Hager was in charge of our day shift; Big Al was handling the night crew; and John Marlow, who had joined the company in the spring of 1983, was filling in as their relief. Hager had been promoted to manager on the Monday following Easter because of a ruckus involving Kevin Russo and Julie Bennett. Julie had been doing the mental work on the day shift, while Kevin had taken care of the physical aspects of the job. Together they did the work of one normal manager. Unfortunately, with the two-person system came the risk of double trouble. With Kevin in the shop I had to be on my toes constantly. He would steal cans of chili, packs of napkins, onions, toilet paper, or whatever else he could sneak out. He then traded his loot for credit at the greasy spoon café around the corner.

It was kind of a game. What Kevin succeeded in stealing was never very much, so I compensated for the loss by assigning him extra chores. He never caught on. He wasn't stealing because he needed the money. He just didn't want to lose his fine-honed criminal talents. In the end, it wasn't his thievery that got him fired. It was the constant arguments that he and Julie had in the shop. The last straw—a full-scale brawl—took place on Easter Sunday. This time he got physical and almost broke her back. I insisted that they take several months off. Hager took over the day shift and Kevin and Julie took off for California.

To handle the odd jobs that Kevin had once performed, I hired "Jeno the Wino" and P. J. Smith. Jeno was one of the Quarter's better-known street characters. I admit that he had his faults, the main one being that he was undependable. But why should he have to conform to a criterion that no one else in the shop adhered to? He was most unreliable when the urge for a drink struck him. At that point he would simply walk out of the shop, buy a bottle of wine at one of the local liquor stores, and head home, which in his case was an alley off Dauphine Street.

P. J., once relatively stable, had become more Jeno-like. He had held his security job for almost two years. At first he loved his work. His assignments included banks, office buildings, and a jewelry store. Then his security company was bought out by a new, much more rigid concern. He protested, "It was too military, too strict. They didn't even want me drinking bourbon in my coffee."

Once relieved of his daily guard duties, P. J. often headed for Bourbon Street. There he didn't have to dilute his Jack Daniels with "godawful coffee." It was during one of his strolls down this street that he befriended Jeno. Within minutes they felt as if they had been lifelong buddies. They began partying regularly every evening. When the partying was over, P. J. would head back to his rented room, and Jeno would return to the alley that he called home.

Jeno called his asphalt-decked, three-sided, open-air domicile "One and a Half Dauphine Street." In the summertime his alley was cool; in the wintertime it was warm. He felt at home there, so much so that he even rejected P. J.'s invitation to room with him. According to P. J., Jeno lived there for over five years. "The alley," he explained, "has its advantages." The rent was right, and the cops ignored it. The only real downfall was that the roof leaked.

Though Jeno was a street person, he had pride. He washed his clothes at one of the Quarter's laundromats. He shaved often. And when he really wanted to clean up, he would go into the men's restroom at D. H. Holmes department store and use the soap and sinks. He made his money watching carts for hot dog and flower vendors when they went to the restroom or to eat. Upon their return they would "drop a dollar on him." He would then move on down the street to the next cart.

P. J. ended up moving into the alley with his buddy. He once recalled, "After I quit being a guard, I just worked odd jobs. No job at all is why I ended up in the alley."

Shortly after leaving his security job, P. J. drank up his last paycheck. Desperate for a drink, he sold his Taurus .38 security pistol to John Marlow, the Lucky Dog vendor on Bienville, for fifty dollars. Not long after consummating the deal, Marlow found reason to show off his recent acquisition. One night, according to P. J., a big burly guy came up

Bourbon Street to Bienville and started running his mouth. John didn't say a word. The man kept heckling him. John calmly informed him that he had better head up the street or he was "gonna introduce him to Roscoe."

"You ain't got no Roscoe," the man mouthed back.

"I ain't?"

John reached into his cart, pulled out the .38, and started chasing him up Bienville. A cab driver witnessing the scene called the police. The responding officer decided that since no shots had been fired and since no one was around to press charges, he would let the incident go unreported. All the cops in the Quarter knew Marlow as someone who had thus far stayed on the right side of the law.

The blue-eyed, blond Marlow was of medium height and slender build. His manner was friendly, polite, intelligent, and usually cordial. When the fair opened, I brought him into the shop to help with the increased work load. He was capable of dispatching and resupplying vendors. And he had mechanical ability. If something went wrong with a cart, instead of my having to fix it he could do the job.

Unfortunately, he possessed a hidden dark side. I had seen it surface briefly the previous fall. I was sitting in my office writing payroll checks when he walked through the door and sat down. He started relating facts about an incident that had occurred the previous night. When he finished, he got up and started to walk out. He stopped for a second, then turned back around. He looked different. His face was expressionless, and his eyes had a strange, far-off look. Suddenly, he took an ink pen from his shirt pocket and attempted to ram it through my checkbook. He then declared in a loud, angry voice that he was going to turn my "f——ing desk over." I jumped from my chair and, while holding the desk down, shouted, "Have you lost your damn mind?"

He threw the shattered pen to the floor and stomped out of the office. I followed. When I called his name, he turned back around. There in front of me was the old smiling, friendly John, not the psycho that I had confronted only moments before. He said, "I really don't know what came over me. I guess it's the stress of working the street. I'm sorry." I was furious, but I accepted his apology. Two days later I convinced him to sell me Roscoe for sixty dollars. I didn't want the pistol, but I damn sure didn't want a stressed-out vendor packing it.

Having to depend on Marlow, P.J., Jeno, and Big Al bothered me. I was confident that Hager could handle his job; the rest of the management team was comparatively weak. But you have to play the game with the hand that Fortuna deals.

By mid-May the hot dog business was booming. It was so good that I decided to add a swing shift in the shop. I telephoned Jim Campbell in California and offered him the new position. Campbell's return gave me additional help; but more importantly, it gave me a backup who could take over when one of the full-time managers burned out. It was going to happen. The only question was, when?

Arriving about the same time as Campbell was a young, heavyset, brown-haired character named Bruce Belsom. Belsom, like so many of his predecessors, was out of work and out of money. He decided to give selling Lucky Dogs a shot. As he recalled, "I met some interesting people at Lucky Dogs. One, unfortunately, was a total nightmare. Her name was Susan. She was working the cart outside the Famous Door. I was working the wagon across the street by the Royal Sonesta. We got together in August. Since I didn't have an apartment at the time, we got a room at the Metro Hotel."

Marlow and Bruce became close friends; but according to Bruce, John never liked Susan. Smitty, Hager, Huggins, and everyone else except Belsom understood why. Susan was not only boisterous and pushy —she had a vicious streak in her.

On the morning of August 20, for example, at approximately 8 A.M. Bruce and John returned to the shop after having a few beers at the Acropolis Bar down the block. Shortly thereafter, all hell broke loose. An argument ensued between Susan and John. No one remembers exactly what started it, but during the shouting match they exchanged colorful terms of endearment. As the disagreement escalated, she ran to the kitchen and grabbed a large crescent wrench from under the counter.

John wrestled the wrench from Susan's hand and struck her with it several times. As the assault was occurring, someone phoned the police. Help arrived within minutes. An ambulance rushed Susan to the hospital, while the police transported Marlow to Central Lockup.

Susan stayed in the medical facility for a week. John was out of jail the next day. The owner of the small restaurant around the corner where Marlow hung out had put his business up as a security bond. John jumped bail. The restaurateur paid the price.

Less than a month after this incident, Susan was involved in a second violent attack. This time she went after fellow vendor Gary Jones because he owed her two dollars for a hot dog that she had given him on credit on his day off. Three nights later she and Gary crossed paths in the shop. She demanded payment, he refused, and they exchanged words. Then she pulled a dagger from her purse and lunged toward him.

Fortunately, the blade missed its mark. But Gary retaliated with a blow to her jaw, and she went reeling to the floor. Just then, Bruce came strolling into the shop. Seeing Gary with his fist clenched and Susan sprawled on the floor, he didn't ask questions. This time he reacted. He went after Gary, and they tumbled to the ground. Gary ended up on top grasping Bruce's neck with both hands. Two other vendors were pulling him off as I arrived. No police were called. No charges were filed. I confiscated Susan's dagger and banned her from the shop for life. Considering her temper, I didn't anticipate it being a lengthy sentence.

She never came back inside, but she would stand out in the middle of Decatur Street and scream in a less than ladylike fashion for Bruce to appear. Reluctantly, Belsom, his head hung low, would walk out the door.

As often happened, one person left our employ and another promptly arrived. Taking Marlow's and Susan's places in our dysfunctional corporate family were Chet and Maggie Anderson. Chet was a retired Marine Corps gunnery sergeant looking for part-time work. I assigned him to take Red Lott's place. Lott was being moved from Jackson Square to an incredible new location.

The fair had made it emphatically clear prior to its opening that it did not want us on its grounds. We had accepted the decision. However, Jed's Lookout, a popular bar and entertainment spot located on the fair's premises, was now requesting a cart. According to Jed's, they had the legal right to bring in subcontractors. Whether Big Brother liked it or not, fair goers would soon be munching on Lucky Dogs inside the Exposition's gates.

In the *Iliad*, Homer said of revenge, "It is sweeter far than flowing honey." Homer had a great set of taste buds.

Shortly after we opened for business in Jed's, I received a collect call from Julie Bennett. She was stranded at a California truck stop. She and Kevin had gotten into another quarrel. He wanted her to turn tricks. When she refused, he walked out. She was now broke and alone. She asked that I wire her enough money for a bus ticket back to New Orleans. Within hours Julie was Greyhound-bound for the Quarter. Given her financial straits, I allowed her to sleep in the empty office in the Iberville shop until she could find a room.

Two days after she arrived, Stafford, out of the goodness of his heart and with the most dishonorable of intentions, invited her to move in with him. Having divorced his second wife, he was desirous of female companionship. Julie accepted. However, less than a month after she moved in, George and his ex-wife reconciled their differences. Julie once again moved back into the Iberville shop. In the meantime, Kevin had shown up in New Orleans to try and recapture Julie's affection. Vowing no more truck-stop tricks, he persuaded her to accompany him back to California.

As Julie and Kevin headed west, a few of our newer vendors were making clandestine supply runs to ma-and-pa grocery stores throughout the Quarter to buy two-liter bottles of soft drinks and retail packs of hot dogs. They intended to sell the products off of our carts and pocket 100 percent of the gross sales. This was theft. Hot dogs and buns are easy to come by, but they are also easy to identify. We use a specific frank that is not available in retail markets. The drink theft, though, caught us by surprise. Within ten minutes after our supplier had delivered our first premix canister, the vendors figured out how to remove and reinstall the plastic safety seals. Once a seal was removed, the tank could be opened and two-liter bottles of the same flavor could be used to refill the canister. Since we charged the vendors by canister weight, they could beat our inventory system by performing their own refills.

We countered their talents with metal seals that were positively tamper proof.

It was bad enough that vendors tried to sell their own products, but, given the chance, some would run with all of the company's money. We had to be especially careful in choosing who would work near the fair. Business there came in quick spurts, and vendors occasionally had several hundred dollars in their possession. The temptation was great. Not long after the fair opened, one of our new recruits abandoned his cart and fled with $147.

The police had enough problems. To them this sort of theft was petty, so they couldn't be bothered pursuing the guilty party. I decided to lend them a hand. I instituted a company-sponsored antitheft program. I taped an old-fashioned "Wanted Dead or Alive" poster to the lamppost at the corner of Iberville and Decatur. There was a one-hundred-dollar cash reward on the thief's head. In less than an hour Paul Hager and an assortment of bounty-hunting street people had the lowdown scoundrel cornered in an all-night diner near Canal Street. The crook breathed a sigh of relief when the cops arrived. He was convinced that for an extra five dollars, his captors would have lynched him. The rest of the vendors took note: thievery would not be tolerated.

The fair proved to be a financial disaster for many of the companies that did business with it. From the beginning, the Exposition was plagued by negative press, partly because it led over a thousand journalists on a tour of the unfinished site just prior to opening day. The result was stories focusing on the Exposition's financial trouble, unfinished exhibits, piles of construction rubble, and the fact that fewer countries were participating than expected. Newspaper articles turned much of the public against the fair before its gates ever opened. The projected millions of visitors never came. Even President Reagan, breaking with tradition, declined an invitation to participate in opening-day ceremonies.

As a result of low attendance, the fair grossed much less than expected and thus failed to pay many of its creditors. Several were forced into bankruptcy. From our perspective, the Exposition had been enormously successful. Its management had done us a tremendous favor by not choosing us as a concessionaire. Had we built special fast-food kiosks, we would have suffered a major financial setback. Construction costs, overrides paid to the fair, and lack of business broke many of those chosen. The same would have befallen us. As it happened, our new carts outside the gates and throughout the Quarter proved to be overwhelmingly profitable.

One of our carts outside of a nationally known hotel on Canal Street, in fact, was doing too well. The hotel's manager called and requested that we remove the unit from the corner. I asked if our vendor had caused a problem with guests.

"No," replied the manager.

"Was the vendor unclean?"

I knew the answer to the question before he responded. Garcia was assigned to the location in question. His black pants were creased, his white shirt was spotless, and he always showered and shaved prior to coming to work. Well, he usually showered. On one occasion, as I worked in the kitchen, I could hear singing and splashing coming from the other side of the wall. Upon investigating, I discovered Garcia in the large galvanized sink in the cart washroom totally nude, sponging himself off in a liquid Joy bubble bath. He had reported for work after partying all night—he hadn't even gone home. Campbell, seeing what was going on, offered to walk over to Woolworth's and buy David a rubber duck. I vetoed the idea. There was no reason to further encourage his behavior.

I knew that Garcia's hygiene was not the reason that the hotel wanted us off of the corner. So what really was behind the manager's request? Reluctantly, he explained that our cart was hurting his restaurant's business. I was stunned: what he claimed was impossible. We deal in wienies; he serves gourmet dishes. Even so, I politely offered to remove the cart if he would put his request and the reason for it on his hotel stationery.

I explained that we wanted to buy a full-page ad in the *Times-Picayune* and announce to the world, at least to the metropolitan area of New Orleans, that our wienie wagon had surpassed his internationally acclaimed chef in serving palate-pleasing products. I then suggested that perhaps he should fire his chef, eliminate his kitchen staff, and allow Garcia to park his Lucky Dog cart strategically amongst the dining room tables. We would gladly split the profits 50/50. The hotel would probably increase its net and decrease its liabilities. The manager chuckled.

He never sent a written request, so I continued assigning Garcia to the corner. I briefly thought about having him wear a chef's hat, a white jacket, and a multicolored ribbon with a medallion as if to signify that he had graduated from some famous culinary institute. But I decided to leave well enough alone.

Financially, the company had the best year in its history to date. But on New Year's Eve I knew that it was time for 1984 to end. As I was making an 11 P.M. money pickup from the carts on Bourbon Street, an attractive, well-dressed, but highly inebriated blond in her early thirties acted on a sudden impulse to grab me in the crotch as we walked past each other. She refused to loosen her Herculean grasp. The woman's plastered husband stopped next to me and leaned on my shoulder. As the world twirled in his head, he quietly stared at his wife's hand. A sober couple accompanying them stood in the crowded street dying from laughter. I stood in the crowded street dying.

The sober gentleman, after gaining his composure, shouted, "Release, release." Obviously, he had trained a bird dog or two in his day. As she relaxed her grasp, I felt life reenter my loins. Without another word, he escorted my assailant down the block as his wife and my grabber's stumbling husband followed close behind.

It was 11:45 P.M. I took a deep breath and then hobbled through the dense crowd toward Barbara Huggins' cart. As I approached, I could hear her hollering to the tens of thousands of party goers jammed onto Bourbon Street, "Go home, people. I don't want to see you no more." She was tired, irritable, and ready for 1984 to end. In minutes, fireworks filling the sky over the river would signify the beginning of 1985. With the new year would come new challenges and, I hoped, the return of my old voice.

9

From Wienie Queens to Washington

1985 began no better than 1984 had ended. On the morning of January 2, a stressed-out, pistol-waving Cuban stormed into our building, enraged because someone had parked a car at the meter in front of his retail store. Snub-nosed .38 in hand, he demanded that the vehicle be moved so that he could park there. Pistol or no pistol, I couldn't be of help to him.

Most of our vendors didn't have a driver's license, much less an automobile. Besides, when we needed to reserve a parking space, we simply chained our old three-wheel Worksman Cycle ice-cream cart to the meter in front of our shop and fed the machine nickels until the delivery truck arrived. The practice infuriated the meter maids, but we had no alternative. We lacked off-street parking, and before the fair the city had eliminated our freight zone.

The city was intent on eliminating the freight zones for the entire block, so I wrote a letter of protest. As a consequence, everyone's freight zone remained—everyone's, that is, except ours. In front of our building they installed shiny new parking meters. Apparently, some bureaucrat in city hall had also read the *Iliad*. He, like Homer, had embraced the idea that revenge is sweeter than honey.

We had lost the battle, but the war raged on. Hence, we chained the bike to the meter. Meter maids attempted to ticket the cycle, but it had no license. On occasion they would storm into our shop demanding that the bike be removed. We refused. There was money in the meter; and the bicycle, according to Webster's dictionary, was "a tubular framed vehicle," "vehicle" being the key word in the definition. We argued that the bike met the legal criteria for utilizing the space and therefore was legally parked. Finally, they left us alone. In response to this new spirit of détente, I stopped Dan Myers from plastering the bike with bumper stickers that read, "Meter maids eat their young."

Meter maids, however, weren't the only ones giving us trouble. Vendors were having customer relations problems: one particular incident got physical. A not-so-gentle gentleman mistook Barbara Huggins for someone else. As she turned from her cart to see who was cursing her from behind, the man struck her forcefully across the face with his open palm. Barbara was willing to accept verbal abuse from inebriated customers, but she wasn't about to withstand physical assault without putting up a fight. She later explained that not even her mother or father had ever slapped her face. Unfortunately, for this gentleman, he had.

Huggins retaliated. She took off her red-and-white-striped vendor jacket, folded it neatly, and placed it on the cart. Then she walked into the middle of the street and knocked the man's lights out. She punched him and kicked him, and as she landed blow after blow she kept telling him, "You're not supposed to hit a woman."

"But I don't hit women," the man declared as he tumbled to the ground.

Barbara replied, "Bull, I'm a woman." The man asked what her name was, and as she responded he passed out.

As Barbara's assailant was being taken by ambulance to Charity Hospital, Julie Bennett was entering a medical center in Los Angeles about to give birth to George Stafford's son. While she was in the delivery room, her boyfriend, Kevin Russo, was raping a thirty-two-year-old woman who had accompanied him to his and Julie's apartment. Russo was arrested five days later.

In May, unaware that Julie had given birth to his child, Stafford remarried his ex-wife. Several days later Julie heard the news via the grapevine. She decided to marry Kevin. The ceremonies were dramatically different. George and his bride were married at the office of a justice of the peace. Julie and Kevin were married in the hallway of a jail. Julie wore a T-shirt and jeans. Kevin wore handcuffs and prison garb. Once the ceremony was over, he was escorted back to his cell to serve a three-year sentence. His handcuffs had never been removed, and he had not been allowed to kiss the bride.

Later, as Julie was filing for welfare assistance, I was filling out the forms necessary to start a new Louisiana corporation, Lucky Dogs International. Our intent was to manufacture and sell Lucky Dog carts. Over the years scores of inquiries had come from a variety of interested parties. In fact, ever since Stephen and Erasmus Loyacano first rolled their wagons onto the streets of New Orleans, the company had received calls and letters at the rate of several a month. The carts had attracted so much attention that the brothers had tried to market their invention in 1949.

They rented a booth at the National Association of Amusement Parks, Pools, and Beaches convention at the Sherman Hotel in Chicago. Interest in their equipment turned out to be far greater than even they had imagined. Over two hundred delegates requested information, some from places as far away as Uruguay, Hong Kong, Guam, Britain, Venezuela, and Spain. Potential for profit appeared to be enormous.

After the show, the brothers decided to move from the less profitable idea of selling the carts to the more lucrative prospect of leasing or franchising them. This idea led to a quandary: what to do if they sold the rights to an area and then for some unforeseen reason their franchisee

An advertisement run by the Loyacanos in *Billboard* magazine in 1949

Courtesy Lucky Dogs, Inc.

could no longer acquire permits to operate in the given locale? This hypothetical scenario became a reality in Caracas, Venezuela.

Six Lucky Dog carts were shipped to the South American city. Board-of-health approval and occupation licenses were obtained, but the police refused to allow the franchisee to place his wagons on the streets. A June 21, 1950, telegram from the Loyacanos' representative in Caracas states, "Police department not desiring more than two or

In the early 1950s, Lucky Dogs was on the cutting edge of fast-food technology
Courtesy Lucky Dogs, Inc.

three people to gather at one time, due to the situation here." Authorities feared that the hot dog stands might serve as cover for dissidents attempting to disseminate the seeds of revolution. Could Lucky Dog carts do to Venezuela what the Trojan horse had done to Troy? The Venezuelan government had no intention of finding out.

As the Loyacanos attempted to move forward in the United States with some type of leasing or franchising program, they encountered ever-increasing problems. Production costs were high; creating a network of distributors was more difficult than they had initially assumed; and they were constantly confronted with vendor problems in their French Quarter operation. By mid-1952 the brothers gave up on the idea of franchising. Now, thirty-six years later, Doug and I began having expansionist thoughts similar to those originally held by the company's founders.

As we were mulling over various ways to promote sales of the carts, Jim Sloan once again vanished from the shop. There was no note, no word, nor any indication of foul play. There was also no sign of the six hundred dollars that he had collected from the other vendors when he checked them in. Most of those who knew Jim figured that he must have been forcibly abducted. I figured that he had probably gone back to his niece's in St. Louis, perhaps for dessert.

Sloan, however, was not the only employee to leave us during this period. Within two weeks of his departure, Chet and Maggie Anderson boarded a Greyhound bus bound for Las Vegas. Sitting in the seat behind them, bottle in hand, was P. J. Two other ex-vendors were already in the glitzy gambling capital. Dan Myers was one. The other was Jim Sloan, a.k.a. "Out-to-Lunch Jim."

Myers had worked with Sloan during one of his tours of duty as a Lucky Dog man. Later, on another trek through town, Dan learned of his ex-boss's less-than-honorable departure. When he discovered the thief working at the Salvation Army shelter in Vegas, he felt obliged to contact us. He also felt obliged to ask if there was a price on Sloan's head. We hadn't put out a wanted poster on him, but I agreed to a finder's fee.

Doug decided that he didn't want Sloan to think that we had forgotten him, so he telephoned the Vegas shelter. Jim was called to the phone. After several unsuccessful attempts at guessing the mystery caller's identity, Sloan suddenly recognized the voice. "I swear I'm planning on paying back every penny of the six hundred dollars that I borrowed." Doug calmly replied, "Tell it to the police. They should arrive any moment." The authorities hadn't been contacted, but Sloan wasn't betting on it. He dropped the receiver and fled.

A few months later we got a second Sloan update. He was now selling newspapers on a street corner in downtown Reno, Nevada. I thought about sending him a birthday card care of the publishing company, but instead I simply asked the informant to pass back by the corner and tell him that Doug and Jerry said, "Gotcha!"

Just as we were solving the Sloan mystery, another unexplainable disappearance occurred. On the morning of July 13, George Stafford pushed out to work a new location across from the Superdome. When I went to resupply him after lunch, the cart was there but he wasn't. Days turned into weeks and still there was no trace of him. I hoped that one of our ex-vendors might send us a postcard saying that they had run across him and that he was all right, but we never received a word.

Someone did, however, send us a copy of the *Daily Iberian*. I wished they hadn't. A bold headline inside the small-town Louisiana newspaper read, LUCKY DOGS LEGENDARY, THOUGH NOT GREAT. The article went on to report, "Lucky Dogs tend to be deep red in color, spicy and inarguably second-rate compared to those found in sausage-savvy cities like New York, Boston, or Chicago. . . . Lucky Dogs squeak by as food with the help of chili, or onions, or mustard, or any combination thereof. Yet they have become legendary, partly for the audacity of appearing in the same block as Antoine's or Arnaud's and partly for the uniqueness of their vending cart."

Surely, one of our guys must have committed some dastardly deed against the reporter. Maybe they shortchanged him. Maybe Dan Myers tried to put the make on him. Or maybe he's the guy that Barbara went face to face with in the street. With our crew I wouldn't rule anything out.

I would have preferred that the writer had called me while he was doing the piece. If it was a colorful and outrageous story that he was after, there were dozens of other angles that I could have suggested. There was the time that Smitty came to the shop wearing red hot-pants, fishnet stockings, pink ballerina slippers, a ruffled tuxedo shirt, a bra, a Prince Valiant–style wig, and smoking a pipe. He insisted on working his cart like that. I told him absolutely not. Board of health regulations dictated that the pipe had to go.

The reporter also could have written about the time that a group of yuppies came to the shop wanting to borrow a Lucky Dog cart for their New Orleans–style scavenger hunt. The cart, along with the other items on their list, had to be at Coliseum Square for the 9 P.M. judging. Besides the cart, the group needed a French Quarter tap-dancer and a street musician. Strictly by coincidence I had to pick a cart up from Audubon Zoo that evening. The park had borrowed it for their "Zoo-to-do for Children" fund-raiser. On my way back to the shop I promised the yuppies that I would pass by the Square. I timed it perfectly. Two blocks from Coliseum a car behind me started flashing its lights and blowing its horn. Inside were two of the scavenger hunters, a young tap-dancer, and a semisober, middle-aged saxophonist wearing a white tuxedo shirt and black pants. I allowed the performers to climb aboard our sixteen-foot flatbed trailer. As I slowly rounded the corner bordering the Square, the musician was blowing his horn, the dancer was tapping, and the cart was strapped center stage. We won hands down.

In marked contrast to the *Iberian*'s article was a feature story that appeared some months later in a nationally renowned publication. This one was highly favorable, but not entirely accurate. The reporter had lost her notes while changing planes in Atlanta en route home. Facing a deadline, she re-created her interviews from memory, quotations and all. After her article appeared in print, she called. All things considered, she queried, what did I think? I remarked that her story was fantastic, but I also thought that she should never cover the Middle East. Creative writing there could have disastrous results.

Her article gave us favorable national attention and would have been helpful if we had continued along the path of trying to sell franchises. But we had backed away from that approach. We first needed to find out if Lucky Dogs could successfully be marketed outside of New Orleans. Our initial test occurred on the outskirts of Toronto. Bramalea Limited, a major shopping center developer in Canada, contacted us about leasing carts. Their intent was to operate the units in their malls. We shipped a cart to Brampton, Ontario, for a trial. I went on location, set up the operation, and trained the crew. Within a week I returned to New Orleans and prepared for our second experiment, a site in central Ohio.

Neither attempt proved successful. In Canada there were twenty-two other food retailers in the mall who sold hot dogs. The lessees complained that it was highly inappropriate for their lessor to compete against them. Bramalea abandoned the experiment and shipped the cart back to New Orleans. In Ohio we encountered a much different problem: a dying mall. With no one to sell to it was senseless to remain open. Our record in malls was a dismal 0 for 2.

Therefore, we decided to explore growth in an area of familiarity, street vending. An investor in Washington, D.C., contacted us about starting a hot-dog pushcart operation in the capital. I was sent to investigate. From all indications, Lucky Dogs could be highly successful in downtown D.C.

The Washington investor didn't have a clear idea of what he wanted to do. He loved the cart, he liked the hot dogs, but he thought that perhaps he needed an expanded menu. At this point I was tempted to suggest to him a hypothetical, though potentially successful, alternative. Chef Paul Prudhomme's internationally acclaimed K-Paul's Louisiana Kitchen is located at 416 Chartres Street. Standing on the sidewalk in front of his restaurant, you could look two-and-a-half blocks up the narrow street and see Paul Hager's Lucky Dog cart in Jackson Square.

The chef at the time was trying to trim his waistline. His wife and employees kept a close watch on what he consumed in the restaurant. On occasion, however, Chef Paul would venture to the Square. There, the world-famous father of blackened redfish, the undisputed king of Louisiana cooking, would satisfy his appetite by dining on Lucky Dogs smothered in chili and onions.

As I mentioned earlier, Paul Hager had been bisexual since his youth, and in adulthood had chosen a gay life style. Kidding around in the shop one day, I made a cardboard sign for Hager's cart that read, "Gay Paul's Lucky Dog Kitchen." The poster was constructed in the spirit of the old "Saturday Night Live" spoofs. Hager wanted to tape it to his cart. At the last minute I vetoed the idea. It might have been too confusing to tourists. The chef certainly would have appreciated the humor. Who knows: had we joined his cuisine with our cart and Hager's name, we might all have made a fortune franchising "Gay Paul's."

During the cold damp days of late 1985 as Hager worked the Square, Roy Williams, our chair leg–toting ex-welder who had rolled the rollers, suddenly decided to move on. Williams had been working outside of Chris Owens' 809 Club at the corner of St. Louis and Bourbon. Four days before Christmas an FBI agent strolled into the shop looking for Williams. His name had popped up in the Bureau's missing persons file.

It seems that Williams' wife had once caught him cheating. He swore that it would never happen again. He lied. Later, during another visit to his girlfriend's apartment, his car was stolen. Roy knew that if he reported the theft, his wife would immediately know that the affair had never ended. He needed time to ponder his predicament, so he went to one of the corner bars. His first drink was followed by a second, then a third, and so on. When he sobered up, he was in a tractor trailer heading south down I-95 with a driver that he didn't know. He decided to just "keep on trucking." The road led to an oil field job and eventually to Lucky Dogs.

The agent approached Williams on the cart and requested that he call home. Williams couldn't gather the courage. The agent therefore contacted the New York Police Department so that they could close their file. Next, he telephoned the man's wife and explained that her husband was alive, but that he did not want his whereabouts revealed. The day after Williams was questioned, he left town.

As Williams was moving from New Orleans to parts unknown, Lucky Dogs during late December and early January was moving its base of operations from 211 Decatur to 517 Gravier Street. Our rent had been raised to the point where it had become financially advantageous for us to purchase our own building. We found a suitable location two blocks south of Canal Street in the central business district.

As we were settling into our new surroundings, I received a call from a California welfare agent. She explained that George Stafford was applying for assistance for his wife, his child, and himself. The agent needed verification of previous employment.

Puzzled, I informed her that George had worked for us for several years, but that on his last day of employment he had simply abandoned his cart and disappeared. Neither we nor his wife had any knowledge of what had happened to him. Now the caller was confused. She said that Stafford's wife was presently sitting in her office. I responded, "That's not possible."

What had happened was that Julie Bennett had called the shop one morning and informed George that he was a father. George at the time was in a state of depression. Remarrying his ex-wife had been a major mistake. As he sat by his cart across from the Superdome, he started thinking about Julie and his new son. Then, on the spur of the moment, he sneaked back home, packed a small bag of clothes, and within the hour was aboard a Greyhound bus heading west.

As George was riding the Greyhound out of New Orleans, a young girl from Tennessee was riding through the Quarter atop a Lucky Dog cart. She and her husband had come to the Big Easy to celebrate their wedding with friends. What started off as a normal evening stroll through the Vieux Carré picked up speed as the fun seekers moved from bar to bar. In the process they also picked up a following. The group grew to such proportions that when twelve college students wearing hats adorned with fake boobs joined their procession, the crew dubbed themselves the "Tit Patrol." After a howling night of gallivanting up and down Bourbon, the fair maiden was placed atop a Lucky Dog cart and pushed back to her hotel.

Several weeks later I received a four-page poem in the mail titled, "The Maiden Voyage of Super Dog I." The writer had given a full account of the patrol's night of merriment. According to the credits, it had been composed by the Corporal, Tit Patrol (USTP Ret.), Poet Laureate of Bourbon Street; and edited by the Commander-in-Chief Bourbon Street Division, Tit Patrol.

Such enthusiasm deserved a response. That afternoon I sat down and penned the following:

ODE TO THE WIENIE QUEEN

Visitors come, and visitors go
Voodoo Queens such as Marie Laveau.
She was devilish, a countess of the night
concocting spells, engaging in fright.
But her powers are remembered second to thee
Oh, Wienie Queen from Tennessee.
The Quarter remembers your presence so well
As you rode your cart from Orleans to Iberville.
Cheers were screamed, obscenities about tail
It's amazing the "krewe" didn't wind up in jail.
Frolic and laughter echoed through the night
As the Queen paraded to her subjects' delight.
As she slipped off the wienie and onto the street
The vendor awoke from his magical sleep.
His Queen now departed, his duty now done
He had to return to the dog and the bun.
His soul had been touched by the Queen and her krewe
Though speaking of dogs they purchased very few.
Now on the corner of a dimly lit street
He listens to sounds of thousands of feet.
He sees in his mind,
He knows in his heart,
Someday she'll return to again ride his cart.
Queen, oh Queen, he begs of thee
Take thy leave from Tennessee.
Return in the night, or return in the day
The crowds will rejoice in the Vieux Carré.

Wienie Queen, Wienie Queen, thou hast cast thy spell
Until you return,
In loneliness he will dwell.

I placed the poem in an envelope and mailed it to yon distant hills of Tennessee.

The following day, as my poem headed towards the Wienie Queen, Barbara Huggins was heading towards the shop. Business was slow, and she had decided that she was going to push her cart in two hours earlier than normal. Paul Hager, as night manager, was upset over her decision and in explicit language informed her of his displeasure. She told him to "stick it where the sun don't shine." Words were followed by a slapping match, and Hager's hand ended up landing on Barbara's face. *Mistake.* Fists flew. I broke up the fight and sent Barbara home.

She left the shop, but when she got to the corner she saw a large wooden sawhorse covering a newly concreted section of sidewalk. She said to herself, "I'm not finished with this yet. I'm gonna hurt somebody." She grabbed the six-foot center section and headed back to the shop after Hager. Chet and Maggie Anderson stopped her at the door, calmed her down, and then escorted her down the street.

Such an incident had become routine to me in my first ten years at Lucky Dogs. It seemed that for every step forward in trying to improve the company's image, the vendors would do something outlandish to set us back two steps. We had new carts, a new commissary, new uniforms, but the same old crew. Deep down inside they were basically kind, loyal, and caring people; but these qualities rarely surfaced. I empathized with Mr. Clyde, the manager of Paradise Vendors in *A Confederacy of Dunces*, who said, "I spent ten years trying to make Paradise Vendors a reputable company, but that ain't easy. People look down on hot dog vendors. They think I operate a business for bums."

Then the June 16, 1986, issue of *Time* magazine hit the newsstands and suggested that some progress on the image front had occurred. The special issue, titled "American Best," had as one of nine topics on the front cover "The Great U.S. Sandwich." I was pleased to read in the opening paragraph the words "Lucky Dogs." *Time* had selected us as one of the great American sandwiches. Damn, we had come light years farther than I had imagined. However, before we had a chance to get too cocky, a letter arrived from Tokyo. The writer requested information about our unique "Lucky Dong carts." OK, we weren't exactly an unmistakable household name. But *Time*'s article was undeniable proof that we had made progress in improving our image.

Not long after the *Time* story broke, a visitor to New Orleans from Portland, Oregon, also took note of our presence in the city. In a letter to the editor of the *Times-Picayune*, the tourist wrote, "As a first-time visitor to New Orleans, I have some observations that seem to contradict several time-honored myths about the city. The cuisine most in demand is not Creole, Cajun, French or the 19 varieties of seafood—it is something called the 'Lucky Dog.' . . . The local time is not Central Standard Time. There are four time zones in New Orleans: pre-party, party, post-party and next party."

Actually, everyone in Louisiana loves to attend parties, festivals, and fairs. And everyone in the state also agrees that food is the key ingredient to having a successful event. When food is involved, there are two requirements that must be met. First, it must be served in large quantities. Second, it must be of superb quality. Trouble begins when Louisianians try to mandate additional regulations concerning food at these events. Once even the state health department and the state legislature became hotly embroiled in an argument over the department's right to regulate food at fairs and festivals. The dispute did not involve us, but our name was dragged to the forefront of the debate.

The legislature for years had exempted more than three hundred special events from public health inspections. The health department and restaurant association opposed such actions. They wanted the exemptions eliminated before tragedy struck. After six months of meetings, the legislature and the health department appeared to reach a compromise. Traditional Louisiana foods—such as jambalaya cooked in iron pots and pigs roasted over an open flame—could continue to be prepared in the old-fashioned manner. Also, home-baked items that were not potentially hazardous—such as cakes and candy—would be exempt.

The new legislation breezed through the House committee. But there the peace ended. The state's chief sanitarian Frank Deffes was quoted in the Baton Rouge *Sunday Advocate* as saying, "When it got on the floor, all hell broke loose. . . . It came as a complete shock to me. I thought that we had worked out all of the problems." The Alexandria *Daily Town Talk* quoted Representative Raymond Laborde, a Democrat from Marksville, as saying, "The reason we have the exemptions is because those health people were shutting down our booths. I couldn't even make my *cochon de lait* [roasted pig]." According to the same article, John Hainkel, a Republican from New Orleans, stood up in the House and stated, "Lucky Dog stands got along fine until those people came around and made them install things. The stands look like spaceships now and the dogs don't taste as good. They don't have that grimy stuff in there anymore." The House broke out into laughter. Someone else took the floor and complained about the quality of hot tamales. Hainkel responded, "You can't get a good hot tamale anymore. They have to make 'em with beef now."

The proposed bill was defeated, 7–68. House Speaker John Alario announced the results to his fellow legislators as "7 to 68 Lucky Dogs." I called Barry Blue and Jo McClean with the health department to assure them that we had nothing to do with the House's action. In recent years, our relationship with the department had been excellent, and I wanted to keep it that way.

Shortly thereafter, I almost got into real trouble with the board of health. Not the local health department, but the board of health in Washington, D.C. Doug and the potential investor in Washington had decided upon testing the market and perhaps doing a joint venture. While I was working on redesigning the Lucky Dog cart to fit the capital's quirky length and height restrictions, our future partner was supposedly obtaining the necessary occupational licenses and permits.

When I returned to D.C., the gentleman assured me that all had been accomplished. He lied. Unknowingly, for three days I operated illegally and could have been arrested. The potential franchisee knew it, but he didn't consider it to be such a big deal. Of course not. I and not he would have been arrested on the street corner. And it would also have been me in the D.C. jail politely asking my new roommate, "Do you mind if I take the lower bunk? Heights tend to frighten me."

I called Doug to inform him of the problem. Instead, he informed me of his. During his routine yearly check-up, doctors had discovered that he had inoperable lymph cancer. They gave him from six months to two years to live. Suddenly my problems seemed trivial.

I put the cart in storage at Star Vending Supply (a commissary that rents space to Washington street vendors) and headed home. I figured that we could complete the test at some future date. For the moment it was more important that I return to New Orleans and oversee our local operation.

Doug wanted a second medical opinion, and a third, if necessary. All the while, business continued as usual. We discussed Washington's potential as a site to continue testing. We agreed that the gentleman that we had been dealing with would be eliminated from all future plans.

To assist in our second test, we hired a New Orleanian, trained him on a cart in the Quarter, then flew him to Washington. There, during July, 1987, both he and I went through the city's mandatory week-long sanitation certification course at the University of the District of Columbia. Upon passing the final examination we became certified street vendors. Disappointingly, there was no prom, no graduation ceremony, no diploma to hang on the wall. Not even the mention of a future class reunion. Our official D.C. vendor clip-on photo I.D. badges simply arrived in the mail.

By being certified I could at least give my co-worker a break two or three times a day. With our badges firmly attached to our shirt collars and the necessary paperwork in order, we were ready to enter the capital's lucrative street vending market.

The same week that I was going through D.C.'s food handlers school, *Rolling Stone* magazine announced that Lucky Dogs had been selected as one of the nation's top nine hot dogs. We didn't get our "picture on the cover," as the lyrics of the famous seventies' rock song go,

Lucky Dogs goes to our nation's capital
Courtesy author

but we did get mentioned inside. The Grateful Dead hogged the publication's coveted spot.

As this *Stone* issue hit the newsstands, we hit the streets of D.C. By lunchtime of our first day the sweltering 100-degree temperature had taken its toll. My vendor resigned. He took a cab to the airport. I took over working the cart. My only possible alternative was to phone my contact at the State Department. After all, he already had a Lucky Dog hat and T-shirt. But at the last minute I decided against it. Odds were he didn't have an official clip-on D.C. vendor's badge.

Doug sent his oldest son, Mark, to assist me for the rest of the trial. Mark couldn't work the cart, but he could drop me off in the morning, resupply me during the day, and pick me up in the evenings. We now had a cart, a vendor, and a chauffeur. The trial continued.

Previously, I had scouted the city and had selected seven corners that I believed would give us a fair test of the market. My first morning soloing I set the cart up outside of the Justice Department's headquarters on Pennsylvania Avenue. According to police regulations, vending sites are awarded on a first-come-first-serve basis. Even so, I chose not to take the premier spot on the corner. I moved to the middle of the block, allowing the regular vendor to work his normal location. An hour or so later an African American woman set up her beat-up, rectangular-shaped, stainless-steel hot dog wagon near the crosswalk.

By 1:30 P.M. I was steaming my second box of dogs. My competition was battling boredom. Customers, given the choice, walked past her filthy stand to buy from my newly manufactured Lucky Dog cart. At 2:00 P.M. her "man" showed up. At 2:02 he began screaming about her pathetic sales. She screamed back and pointed in my direction. He turned and stormed the seventy yards over to my cart, squinting angrily at me in the sunshine. The veins in his neck were swelling, and in a hostile voice he shouted, "I like steak on my table."

I responded that I too enjoyed the taste of a juicy sizzling piece of beef now and then.

At that point he informed me in rather explicit street language that I had totally misinterpreted his meaning. To ensure that I clearly understood his intent, he directed me to vacate the premises or he would feel compelled to evenly distribute my body parts across the hot pavement.

It was 103 degrees, and not the slightest breeze was blowing. I was tired, sweaty, and upset because my co-worker had bailed out. The only shade I enjoyed came from my cart's umbrella, and that wasn't much. Making matters worse, I now had a skinny, six-foot-tall, mean-looking s.o.b. in my face screaming that he was carnivorous. After babbling a few minutes he finally reached a decision. He was planning on coming back with his "brothers," and they were going to perpetrate unspeakable actions against my person and my cart.

I advised him against such actions. I asked in a heated voice, "Do I look like a normal street vendor? Does this cart look like something that a regular vendor could afford? Of course not! It's owned by a powerful southern mafia figure named Doug Talbot. Talbot controls the French Quarter, the Gulf Coast, and is now muscling in on the D.C.

area. [Warming to my role.] F—— with his money and he'll have your heart ripped out and fed to you before you gasp your last breath. Look around. We're being watched at this very moment. His henchmen make certain that I don't run. I owe the man. They watch me like a hawk."

The man began looking around as paranoia took hold of him. He saw mafia henchmen on every bench and behind every bush. I told him that he better buy a dog and a drink or the boys were going to be pissed. While he ate a jumbo, he nervously asked, "Is he selling shit [drugs] off the cart?"

"What do you think?"

"I think the man's into big shit."

"You're a bright guy. I hope that you remain that way."

He started making broadly visible gestures to show that he was sorry for bothering me. Afterwards, he walked over and whispered something to his girl. She closed up her cart and pushed it off. The rest of the afternoon was rather pleasant.

The following morning I set up to one side of the White House in front of Waldenbooks. Total business for the day was a little over $230. There were no hostiles to deal with, but also very few customers to serve. The manager of the bookstore was so thrilled with the cleanliness of our operation that he purchased two dogs.

My permit restricted me from operating on the mall in front of the Smithsonian's Air and Space Museum, the best spot in Washington. But I was able to test locations outside of the U.S. Mint, the National Zoo, the National Archives, the FBI building, and behind the Smithsonian Institution. All of the sites that I selected drew millions of tourists each year. Among these five locations, the only one where I ran into noticeable resistance was outside of the FBI building.

Mark dropped me off and I pulled the cart up on the sidewalk, positioning it between a large circular planter and the cloth-covered stand of an eighteen-year-old fruit vendor. My cart was nine feet from the concrete planter on my left and seventeen feet from the fruit vendor's table on the right. D.C. law states that no vendor can operate within ten feet of another vendor. My tape measure assured me that no one else could park between the planter and the cart or between the fruit stand and the cart.

As I was lighting the burner, the young Italian-looking produce vendor with a New York accent walked over and remarked, "If you were a woman they'd probably just rough you up, but being a man they're gonna kill you."

"Who," I asked, "is going to do this atrocious act?"

"Philip," came the reply. "This is his corner and he ain't gonna like that you done took it."

I countered, "According to the law, it is first-come first-serve."

"Philip don't care about no law."

As we talked I continued to set up my cart. Everything was in place, but I still had two ice chests with my backup supplies and an extra box of hot dog buns sitting exposed in full view. The young fruit vendor had a white-draped table with his produce displayed on top. I suggested a bargain. If he allowed me to store my supplies under his table, then I would supply him with all the free hot dogs and soft drinks that he could consume during the day.

"Philip ain't never given me nothin', and he's been here a year. He ain't never 'preciated what I've done for him. Yeah. All right. It's a deal. Here, you want some grapes? Try these."

I had made a friend. At least now if Philip murdered me, there would be someone on the street to mourn my demise. Of course, while doing so, he would be consuming limitless free drinks and free Lucky Dogs.

Within fifteen minutes after I opened for business, Philip drove up in a rusty old green Volkswagen beetle pulling the standard stainless-steel New York–style hot dog cart. He didn't look that tough. He was maybe in his early twenties, in good shape, probably of Filipino descent. He slammed on his brakes, flung open his door, and ran up to me shouting, "What the f—— do you think you're doing? Get your f——ing ass off of my corner."

I noticed that in the capital, just as in the Quarter, the "f" word seemed to be the expletive of choice in heated discussions. I calmly explained that according to Washington's vending code, it was not his corner. If he so desired, he could read the code for himself. I just happened to have a copy with me. Next, I explained that I intended to be on this spot only for one day. Leave me alone and it might be a year before I returned, if I ever returned at all. Mess with me and I would be here every day of the week.

At that point he calmed down, but he was choked up. "You don't understand. Today's my birthday. I was gonna work on my birthday, and you took my corner."

Not wanting to sound unsympathetic, I explained what I was doing in Washington. I suggested that he work the spot in front of Waldenbooks; there he could net perhaps a hundred dollars for the day. Tomorrow he could have his normal corner back. But my suggestion didn't appeal to him. He responded, "F—— it. I'll blow the day off and go to the beach."

Ten minutes after Philip left, an extremely rough-looking Filipino pulled up by the curb on a Harley-Davidson chopper.

"What the hell are you doing here? This is my brother's corner."

I was impressed: two complete sentences and not a single "f" word. I responded, "Don't tell me that you forgot. Today's Phil's birthday. He took off and went to the beach." As if on cue, the biker roared off down the avenue—probably in search of a Hallmark card shop.

Sales outside of the FBI headquarters were brisk. Secretaries bought the fresh fruit. The more macho male agents proved to be the meat-eaters. They, too, probably liked steak on their table, but for the moment they relished the taste of Lucky Dogs.

The only negative aspect about the spot was that a grungy man was sitting on a bench about twenty feet from me babbling in a very loud voice. He was your typical street person: clad in dirty clothes without shoes, he hadn't washed his hair or shaved in months, and his only possession was an old wadded-up blanket that he regularly raised over his head and shook at the sky. Between shakes he would jump up and run to the outside wall of the FBI building and shout something about the imperialistic mother country having to pay for her sins against the world. His words were barely coherent.

The man, however, did have energy and a great set of lungs. Plus, he could stay focused. All he needed was a little guidance and a mini-course in marketing. I called him over after listening for an hour to his annoying gibberish, and made him a business proposition. If every other time that he rushed the FBI building he would simply scream, "Buy a Lucky Dog, they'rrre great!" then I would, in turn, furnish him with all of the free dogs and sodas that he could consume. I even gave the fruit vendor as a reference. The man became highly indignant and began yelling that the demons of corporate America were not going to silence him with promises of dogs and cola.

By the time the sun was directly overhead, mother nature had done what corporate America could not. She had fried his brain and dried his palate. Blanket in hand, he shut up and wandered off to look for refuge under a shady tree.

The seven-day experiment proved that the carts would be successful in Washington. The difficult task would be to form a master company because D.C.'s laws were written according to a one-vendor, one-cart concept. We decided to hold off on forming the new corporate entity until we knew more about Doug's condition. He looked healthy and felt fine, but there were still the unpredictable effects of the inoperable lymphoma.

Meanwhile, working the streets in New Orleans was getting tougher. Ignatius J. Reilly in *A Confederacy of Dunces* had reasoned: "The human desire for food and sex is relatively equal. If there are armed rapes, why should there not be armed hot dog thefts?" In reality, there were. One attempt occurred in the most unlikely of places, Jackson Square.

Chet Anderson was working his cart when, just after dark, two thugs walked up and demanded that he give them free hot dogs. Chet had spent two years in a North Korean POW camp. He had taken everything that his captors had thrown at him and he had survived. He wasn't about to let two street punks defeat him now. The scumball closest to Chet pulled a knife. Anderson grabbed his wooden bar stool with both hands and invited the would-be thieves to take a hot dog if they were brave enough. They scurried off like frightened rats.

Another armed attempt to hold up a hot dog vendor involved a well-known head of a New Orleans petroleum corporation. The executive happened to be in the Quarter late one evening. Prior to driving home, he stopped at the corner of Toulouse and Bourbon to buy a Lucky Dog from Myers. Myers was just starting to put the onions on the chili dog when a shady-looking character walked up and pulled a knife. He demanded the vendor's cash and the oil executive's wallet. All went according to the thief's plan until he got greedy. To his wish list he added the steaming chili dog that Myers had just made. At that point, the executive became upset. He pulled a pistol from beneath his jacket and shouted, "I'll be damned if you're taking my Lucky Dog." The robber fled.

Other unscrupulous attempts to take the company's money were more old-fashioned shakedown scams. The first one involved a couple from Pennsylvania. When I returned from lunch one afternoon, Hager informed me that I was to call room 1216 at the Marriott Hotel concerning a problem with our hot dogs. The message continued that if the party was not there, I was to contact a specific attorney in Pittsburgh. There was no answer at the hotel room, so I called the second number. All I had was the caller's first name, John. The lawyer's receptionist immediately knew the man to whom I was referring. She hadn't spoken to him in weeks, but she was certain that it must have been he who had called. Obviously, he was a regular client.

Later that afternoon I made contact with the gentleman. He insisted on meeting immediately. Supposedly, his wife had purchased a hot dog from Chet Anderson, suffered a reaction to the nitrates, and been rushed to the hospital in an ambulance. He now wanted to discuss our legal responsibility.

We met at the Bienville House's coffee shop on Decatur. Sitting across the table from me, the steelworker, wearing a black T-shirt with a pack of cigarettes pushed up under the left sleeve, insisted that his wife had almost died because of our product. He suggested that a settlement in the ten- to fifteen-thousand-dollar range might persuade him to remain silent. I informed him that nitrates were not our responsibility. Ultimately, such a complaint would fall under the legal liability of the meat manufacturer. I added that the state food and drug inspectors, at our request, were collecting samples of our hot dogs as we spoke. If he wanted to call the television stations, that was his prerogative; but we could take no action until we found out the lab results.

Within days the state officials informed us that the nitrate level in our dogs was far below the maximum limits. Medical experts assured us that the hot dog alone could not have caused the reaction.

I believe that prior to eating the hot dog, the woman had gone to the A&P grocery store on the corner of Royal and St. Peter and bought a couple of packs of processed sandwich meat. She knew exactly how much to eat and how long it would take for the reaction to occur. She allotted herself enough time to walk the one block to the Square, where her husband had already purchased the Lucky Dog and was awaiting her arrival. Witnesses said that she had barely finished eating the dog when the ambulance arrived. It had to have been called beforehand.

When I spoke to the attending physician at Charity, he remembered that the husband had been adamantly opposed to an emergency tracheotomy. The woman's reaction cleared up just in the nick of time. As a matter of fact, when I had called the Marriott that afternoon, the supposedly deathly ill lady and her husband were taking a leisurely cruise down the Mississippi River on the steamboat *Natchez*. It was not until after their boat ride that the husband learned of my call and contacted me.

The medically dangerous scam had probably been pulled off successfully dozens of times across the country. Restaurants will go to great lengths to avoid negative publicity. But the couple had misjudged us. I mailed a copy of the report from the State of Louisiana Food and Drug Unit to their Pittsburgh attorney. I never received a response. Case closed.

The second trumped-up incident involved a navy doctor who was staying in town for a medical convention. He claimed that Stafford had gotten irate and thrown a cup of Pepsi on him. He wanted to talk to me about the episode and discuss "justice." If we could not come to an agreement, then he would go to the press about the rude way that he was treated in the city. When he arrived, I noticed that his clothes had no signs of stains. Yet he continued insisting that he wanted "justice."

Justice in his view lay between five hundred and seven hundred dollars, a bargain compared to the steelworker's demands.

I called Doug at home. Doug told the doctor that he needed half an hour to consider the settlement. During that time we called City Councilman Mike Early, Orleans Parish district attorney Harry Connick, and the base commander at the Belle Chase Naval Air Station. We wanted to alert the proper authorities about the attempted blackmail and to find out the name and telephone number of the base commander in Florida where the doctor was stationed.

The doctor returned expecting to find a crisp stack of green justice. Instead, he found that we were considering taking legal action against him. At that point he decided that perhaps it was in the best interest of all parties if we just forgot about the unfortunate incident.

The doctor, his wife, and their two young children had come to the city in an old, faded red Toyota Celica. They had stayed at the New Orleans Hilton overlooking the Mississippi River. The view from their room was fabulous. Their bill was also probably stunning, considering his military wages. The physician obviously had spent more than he could afford and, like the previous shyster, tried to extort money from us to finance his weekend. Thankfully, like his predecessor, he, too, had failed. Fortuna's wheel once again seemed to be spiraling upward.

10

Between Hot Dogs and History

A new year brings both new hope and new problems; 1988 immediately brought the latter. I had hired an ex-navyman as our relief manager. The gentleman, it turned out, had left the military, but not his military ways, behind. As a result, he spent most of his time ordering vendors to do his work. Because of his bossiness the crew nicknamed him "the general." They even saluted him when they reported for their carts. The general did an excellent job as manager, but that was not the position he wanted. He wanted my job. God only knows why, but he did. It got to the point where he would call Doug and try to torpedo me behind my back.

Finally, Doug had had enough. He called me and wanted to know what action I was going to take against this back-stabbing Judas. I replied, "None." I wanted him to keep working. From my point of view, the general was doing an excellent job. In trying to impress Doug, he was painting the inside of the shop, repairing the carts, and assisting in the training of new vendors. As long as he was doing his job, I saw no reason to release him.

He did go a bit far one morning when he came to work with three gold stars pinned on either shoulder. At lunch I went to Woolworth's and bought a pack of big stick-on gold stars and put four on each of my shoulders. I walked into the kitchen under the pretense of checking the inventory. He just smiled. Military guys understand that four stars outrank three.

After eight months the general requested an honorable discharge. He moved to Colorado. I kind of miss the guy, especially when the shop needs to be put back into shipshape condition.

As the general was leaving, the Republican National Convention was preparing to open in New Orleans. Its organizers asked that we participate in the *Times-Picayune*'s "Grand Old Party" in the New Orleans Convention Center. It was to be the big event for the thousands of press corps members covering the convention. Approximately thirty major restaurants were involved, plus us. Entertainment included three stages with live bands and a Mardi Gras parade to close out the gala affair. No expense would be spared.

In town for the convention was Ronald Reagan, Jr., the president's son, who had been hired as part of the "Good Morning America" staff. One of his feature stories called for him to interview a Lucky Dog vendor on Bourbon Street and to ask him his opinion on the upcoming presidential election. I arranged for him to interview Chet Anderson, our vendor who had once been a Korean War POW. Everything had been cleared through the captain of the Vieux Carré police district since the show wanted to shoot the interview on the street.

Chet was standing outside the Old Absinthe House bar on the corner of Bienville and Bourbon, going over in his mind how he wanted to respond to the questions that they were about to ask. His shirt was clean, his pants were pressed, and his cart sparkled. The cameraman had a problem, however: he wanted a shot of the cart with the length of Bourbon Street in the background. In order to create this scene, the wagon had to be pulled out into the middle of Bourbon. It shouldn't have been a problem since at night the street is a pedestrian mall.

Unfortunately, the beat cop must not have been aware of his captain's prior approval. As the cameras rolled, so did the patrolman's tongue. He stormed onto the scene ordering the film crew to move their equipment out of the street or he was going to haul all of their asses to jail. When the director tried to explain that the interviewer was the president's son, it didn't impress the officer. Odds are, the cop was a Democrat.

Chet called me at home panicked over the situation. I called the captain and he radioed the patrolman. A crisis was averted and the crew was allowed to continue filming. By now, though, Chet was so nervous that when questioned he told Reagan, Jr., that Lucky Dogs was a "New Orleans transition." He meant to say a "New Orleans tradition."

Chet's faux pas was not the only one made by a vendor during an interview that evening. A radio station doing a live remote stopped by Myers' cart on Toulouse and Bourbon. The question asked was, "What

James "Red" Lott manning his cart at the *Times-Picayune*'s "Grand Old Party" during the 1988 Republican convention
Courtesy author

makes your Lucky Dogs different from all of the other ones served on the street?" Myers meant to say, "It is because of all of the different kinds of condiments that I put on them." Instead, he uttered, "It is because of all of the different kinds of condoms that I put on them." To the hordes of listeners who called the shop with their humorous remarks, I calmly explained that Myers simply adhered to the practice of safe vending.

As Myers was delighting an audience via the air waves, down the street at St. Peter and Bourbon, James Hudson was dodging mustard. A group of sorority girls pulled up to his cart in a new white convertible. One of them yelled, "Let's get the hot dog man." Suddenly, they jumped from their car and grabbed Hudson's mustard squeeze bottles. Seconds later they opened fire. Mustard was flying and girls were giggling and laughing. Hudson, out of self-defense, grabbed his ketchup squeeze bottles and unleashed a volley of red. They began chasing one another around the cart and car. Red and yellow streams of semiliquid substances were airborne in all directions. The girls kept squirting and chanting, "We got the wienie man. We got the wienie man." James was returning fire and screaming back, "But I got you, too."

Hudson was covered in mustard. The girls were covered in ketchup. The convertible and cart were covered with both. In a matter of minutes the ammunition was depleted. The girls dropped their bottles, jumped back into the convertible, and sped away.

Stafford, who had recently returned to the Quarter, was once again working a cart. A customer informed him that one of his co-workers was presently involved in a food fight. George hurried to the scene. Surveying the mess on the pavement, on the cart, and on Hudson, all he could say was, "You better not let Jerry hear about this or you'll be canned." I didn't have time to can Hudson. I was still too busy answering the phone at the shop. Myers' radio comments had brought on a flood of calls, some of them outrageous.

By the following week, the delegates to the 1988 Republican National Convention had left town. Life in the Quarter was returning to normal. And what was normal? Gravel Voice Eddie was holding open the door of the Fallen Angel and inviting passers-by to "step inside and see da most beautiful babes on Bourbon." A few feet away Rose Cart Bill was asking a distinguished-looking gentleman, "Idn't ya old lady wordt the price of a flower?" Down the street Wheelchair Al was sitting outside of the Famous Door begging for spare change. On a good night Al could panhandle over two hundred dollars. Booze, friends, and barmaids got most of it before dawn.

At St. Peter and Bourbon young black tap-dancers were exhibiting their skills. Appreciative onlookers tossed dollar bills into their collection hat. Close to the curb, shoeshine hustlers were calling out, "Mister, mister, betcha ten bucks I know where you got dem shoes." When the unsuspecting mark fell for the line, the hustler would say, "On yoh feet on Bourbon Street." The shiner's associates then verbally intimidated the tourist to "pay up."

Just behind the hustlers, out of Preservation Hall, drifted the sounds of New Orleans jazz. In front of Crazy Shirley's corner bar, less than a hundred feet from Preservation Hall, stood Stafford barking out, "Getcha eight inches of fun on a bun." The one-liner has been passed down from vendor to vendor since the 1940s. In this age of political correctness some of us have tried to eliminate it, but like Lucky Dogs, it has a life of its own.

On that late December evening as I watched Stafford work the crowd, I thought about how interesting 1988 had been. In contrast, 1989 would prove to be a year to forget. Big Ben Bullard, the gentle biker and former Lucky Dog manager, would be killed in a traffic accident in Texas. A few months later Daniel Horacy, Ben's ex-roommate and also a former Lucky Dog vendor, would die in a motorcycle accident in Alabama. At almost the same time Sherry, a new vendor, would die in a motorcycle accident in New Orleans. Then in September our vendor on the Moonwalk would die of complications from pneumonia. This was followed in October by the loss of David Garcia to a liver ailment. The only bright spot of 1989 would be that Doug's cancer went into remission.

Fortuna gave us a new spin of the wheel in 1990, however. With the new year came a unique opportunity. Alain Sidney-Louis of Fort-de-

France, Martinique, had seen our carts during a visit to the Quarter. The large wiener-shaped wagons intrigued him. According to Alain, street vending was thriving in his homeland even though the vendors' carts were deplorable pieces of equipment. He figured that if their dilapidated plywood wagons could turn a profit, then a fleet of attractive Lucky Dog carts could gross a fortune.

Alain already owned a retail clothing store and a general merchandise outlet in Fort-de-France, another retail business on the nearby island of Guadeloupe, and a furniture factory in the Dominican Republic; but he still had a desire to dabble in dogs. After considerable discussion, he and Doug concluded that a cart should be sent to Martinique. Naturally, someone would have to visit this West Indies island to train personnel, to handle any mechanical problems that might have developed during the cart's shipment, and to assess the French territory as a potential market. It was a tough assignment; but I threw my sunglasses, shorts, and copy of something like "Learn the Entire French Language in Less Than Twenty-Four Hours" in my luggage and took off for the airport. I wanted to get airborne before anyone changed his mind about the experiment.

From Miami to Martinique, Air France made only one stop, in Pointe-à-Pitre, Guadeloupe. As flight attendants instructed us to exit the plane, an elderly Englishman sitting next to me asked if I had ever flown into Guadeloupe before.

"No," I responded.

"I have, and if I may, I would like to offer a bit of advice. Carefully inspect your luggage when you arrive at your destination."

The man knew of what he spoke. My bags were ravaged and half my clothes stolen. The only shoes that I had were the loafers on my feet. My new pair of Nikes, two Lucky Dog T-shirts, and most of my pants and dress shirts were gone. A severe storm had recently devastated Guadeloupe, and unbeknownst to me as I stood in the airport terminal, I was generously contributing to the island's "Hurricane Juan relief fund."

My benevolence amazed even me. What also amazed me was that the customs officers in Martinique became monolingual when I discovered the theft. I would have given them a piece of my mind in their native tongue, but the thief had also absconded with my French/English dictionary. Seeing no reason to inspect my luggage, they motioned me through customs. The agents understood that someone with a far greater interest than theirs had already scrutinized my belongings.

It was evening when my plane touched down in Fort-de-France. Alain drove me directly to L'Hôtel Le Bon Appart. It was a quaint eight-room downtown inn. Unfortunately, no one in Le Bon Appart spoke English and I did not parlez français. In spite of the language barrier, the proprietor, a Frenchman named Fred, proved to be a pleasant fellow and a thoughtful host. He welcomed me with a smile and a tall glass filled with a cool native rum drink. We talked for ten to fifteen minutes: I spoke English; he spoke French. I haven't the slightest idea what he said and I don't think he understood a word that I uttered, but that didn't matter. After finishing the drink, I shook his hand, said good-night, and carried my rather lightened luggage up three flights of circular stairs to my room.

The accommodations were charming, native Martinique. The walls were mahogany planked, and the ceiling was supported by exposed wooden beams. This was the type of small, off-the-beaten-path hotel where someone such as Hemingway might have stayed. I tried telephoning Jane. The operator spoke only French. I would have no contact with the English-speaking world until Alain arrived the next morning for breakfast. Settling in, I turned on the television. Steve McQueen, every red-blooded American man's man, was speaking fluent French in the classic war movie *The Great Escape.* I sat back, relaxed, and tried to figure out what he was saying. Damn, I missed my French dictionary.

The following morning it took an import broker three hours to cut through the red tape before our cart could clear customs. As we waited, a depressing thought entered my mind. What if the transport ship had called on a port in Guadeloupe? If it had, there might be nothing left in our wooden crate except bubble wrap and packing peanuts. Finally, though, at 11 A.M. the authorities issued the proper papers and the crate, cart included, was released.

Alain was enthusiastic and suggested that we immediately open for business. I, on the other hand, maintained that we should wait until all of the proper permits had been acquired. Alain capitulated, and we transported the cart to the office of the local board of health.

The inspector looked between the wooden slats of his white Venetian blinds at the hot dog–shaped vending unit sitting in his oyster shell parking lot. "Ah, verdy nice," he said, as he started filling out the permit.

"Wouldn't you like to inspect the cart?" I asked. "It has an insulated meat compartment, a sneeze guard, and four sinks."

"Sinks. Why sinks?"

"For washing your hands and for washing, rinsing, and sanitizing cooking utensils."

"Does that not increase the cost of the cart?"

"Considerably," I answered.

"Then why have them?"

God I liked the way this man thought. If only he could get transferred to the Department of Health and Human Resources in New Orleans.

By 2 P.M. the cart, with its full array of health and city licenses, was legally operating on the street outside of Alain's retail store, less than two hundred yards from the emerald green gulf waters. Yachts and schooners filled the harbor, and the gentle trade winds blew ashore. A steady stream of tourists and locals alike gave nods of approval as they strolled past the island's newest addition.

Sales the first day were slow, but not disappointing. By the time we began operating, the lunch rush was already over, but that didn't matter. For the moment our focus was not on sales, but on training personnel in the proper use of the equipment. The two young men assigned to the project both spoke fluent French and English. One potential vendor, in his mid-twenties, wore a military pin identifying him as a French fighter pilot. The other trainee wore a gold chain around his neck from which dangled two Bengal tiger teeth. I figured that a combat pilot and a guy brave enough to pull teeth out of a tiger both ought to be tough enough to work a Lucky Dog cart on any street corner. Initially, I focused the men's training on the mechanical workings of the unit. Later, we concentrated on the more complex tasks of steaming buns and squirting mustard.

The following day would be our true test. Alain announced that the cart would be taken to the city's soccer stadium to sell Lucky Dogs at a game billed as the soccer championship of the Caribbean. In the islands, no sports title is more coveted. Making the event even more dramatic was the fact that tiny Martinique was in the finals playing heavily favored Cuba. The communist country had a strong, well-seasoned team, while the small French territory had a young squad filled with enthusiasm but lacking playoff experience.

Later, as we drove to the arena, I asked Alain how he had managed to secure permission for us to operate at such a prestigious event. His answer: "I haven't yet, but do not worry. I have a plan." We pulled up to the stadium's main entrance and he spoke to two gentlemen in French. When the truck transporting the cart arrived, security waved it through the gate. The wagon was unloaded and positioned inside the arena against the eight-foot-high chain-link fence that separated the fans from the field. It was the premier location. Alain's plan, whatever it was, had worked.

As the Lucky Dogs steamed, twenty thousand soccer enthusiasts poured into the stands. Minutes later the teams took to the field for pre-game warm-ups. I seized the opportunity to snap a few photos of the cart. Suddenly, the fans in the concrete bleachers behind me became vocally hostile. Alain started laughing. The more boisterous they became, the more humorous he found it.

"What's the problem?" I asked.

"You," he chuckled. "They believe that you're an American spy taking photographs of the Cuban dignitaries and of the Cuban soccer team. Put your camera away. I'll explain why you're really here."

Once the Nikon was out of sight, the crowd calmed down. Business was excellent, especially at half-time. My co-workers translated the orders and handled the francs while I manned the steamer. Fans, socialist and communist alike, stood in line to purchase hundreds of democracy's dogs.

The game ended in a tie, but to Martinique's ecstatic fans it was as if

David had again slain Goliath. Alain was especially proud, for his cousin had scored the last-minute goal to tie the powerful communist team. Martinique's players were immediately elevated to the status of national heroes.

The following afternoon, as my newly trained recruits worked the cart, Alain and I went to lunch. Joining us in the quaint French restaurant was a tall, well-dressed gentleman in his mid-forties with a Middle Eastern accent. As a luncheon companion he was extremely cordial. Conversation revolved around the previous night's game and Alain's new business venture—nothing out of the ordinary. Then after lunch, as the gentleman rose to leave, he leaned toward me and said, "I hope that you do not believe all the vicious propaganda that you hear about the PLO." With that, he turned and walked away. I asked Alain what he had meant.

"Exactly what he said. He is the Palestine Liberation Organization's chief representative in the Caribbean."

"Great. Last night I was accused of being a spy. Today I have lunch with a terrorist. I don't want to think about tomorrow." Alain just laughed.

Finally, after three days of supervised training, our two-man crew declared themselves ready to solo. I had doubts as to how successful they would be. These guys were conscientious, dependable, and sober. Neither wore hot pants or spiked heels. They had none of the traits of our better vendors back home. Alain suggested that we give them a chance anyway. While they worked the cart, we flew to the islands of Guadeloupe and Saint Martin, and surveyed for other potential expansion sites.

Tiny Saint Martin showed the most promise. Half under French control and half under the control of the Dutch, it is a land of much luxury and thriving commerce. Cruise ships fill the harbors. Quaint shops and boutiques feature fine silverware, jewelry, perfumes, fashionable clothing, and other elegant items. Kentucky Fried Chicken and Burger King had already infiltrated the market, but there was still room for several Lucky Dog carts.

Guadeloupe, by comparison, was much poorer. I questioned whether its population could afford our prices. There was also another problem. Somewhere on the island was a thief wearing new Nikes and a Lucky Dog T-shirt. I kept an eye out, but the scumball never surfaced.

From Guadeloupe I departed for the States. I toyed with the idea of taping a note to the outside of my luggage stating, "Gave Generously upon Arrival," but refrained from fear that a humorless baggage agent might reroute my suitcase to Devil's Island.

The trial period on Martinique was scheduled to continue for another thirty days. At its conclusion Doug and Alain were to decide whether to pursue expansion or to end the project. The French government, in the meantime, halted all shipments of meat traveling from the United States to Martinique via Air France. Whether this new policy was coincidental or a result of my talking with the airline about making regular shipments from Miami to Fort-de-France, I am not certain. Whatever its cause, it left us with only one option: shipping our product by sea, and this was not feasible. A single refrigerated shipping container would hold slightly over 100,000 hot dogs, far too large a quantity for our one-cart operation.

As I worked to overcome the shipping dilemma, Alain was supposed to continue the test. Suddenly, however, I discovered that his phone in Martinique was no longer in service. I tried reaching him at his store in Guadeloupe and at his furniture factory in the Dominican Republic. I tried reaching him through his U.S. freight-forwarder in Miami, but she too had lost contact with him. To this day we have no idea what happened to Alain or to the cart. In our dealings with him he had always proved to be honest, intelligent, and very likable. Could he have fallen victim to the French Secret Service? I have heard that the French don't like McDonald's, but would they engage in commercial espionage to undermine *le chien chaud*?

The expense of returning to Fort-de-France, locating the wagon, and shipping it back to New Orleans would have exceeded the cost of the equipment. The possibility also existed that the cart was no longer on the island. Who knows: it might have been hijacked and smuggled out of the country, and could now be selling Arafat Red Hots somewhere in the Middle East. I can see it now: "Lucky Dogs—official hot dog of the PLO."

Thanksgiving and Christmas passed, and New Year's Day, 1991, was upon us. The shop was packed with vendors frantic to hit the streets, each wanting his supplies twenty minutes ago. A few were furious that their helpers had gotten drunk and failed to show for work. Big Alice was cursing about needing onions, and Smitty was mumbling something about hot dog tongs. Stafford's helper accidentally dropped a full pan of chili. The mess covered the floor, and while we were cleaning it up, someone stole two packs of hot dogs off of the kitchen counter. Five or six other vendors were complaining that their carts had not yet been cleaned; Jack, our maintenance man, was shouting back that he was washing them as fast as he damn well could. In the midst of this bedlam the phone rang. It was Professor Stephen Ambrose. He said something about wanting me to speak at UNO on Andrew J. Higgins, the industrialist who was the focal point of my master's thesis.

Although the surrounding confusion prevented me from thoroughly comprehending what he said, I accepted his invitation. I assumed that I was to give a short informal talk before his modern military history class. I was wrong, but it wasn't until several weeks later that I discovered the magnitude of my mistake. To be honest, after New Year's I even forgot about the call.

Then in February I received a program from UNO's Eisenhower Center for Leadership Studies concerning their upcoming War in the Pacific Conference. Listed as speakers were Major General David M. Jones, whose topic was "The Doolittle Tokyo Raid: A Personal Memoir"; George Gay, the lone survivor of Torpedo Squadron 8, speaking on "Witnessing the Battle of Midway"; Ronald Spector of George Washington University, covering "Japanese Naval Strategy in World War II"; and Kenneth J. Hagan of the U.S. Naval Academy, lecturing on "American Submarine Warfare in the Pacific." There were several other nationally known historians on the program—and me.

I telephoned Ambrose, thanked him for his confidence, offered to serve Lucky Dogs free of charge to the conference's attendees, and politely declined the invitation to lecture. He insisted that it was too late to withdraw. The program had been finalized. I was to deliver a twenty- to thirty-minute speech on Higgins and the evolution of amphibious

Lucky Lamar satisfies another Lucky Dog addict at his Bourbon Street stand
Courtesy David Richmond

landing craft at 3 P.M., Friday, April 12. The only reason I didn't panic
was that I didn't have time to; Mardi Gras was only two weeks away
and I had too much to get done before then.

For Lucky Dogs, the final five days of Mardi Gras have the greatest
financial impact. It is then, weather permitting, that we make up for
the pitiful sales of January and early February. On the Friday prior to Fat
Tuesday, the crowds in the Quarter begin to swell. The historic district
bulges with tens of thousands of revelers. By Mardi Gras afternoon, customers are standing in line fifteen deep waiting to buy Lucky Dogs.
Vendors and their helpers keep their carts out around the clock. Time is
irrelevant. The crowd needs fuel for their bodies so that the madness
can continue. During these fantastic final five days of Carnival, some of
the zaniest events in the company's history have occurred.

There was the time that a highly inebriated gentleman stumbled into our shop leading an appaloosa stallion by the reins. For a measly ten dollars he offered to part with his precious steed. Stitched on the saddle blanket were the letters NOPD. Apparently, our wrangler had discovered the horse tied up in the Quarter and enacted the old finders-keepers statute. When I rejected his generous offer, the drunk led the animal out of the shop, mounted him on about the fifth attempt, and then began making his way down Decatur toward Jackson Square. As the well-trained animal slowly weaved his way through the crowd, his not-so-stable rider clung to the saddle horn and bellowed out Roy Rogers' old tune "Happy Trails to You."

Then there was the Mardi Gras season when Dee Rigby showed up looking for work. She pulled up in front of the shop in a white El Dorado convertible. It was like a scene out of the movies. The car door opened and a pair of legs slowly slid out. Smitty, Father Larry, and Stafford happened to be looking out toward the street. When they saw Rigby, they started hooting and hollering.

Wearing a tight blue dress, she strolled into the building and headed straight for the kitchen. I was at the counter. She fluffed her hair with her hands and said, "Hi, Jerry. Bet you don't remember me."

She looked vaguely familiar, but I couldn't place her. Then she said, "It's me, Donald. A lot's happened since I last worked for you."

I thought, Damn right.

Frankly, s/he looked better as a female, and her sales proved to be much improved over his earlier attempt at vending. Stafford later bragged, "Yeah, I knew right from the get-go that she wasn't for real. I knew she was a guy."

Bull. All the guys in the shop almost killed one another to get to the kitchen counter to stand next to him/her.

There was also the Mardi Gras night that an attractive young female disrobed on St. Peter and Bourbon and tried to have sexual intercourse with the protruding section of Stafford's hot dog cart. To the jeers of the crowd, the police covered her with a blanket and escorted her away. Later the same night, on Canal Street women were climbing on top of our cart outside of the Marriott Hotel. They wanted to be above the crowd so that they could bare their breasts to the masked riders on the

Carnival floats. Such exposure would be rewarded with enormous numbers of beads: every parade goer's objective during Mardi Gras. One lady that we forced from atop the cart loudly informed us that she had far more invested in her chest than we had in our hot dog stand. The ninety or so guys pushing and shoving to get close to our wagon tended to agree with her.

For years, two nomadic Canadian brothers joined our crew for Mardi Gras. With green cards in hand they always arrived a month before Carnival to be certain of getting a cart. Once the season was over they would head for Mexico, where they could live like kings with their recently earned money. When their cash reserves dwindled, they returned to Canada and worked the ski resorts until it was time once again to migrate south for Mardi Gras.

On this particular Mardi Gras night Stafford found the cart of one of the brothers abandoned on Canal Street outside of a hotel, blocks from its assigned corner. The Canadian's unpaid bill for the day totaled slightly over four hundred dollars. I wasn't concerned because I had over fourteen hundred dollars of his personal money locked in the company's safe. His brother, however, was extremely worried. It wasn't until the morning of the third day that the missing vendor surfaced.

An attractive American divorcée had invited him to her room to discuss international relations. As a guest in her country, he felt it his moral obligation to accept. He pushed his cart to the Sheraton and left it sitting out front, figuring that eventually we would discover it. In his opinion, had all of his dogs been stolen and all of his savings been depleted to pay his bill, it would have been a small price to pay to help bring two nations closer together. Détente was so successful that the two ambassadors made plans to meet the next Mardi Gras. Same cart, same corner.

Even vendors who stay on their carts during Mardi Gras run into unforeseen problems. On one rainy Fat Tuesday night, Smitty's money got soaked. Unbeknownst to us, he tried to dry it in the shop's microwave. By the time the buzzer went off, his cash resembled burnt toast. The pile of crispy cotton fibers had to be sent to the Federal Reserve Bank and exchanged for less brittle bills. Smitty's faux pas seemed a fitting

end to Mardi Gras in that it occurred a few hours after midnight: officially, he had microwaved his money on Ash Wednesday.

With Mardi Gras over I began to concentrate seriously on writing my
speech for the War in the Pacific Conference. I researched, I wrote, and
I practiced delivering it over and over. I felt confident that I was prepared. However, the morning of the conference I had butterflies in my
stomach. I knew that in the audience would be professional historians
and decorated veterans who had served in the war.

I thought that perhaps if I just sat outside the conference room and
didn't listen to the expert lecturers speaking before me, then I might
not get quite so nervous. I sat down in a chair in the large foyer next to
an elderly gentleman. He seemed polite and cordial. He saw my notes
and asked in a German accent if I was one of the speakers. "Yes," I
replied.

"On what topic?" he asked.

"The Higgins landing craft," I responded. "They were instrumental
in the Allies' D-day invasion and in the victory in the Pacific."

"I am quite familiar with them," he replied. "I am Colonel Hans von
Luck. I was commander of the 125th Regiment of the 21st Panzer Division at Normandy. I am looking forward to your lecture." I thought,
Not only do I have the Allies, I also have the Axis powers in the audience. Why didn't Ambrose just let me serve Lucky Dogs like I wanted
to?

In the end all went well. I knew this because Major John Howard of
D Company of the Oxfordshire and Buckinghamshire Light Infantry, a
gliderborne outfit in the British 6th Airborne Division, told me so. It
was Howard's gliders that landed behind the enemy lines in Normandy
hours before the first Higgins boats hit the beach on D-day. It had been
Howard's responsibility to make certain that Pegasus Bridge remained
intact so that the invasion forces would have access to move from the
beach into the French heartland. I appreciated Howard's compliment.

Now that my speech was over I changed from a suit back into jeans
and tennis shoes and headed for the shop. It was time to turn my attention from history back to hot dogs.

11
Special Officer Smith

In September, 1992, Chet and Maggie Anderson were hawking their dogs in the Square. One of their customers happened to be a reporter from *Newsweek*. The writer asked Chet his opinion of President Bush's handling of the economy. Two weeks later, in the magazine's September 21 issue, there appeared an article on the sagging U.S. economy. Did the article feature an economics professor from Harvard or Yale? No. Did it feature economists from Washington's renowned brain trusts? No. Under the bold caption "What's a President to Do?" appeared a full color, third-of-a-page picture of Chet making a hot dog.

Bush probably looked at the *Newsweek* article. Before doing so he should at least have asked Ronald Reagan, Jr., about Anderson's credibility. Reagan would have told him about Chet's "New Orleans transi-

tion" blunder and maybe the president would have responded skepti-
cally to Chet's state-of-the-nation summary. Chet was quoted in the
piece as saying, "This is the best year I've had in the hot dog business.
If I were asked to make a sacrifice to help the national economy, I
would do it in a minute." Unfortunately, retired Marine Corps gunnery
sergeant Chester Anderson did not represent the feelings of the majority of the nation. Bush lost. Since then, no one has been to the Square
seeking Chet's advice.

In the fall of 1992, while Anderson was making news, Big Alice was
caught riding through Texas in a stolen car. Since she was unaware that
the vehicle was hot, the judge gave her probation. At the same time,
"hugger muggers" were cruising the Quarter. These women had replaced the traditional streetwalkers who had been working the historic
district since shortly after the French explorers Iberville and Bienville
landed on the banks of the Mississippi. The muggers would zero in on a

Chester and Maggie Anderson work their cart in Jackson Square
Courtesy Patti Perret

lone intoxicated gentleman, and after a few minutes of flirting they would lead him into a shadowy doorway. As one woman distracted him with passionate advances, the other would lift his wallet. A few seconds later they would abandon him and head for their next mark. A mugger once confided to me as she stood on the corner eating a Lucky Dog, "Honey, being a prostitute ain't what it used to be. I was out here trying to sell it and all the young bitches were out here giving it away. I hads to change with the times."

Changing with the times is exactly what Lucky Dogs was attempting to do. Crime and competition for the entertainment dollar was causing the Quarter to lose a portion of its patrons. To continue being prosperous, we needed to expand beyond street vending. Our first real success in this direction came in the fall of 1992 when we began operating in the New Orleans International Airport. Instead of parking outside on Bourbon Street, three of our carts were now inside on carpeted concourses. Customers were businessmen, pilots, stewardesses, and sober tourists. Our labor was paid by the hour, not by commission. It was, overall, a much more upscale operation. We had made progress in our expansion attempt, but we were still looking for other areas with potential for development.

The advent of casino gambling in Louisiana and along the Mississippi Gulf Coast created the perfect growth opportunity. All we had to do was convince the casinos to allow us to operate inside their multimillion-dollar gaming palaces. Odds were against it, but it was worth the gamble. If successful the payoff would be a very profitable future. As the Cajuns in south Louisiana say, "Laissez les bon temps rouler." Let the good times roll. And roll they would.

Gaming first came to Mississippi. As Louisianians hotly debated the moral issue of legalizing gambling, Mississippians were busily constructing a mini Las Vegas on their coast. Once their casinos opened, fewer and fewer potential wienie eaters came to the Quarter. We needed to find a way to go to the gaming palaces with them. But how?

Then Fortuna blessed us. Louisiana's legislators, not wanting to be upstaged by their eastern brethren, passed a progambling bill. New Orleans would be allowed a single land-based casino. The remainder of the state's gambling activities would be restricted to fifteen riverboats.

The Hilton's *Queen of New Orleans* called, requesting that we place a cart aboard their soon-to-open vessel. They liked our product. They loved our name. Following the Hilton's lead, Christopher Hemmeter contacted us. The multimillionaire resort developer had been chosen by the city to develop its land-based gambling establishment. Hemmeter was interested in placing Lucky Dog carts throughout his Grand Palais Casino to catch the overflow business that he projected his buffet-style restaurant would generate.

While the casino industry was beginning to make inroads into the Louisiana market, I was writing the last chapter of a biography on Andrew Jackson Higgins. During graduate school I had considered writing about the boat builder, but the idea had not reentered my thoughts for almost fifteen years. Then in 1991, a few weeks after the War in the Pacific Conference, Professor Ambrose invited me to lunch. During my college career, I had taken four of his courses, served as a graduate assistant for one of his classes, and worked closely with him as he directed my thesis. Now as we sat across the table from one another, he suddenly quizzed me: "Do you want to work on your doctorate or write a book?" I reverted back to the pass/fail, student/teacher relationship. Driven by the fear of failing lunch, I selected option B. He never offered an option C, "none of the above."

I admit that lecturing at the conference had rekindled my interest in history. And it reminded me that over the years I had always felt that I had left something unfinished. My master's thesis did not fully tell the story of the wild, colorful World War II boat-building genius, and thus far neither had the professional historians. I accepted Ambrose's challenge: I decided to write the book. I felt obliged to: he had picked up the lunch tab.

My nights and weekends from spring, 1991, until mid-January, 1993, were devoted to research and writing. In May, 1993, LSU Press accepted my manuscript for publication. If I had accomplished nothing else, at least I had proven to myself that I had the perseverance to see the project to its conclusion. My labors, however, had reaped another great benefit. While I worked on the book, I never thought about Smitty, Big Alice, Dan Myers, Father Larry, or any of the other characters whom I associated with at Lucky Dogs.

Unfortunately, the relief was only temporary. Each morning when I reported to the shop some new wacky problem greeted me. The morning of May 6, 1994, the day that I received my advance author's copy from LSU Press, proved to be no different. The zany situation awaiting me that day involved Larry Griffiths. Griffiths by trade was an engineer. He had once been a part of the military arms complex, and his resumé included working on designs for a minesweeper for the U.S. Navy and working on the booster assembly project for the Apollo spacecraft. For Larry, détente meant corporate downsizing and a pink slip. Overage, overqualified, and taking lithium, he was bypassed by companies looking for younger engineers, who required smaller salaries and apparently represented less of a risk. Griffiths thus joined our ranks.

On the day in question, Griffiths reportedly had been brandishing a club and threatening his landlord. Prior to the club-waving incident, he supposedly had thrown a water pitcher through his landlord's front window. The police had been summoned, but Larry took off before they arrived. He headed for the shop.

Calmly, he strolled in and informed me that he was taking a leave of absence to pursue a career in professional softball. On his head was a funky old faded red University of Wisconsin baseball cap. As we spoke, Dan Myers walked up behind us. Griffiths quickly wheeled around and asked, "You ever played ball?"

"In high school," responded Myers.

"Humph, hardball. You're on Jerry's team." He then looked me square in the eyes and said, "If you run across any top-notch softball players, send them to my recruiting office in the Place St. Charles building." Next, he took a pack of rolled-up posters that he had in his hand, swung it like a bat, and yelled, "Play ball!"

"Damn," he muttered as he missed the imaginary pitch. Having struck out, he turned and headed out the front door. Later that afternoon, the police called to let us know that they were taking Larry to

Larry Griffiths sporting his University of
Wisconsin baseball cap
Courtesy author

Charity Hospital. They had discovered him directing traffic in the in-
tersection of St. Peter and Bourbon, and from what I understand he was
doing a fine job. Even so, the officers felt that he should spend a day or
two under professional observation.

On Friday, March 3, 1994, as Larry headed down the hall in the west
wing of Charity to be evaluated by doctors, I was heading for a political
event. A friend of a friend of Doug's was running for political office.
Doug had been talked into donating a cart and hot dogs for one of his

rallies. Our key personnel were already scheduled either for the shop or on the *Queen*. There was no one left to work the event but me.

At 3 P.M. I arrived at the site and found an empty lot, a man cutting the last portion of it with a push mower, and another fellow picking up trash around its edges. Two other T-shirt–clad gentlemen stood by the curb watching. One of them motioned where he wanted the cart stationed. As I followed his instructions, the other onlooker strolled over and began relating his life history.

He had been a drug pusher. The navy, he claimed, had straightened him out. He now owned a home, had kids, and was determined not to let the problems that had nearly destroyed his life take over his neighborhood.

By 5 P.M. a small crowd started gathering, mostly drawn by the rally's entertainment: a disc jockey blaring out such classic rap lyrics as "Black m—— f——, get your AK-47, m—— f——, m—— f—— ..." The song's second verse made mention of killing the "white m—— f——." Personally, I would have preferred something a little less inflammatory. Perhaps a few old Ricky Nelson tunes or maybe something by the Beach Boys.

By 6 P.M. the crowd had grown to over 250 people and I had served over 300 Lucky Dogs. The candidate arrived late, delivered his speech, then afterwards milled about in the audience shaking hands and patting backs.

Almost at dusk a seedy element slowly began filtering in. A tall, slender, rough-looking character arrived. People moved out of his way. He swaggered toward the center of the property to dance with the teenage girls. They ignored him. He danced by himself. The crowd was now more into free beer than good government. By 6:30 the sun had gone down and the candidate left for his next campaign stop. The disc jockey announced "last song." Naturally, it was "Get Your AK-47."

My new buddy, the reformed pusher, was looking out for me. He instructed his "brother" to keep playing music "until the wienie man had gotten his wagon outta there." Quietly, he and his friends pulled the cart down the side of the crowded lot and then loaded it into my truck.

I appreciated their help and their concern. Had it not been for them, I might have ended up in Charity Hospital a floor below Larry.

Gone are the days of Sunday afternoon flag waving and apple pie political rallies. Gone are the innocent lyrics of the Beach Boys. Gone, too, was the blue Ford pickup with me at the wheel and the Lucky Dog cart in the back.

When I arrived at the shop, Paul Hager was waiting for me. He and Griffiths lived in the same building. Hager thought that I should know that his landlord, while cleaning out Griffiths' apartment, had found scribbled on a sheet of paper, "I am going to kill Jerry the Lucky Dog man." Along with the note were four .357 magnum bullets, but no gun.

The next morning I received a collect call from Charity Hospital. Griffiths wanted me to lend him money for cigarettes. He also wanted confirmation that he could have his old corner back once he was released. He had no recollection of directing traffic, of wanting to start a professional softball team, or of wanting to murder me. He was once again on his medication and he sounded normal. I sent P. J. over with a few dollars and the promise that we would discuss his employment status after he was discharged.

At 6:30 A.M. on Sunday, May 8, the phone rang. It was Professor Ambrose.

"Have you seen this morning's newspaper?"

"No."

"Look on page 13 of *Parade*."

So I did. There, under Herbert Kupferberg's "What's Up This Week" byline was the heading "The best books about the most crucial 24 hours of World War II." Kupferberg had written nine short book reviews. The first one I noticed presented Cornelius Ryan's classic, *The Longest Day*. Next I saw Ambrose's recent bestseller, *D-Day, June 6, 1944: The Climactic Battle of World War II.* And the third to catch my eye was *Andrew Jackson Higgins and the Boats That Won World War II*—my book. I was stunned. And then I felt an incredible wave of personal satisfaction.

Of course, the higher one's ego soars, the further one has to fall. Less than four hours later, as I stood in the shop's kitchen, I noticed that Dan Myers had a copy of the morning paper in his hand. I pulled out the *Parade* section and showed him the review. I expected maybe a "great" or a "wow." Instead, I got, "Yeah, nice. Now slap a piece of dry ice on the page and wrap it up so I can put it in my meat chest and push outta here."

Later, as the rest of the crew searched for copies of *Parade* for their dry ice, Fortuna smiled on me again. I was invited by Benis Frank, chief historian of the Marine Corps Historical Center, and Edward J. Marolda of the Naval Historical Center to be one of the speakers at the World War II in the Pacific Conference in Washington, D.C. The symposium was opened with a welcome by Secretary of the Navy John H. Dalton.

On the evening of the conference's banquet I was seated at a table filled with very friendly military brass and one young, extremely cocky professor. He dominated the conversation with his self-proclaimed brilliant analysis of the war. Hell, the generals and admirals that we were dining with had fought in the battles that he was lecturing about. They began ignoring him. I tried the same tactic, but it didn't work. He leaned over and asked me, "Have you ever been to Washington before?"

"Yes," I replied.

"For research purposes?"

"In a sense."

"At the National Archives?"

"Sort of."

"Sort of?"

"Well," I explained, "I was actually on the outside of the building. I was a licensed Class A Central Sidewalk food vendor, and I was trying to find the best locations in D.C. to hawk hot dogs."

He recoiled. "Am I to understand that you peddled wieners on a street corner out of one of those hideous-looking vending carts?"

"Don't be ridiculous. I used a Lucky Dog cart, the Rolls Royce of street-vending equipment. A word of advice, however. If you ever vend in D.C., keep a frozen steak in your ice chest and a birthday card in your cart. This might not mean much to you now. But if you work outside of the Justice Department or the FBI building, you'll thank me for the suggestion."

"Really," he uttered halfheartedly. Then he abruptly turned and attempted to start a conversation with the admiral seated on his other side. Thus we underimpressed one another. From my point of view, the guy didn't have the right stuff to be a good vendor anyway.

When I arrived back in New Orleans, it was business as usual. We had an incredible overabundance of buns in the shop; Father Larry was attempting to open a confessional in one of our store rooms; and Hager and Knight were in the midst of a heated argument. By the time the other vendors and I got to the kitchen, Paul had his hands around Big Alice's neck and was trying to choke her to death.

Right after we broke up this brawl, Barbara Huggins called. A drunk had tossed a beer bottle into the air and it had landed on her helper's head. After being struck he dropped to his knees and appeared dazed. She held up six fingers and asked him how many he saw. He replied, "Nine." She screamed out, "Lord! Lord! Somebody get an ambulance. I think he's brain damaged." Minutes later she called back to inform us that he wasn't hurt. He just couldn't count very well.

Meanwhile, on Bourbon Street a stripper was using one of our company T-shirts in her act. I requested that she refrain from wearing any part of our uniform in her bun-baring extravaganza. She agreed to take it off. I tried to explain that that was the problem.

While I was working on getting the Quarter operation back under control, Doug was contacted by Mike Early, a former New Orleans city councilman. Early knew a politically well-connected individual in Mexico City who was interested in going into street vending. Mike thought perhaps there was an opportunity for a joint venture between a group of investors that he represented, the ex-Mexican official, and us. Would we be receptive to investigating the opportunity? Certainly.

Early and I flew to Mexico and spent three days canvassing the area. The last night there I ventured to a gift shop not far from our hotel. On the way back I was afforded an opportunity to change forever the street culture of the Central American city.

As I walked down the sidewalk, a tatterly clad shoeshine boy called out, "Mister, mister, you need a shine?" The lad's marketing technique was embarrassingly amateurish. It left me with the option of simply responding "no." At that point he would have no recourse but to seek another potential client.

Since the young entrepreneur understood English and since I was filled with the spirit of NAFTA, I considered it my moral obligation to stop and introduce him to a North American technique that would decrease his overhead and increase his profits. I convinced him to replace his old worn-out line with the catchier, "Mister, mister, I betcha twenty pesos I know where you got dem shoes." As a bonus, I also introduced him to the "will work for food" racket and the squeegee kid routine.

With any luck, I figured, there might soon be another major change in Mexico City. The people of Zona Rosa might be hearing the Spanish equivalent of "Getcha eight inches of fun on a bun." A city with twenty-two million inhabitants certainly has potential. We reported back to Doug that the market could reasonably support sixty carts. If we were correct, Mexico's operation could dwarf our Quarter business. Unfortunately, we would never have the opportunity to find out. A sudden drastic devaluation of the peso forced us to put our expansion plans there on hold.

Upon on my return home, I had an important dinner with longtime vendors Chet and Maggie Anderson. Chet had survived the Korean War and POW experience, but having been stationed in the desert of the Southwest during the early tests of the atomic bomb had finally caught up with him. He was suffering from cancer that he believed to be directly related to the nuclear tests. The VA Hospital in New Orleans was treating him, but he and Maggie decided to move up north where they could be near their children and grandchildren. Before departing, they insisted that we go out to eat.

They selected the Star Steak and Lobster House on Decatur, four doors from where our old shop had been housed. The restaurant, once occupied by the Acropolis Bar and its trade of wild drunken seamen, had been renovated and was now catering to a much more respectable clientele. As the Andersons and I walked down Decatur to dinner, we passed no prostitutes or seamen, only businessmen in suits and tourists. Rosenberg's shoe company, Lucky Dogs' old neighbor, had ceased operating, and its building was now occupied by the House of Blues. The Pair-of-Dice Bar on the corner of Decatur and Bienville had also closed. Ryan's Irish Pub now anchored the corner.

The upscaling of the street had brought more tourists to the area and forced characters like Frenchy to move to the fringes of the Quarter or further up the unrenovated sections of Magazine Street. The old Decatur was gone forever, and, before long, so too would be Chet and Maggie.

In late November, 1994, it appeared that P. J. might also be going— not out of town, but to jail. One afternoon Stafford came to the shop and reported that he had just seen P. J. in the back of a police cruiser on Canal Street.

An officer had noticed Smith walking down the street drinking wine from a bottle wrapped in a brown paper bag. The policeman asked him for identification. P. J. couldn't produce any. The officer then put him in the back of his patrol car and began questioning him. He asked for his name. P. J. gave it to him. He asked for his social security number. P. J. gave that to him also. Then he asked for and received his date of birth. With those three pieces of information, the officer called his dispatcher and had the station run a computer check on his detainee. Bingo: "Paul Jackson Smith—special officer." The policeman was stunned, but not nearly as much as P. J. was when the patrolman opened the cruiser door, handed him back his bottle, and then apologized for interfering with his undercover work. P. J. accepted the apology, took his wine, and headed for the shop.

Minutes later he was helping Huggins push her cart to the Quarter. As they crossed Canal Street, there, standing on one side of the bus lane, was the officer talking to two bike patrolmen. As P. J. passed, the policeman who had almost arrested him gave a sly low wave with his right hand. Special Officer Smith nodded, took a sip, and kept on pushing.

P. J., Huggins, and the Lucky Dog cart headed down Bourbon Street, a few blocks away from a major renovation site. Work was finally beginning on the fifty-million-dollar project to turn the city's Municipal Auditorium into a temporary casino. According to a Harrah's spokesperson, the facility would employ 2,500 people, feature 3,000 slot machines and 85 gaming tables, and receive an estimated 4,200,000 annual visitors.

Important to us was the projection that 75 percent of casino patrons would purchase a fast-food item. Five concessionaires were to be selected; each would operate a single one-hundred-square-foot food service area to help complement Harrah's buffet operation. We were hoping that Lucky Dogs would be chosen, even though Hemmeter was no longer in control of the decision-making process.

While we awaited word, it was business as usual in the Quarter. And in this case that business proved to be unfortunate for James Hudson.

Hudson, the once young kid from southern Mississippi, had grown to maturity hawking Lucky Dogs on Bourbon Street. On this particular autumn evening, a rough-looking character walked up to James's cart and demanded a couple of free hot dogs. Hudson responded, "Man, I can't do that. I have to pay for everything that's missing." The gentleman muttered something under his breath then walked off. A few minutes later James felt a powerful blow to the back of his head. Blood gushed from the wound and started to flow down the back of his head to his neck. The disgruntled moocher had returned and struck him with a tire iron. The grazing blow gashed Hudson's scalp, but luckily didn't crack his skull.

The perpetrator fled. Hudson took off in pursuit. Three blocks later he tackled the man. A flower vendor working the street had seen the attack and had also taken off after the assailant. He was trailing James, shouting, "Get 'em, Hud. Get 'em, Hud." Bringing up the rear was a police captain who had been eating supper in a nearby restaurant. He, too, had witnessed the assault.

Hudson was weak from the loss of blood, but he had the man on the ground when the captain arrived. After a few stitches and a couple of days of recuperation, James was back on his corner. He was hoping for good business and a peaceful crowd. At least he would have one of his two wishes granted.

Not long after the above attack, he and his wife, Lisa, were working the cart. (They had met in January, 1989; after four days James proposed and Lisa accepted.) A sailor walked up, grabbed Lisa, and tried to kiss her. James said, "Hey, man, that's my wife."

"So what?" the guy responded. Then he tried to kiss Lisa again. James said, "For the last time, back off." The man released Lisa, but as he did he proceeded to take a swing at Hudson.

James dodged the punch then landed a devastating right to the sailor's face. The man dropped. A few minutes later the seaman lifted his hands and cracked his nose back into place. He got up and said, "Let's just shake and forget the whole thing." As James extended his right hand the sailor took another quick swing. Hudson ducked, then came up with a brutal left. His punch broke the man's nose in the opposite direction. Moments later MPs hauled the bloodied sea dog away.

As Lisa worked the cart the following afternoon she saw nine guys in navy uniforms walking toward her. She sensed that they were looking for James. She was right. The leader asked, "Was it your husband who beat up the sailor last night?" When Lisa reluctantly answered that he was, the leader replied, "We just wanted to tell him thanks. The guy he busted up is a real asshole. He's our ship's heavyweight champion. Every time we make port, he goes ashore and starts a brawl. Then he comes back on board and brags about how he trashed some poor sucker. You have no idea how great it is that somebody finally knocked the crap out of him. No disrespect meant, but the fact that it was a hot dog vendor makes it even better."

James wasn't our only vendor having problems with men in uniform. While pushing his cart back to the shop, Smitty ran into a police motorcycle that was parked on one side of Bourbon Street. The officer was still on it. The patrolman vented his anger then sent Smitty on his way. Not three nights later Smitty accidentally rammed his cart into the bumper of a patrol car parked on Canal Street, waking up the criminal who was asleep on the back seat. The officer, who had stopped at Burger King for a cup of coffee, was furious. But, since there was no damage to the cruiser, he, too, dismissed Smitty with just a warning.

Smitty had been lucky with his vehicular encounters. Bill McCarty didn't have the same good fortune. Very early one morning a drunk driver ran over him as he was pushing his cart back to the shop. Mac had to spend six weeks in the hospital. He was unable to work for almost a year.

Chet and Maggie had retired and headed north, and McCarty was recuperating and so off the schedule. Just as I was beginning to think that the old crew was history, I received a call from Jim Campbell. Ten years had passed since Campbell last worked for Lucky Dogs. He and Pepper

Jim Campbell (*left*) and Joe Mayfield (*right*) surveying Bourbon Street in March, 1995
Courtesy Times-Picayune/*Kathy Anderson*

had been divorced for nine. He had remarried and for the past seven years had given up drinking and been steadily employed, most recently by the Small Business Administration. He was now calling because he was tired of suburban life, tired of having to wear a suit. He wanted to wear tennis shoes and jeans once again and feel the freedom of the street. He wanted to come back to the Quarter and sell Lucky Dogs.

I tried to talk him into staying in California, staying with his wife, and continuing to live a normal life. He wanted no part of it. He said, "I miss the old life too much. God I want to come back. Those were exciting and good years. It was kind of a romantic life style, a different life style, a life style most people never have. They never touch it. It was always an adventure. It was Woodstock every day. I don't want to stay here and rot behind a desk. Save me a corner. I'm coming home." The next sound I heard was that of a dial tone.

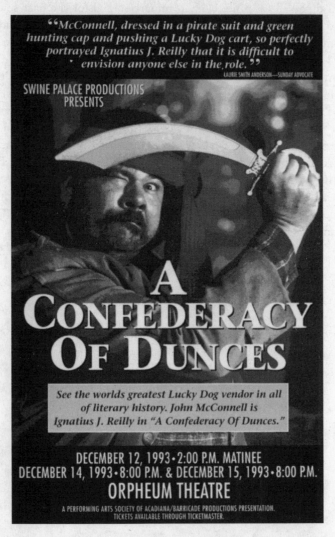

Playbill from a contemporary stage production of John Kennedy
Toole's Pulitzer Prize–winning novel, *A Confederacy of Dunces*
Courtesy Swine Palace Productions

12

The More Things Change...

> He's sitting in his room right now writing some fool-
> ishness. I says, "What's that you writing now, boy?"
> and he say, "I'm writing about being a weenie vendor."
> Ain't that terrible? Who want to read a story like that?
> —Irene Reilly, in *A Confederacy of Dunces*

In the early months of 1995 construction crews were logging overtime trying to meet their completion deadline for Harrah's New Orleans project. For our part, we were trying to convince Harrah's that Lucky Dogs was more than your typical ma-and-pa street-vending operation. We wanted them to see us as a New Orleans tradition. If we were successful, they might select us to be a part of their local concession package.

Unfortunately, during this same period two local college students were putting the finishing touches on their version of a David Letterman top-ten list. Impressed with their creativity, they placed an ad in *Gambit* magazine announcing Mardi Gras T-shirts, featuring their top ten reasons for attending Carnival. Reason number ten: "2 things that smell bad, but relieve you, that you never want to experience again—Port-o-Lets & Lucky Dogs."

Damn college kids. I kept dreaming that we finally got to make a presentation to Harrah's, and their executives were sitting there in Port-o-Let and Lucky Dog T-shirts. Out of curiosity, I asked one of our vendors, who worked as a part-time tarot card reader in Jackson Square, her professional interpretation of my dream. She responded, "You ain't got a prayer of making it in the casino. Now, that'll be five dollars for psychic consultation of a commercial nature."

I wasn't worried about her prediction. Father Larry promised that for a "ten spot" he would "light a couple of candles, pray the rosary, and guarantee success." For a business reference he gave me the name of some Cuban lady in Miami.

While we patiently awaited a reply from Harrah's concerning our concession application, impatient Jim Campbell left California and returned to Lucky Dogs. Campbell was determined to recapture the wild and free life style of the 1970s. Instead of wearing a three-piece suit, he once again had on faded jeans and a striped vendor's shirt. Instead of sitting behind an office desk, he was once again sitting on a wooden bar stool next to his hot dog cart. Instead of living in California with his present wife, he was back in New Orleans with his ex-wife, Pepper. Fate had brought Pepper back to town. Thirst for a cold draft beer had brought her to Bourbon Street. There she rediscovered "her ex–old man" hustling dogs. It was the seventies all over again—almost.

There was the complicating factor that both Jim and Pepper had remarried: Jim once, Pepper twice. Pepper's present husband, Mike, was serving time in New Orleans Central Lockup for striking her during a drunken domestic squabble. Her second husband, Lee, in the meantime had wandered into town. He was crashing on her couch until he could find a cheap room. Now, her first husband, Jim, had reappeared.

For three weeks I had Jim, Pepper, and Lee all working at Lucky Dogs. Even more bizarre, they were sharing an apartment. Pepper, on occasion, would leave her ex-husbands at home and visit her present one in jail. It was as though time had warped back to the free-love, live-and-let-live late sixties and early seventies. Campbell might not have recaptured the past, but he was coming damn close to re-creating it.

However, the old adage "three's a crowd" proved to be true. Thus, Lee ventured west. Mike, soon after being released, also took off for California. At about the time that Mike was leaving, I received a call from Tim Nelson, Harrah's local food and beverage director. Nelson informed me that we had made the casino's short list of fifty-six concession finalists (from the long list of approximately eight hundred applicants). Now, like the other finalists, we were to make a thirty-minute visual presentation. When we arrived, Harrah's representatives were all in suits; there wasn't a single T-shirt–clad executive amongst them. Fortuna had done well.

Other good news came from Hemmeter. After failing to receive the state license to operate the land-based casino, he had been awarded a riverboat gaming permit for New Orleans. As a result, he called us requesting that we place a Lucky Dog stand in his soon-to-open River City gaming boat terminal. We jumped at the offer.

Thirty-two days after we began operating at River City, fireworks and a laser light show signaled the grand opening of Harrah's temporary casino. The Big Easy was back into big time gambling, and thankfully Harrah's, in spite of the college kids' ad, chose us to be part of it. Father Larry, of course, claimed full credit for our having been chosen.

But as Ignatius well knew, good fortune is not to be relied on. Sometimes, according to that obese misguided genius, Fortuna will spin us downward, but on the way down she will halt her wheel and momentarily we "find ourselves in a good, small cycle within the larger bad cycle." Apparently, this is what happened to Lucky Dogs in the spring of 1995. Then, just as surely as spring gave way to summer, the good cycle gave way to the bad. In June rumors of River City filing for bankruptcy became common. Locals avoided the complex because they felt

Editorial cartoons by Pulitzer Prize–winning Walt Handelsman concerning Lucky Dogs and gambling

Courtesy Walt Handelsman/Times-Picayune

that it was located in an area known for wharves, not entertainment. Tourists also failed to visit the casino in appreciable numbers. Plus, it never drew enough of the elite clientele that it desired.

I happened to be in the terminal early one Sunday morning when a middle-aged woman, curlers still in her hair, walked in and announced, "Jesus gawd, darlin! They ain't even got their buildin' done." This proclamation was followed by a question to one of the nearby construction workers, "Honey, tell me: do they gots nickel machines?" As he spoke she noticed our cart. "Awww heart, ain't that cute? They even gots one of dem funny looking little hot dog wagons." Curler-headed nickel-slot players in house dresses couldn't have been the type of clientele that Hemmeter truly wished to attract, not after having spent $223 million in developing the complex. In the end, the casino didn't even lure enough penny ante gamblers to stay afloat.

Hemmeter, unfortunately, was not the only one in New Orleans having creditor problems. Big Alice had serious troubles of her own. Desperate because her boyfriend had drunk up her rent money, she borrowed $250 from a Bourbon Street loan shark. Payment was now overdue, and the shark was calling the shop threatening to kill her if she didn't immediately "fork over" his money. She couldn't. She was busted. Adding to her predicament, she was being evicted because her rent was three weeks overdue. I earlier had loaned her enough money to take care of the situation. Foolishly, though, she had given it to her boyfriend to pay their landlord. The money never made it to the landlord. It did, however, manage to make its way into the cash drawers of several Quarter taverns.

When I walked into the shop that humid June morning, Alice was hysterical. She kept wailing, "He's gonna kill me." I calmed her down with promises of help. I told everyone there that if the gentleman called again, I wanted to speak with him about resolving the matter.

The shark called. Stafford answered the pay phone and proclaimed, "Come on down. Jerry said he's gonna pay you." Before I knew it I had a tall and powerfully built, broad-shouldered black man standing in my office with his large right hand, palm up, extending toward me. This was not what I had envisioned when I offered to assist. I'm not really certain what I had envisioned, but I was positive that this wasn't it.

Alice Knight giving one of her "If I make this you
better buy it" looks
Courtesy author

The moment called for immediate action. But what kind of action?
I took one more look at his massive size and instantly decided upon a
path of delicate diplomacy. I began by apologizing for his having been
misinformed, and I assured him that we would help solve his problem,
but that I could not immediately reimburse him all that he was owed.

I had an advantage in our discussion. I knew that he was financially hurting. According to Alice, the gentleman's wife had been arrested for solicitation. Normally, she would have been out on bail within hours. This time, however, for whatever reason, she was having difficulty getting released. Because of her incarceration, her man was suffering a severe cash-flow problem. As a result, he was pressuring Alice for payment. A dead Alice would be of no benefit to him, but neither would a live one walking Bourbon Street destroying his enforcement credibility.

I tried to sell the shark on the idea that we both needed Alice. If harm befell her, we would lose our cart washer and he would lose his $250. I suggested that as reasonable businessmen we work this out to our mutual advantage. I offered to deduct $50 per week from Alice's paycheck and hold it for him. In essence, I would assume responsibility for the loan. Additionally, as part of the agreement he could spread any rumor that he deemed necessary to maintain his reputation as a "bad ass." Alice would agree not to challenge it. However, in return he had to promise to freeze the loan at $250. There could be no additional interest charges, and no further harassment.

The idea appealed to him. It gave him instant cash, guaranteed his full repayment, saved his reputation, and stopped him from having to bloody his fists. We shook hands, I gave him his first installment, and he calmly left. Alice breathed a sigh of relief. So did I.

For the next four Fridays the shark came a-calling. Never once did he utter a harsh word. After receiving the final payment he told Alice, "Everything's cool."

Big Alice had overcome her financial problem, but unfortunately the owners of Harrah's temporary casino could not overcome theirs. At 4 A.M. on Wednesday, November 22, 1995, the casino closed its doors for good. Unfortunately, the part-time tarot card reader had been right. When I confronted Father Larry about the closure, he proclaimed, "Hey, the Hamilton only assured that you would get into the casino. If it was long-term success that you wanted, you shoulda dropped a couple of Ben Franklins in the collection plate."

Things locally were depressing. Sales in the Quarter were down, and now the casino had closed. But a bright spot formed on the horizon: Harrah's new casino on the Skagit Indian reservation in Bow, Washington, had decided that it wanted a cart. Grand-opening ceremonies were scheduled for mid-December, 1995. We only had a few weeks to be operational, but we felt we could achieve this goal.

Doug's twenty-six-year-old son Kirk and I arrived in Bow on December 13. We had no labor, no supplies, and we were uncertain if our equipment would be air-delivered on time. We cleared all of those hurdles, but then ran into an unforeseen one. The Washington State gaming commission would not allow the casino to handle our nightly gross. To overcome this obstacle, we opened a bank account in the nearby town of Sedro-Wooley. We assumed that the problem was solved. We were wrong, but it would be days before the error was discovered.

Kirk and I left Washington on December 19, heading for Harrah's in Reno. The Nevada casino also wanted a cart. Our brief stopover would give us ample time to apply for the necessary occupational license. It would also give me an opportunity to play Sherlock Holmes. I wanted

On the Hilton's *Flamingo*
Courtesy author

to track down Jim Sloan. If he was still hawking newspapers in "The Biggest Little City in the World," I hoped to sneak up behind him, tap him on the shoulder, and say "gotcha."

We were too late. An old codger selling dailies out in front of the Cal-Neva casino informed me that Sloan had died of pneumonia the previous January. We would never find out why Jim stole the six hundred dollars from the shop and fled to Vegas.

By the time Kirk and I reached New Orleans on December 23, troubles had arisen on the Washington Indian reservation. According to Harrah's, the tribal police would not allow our employees to transport our daily cash receipts off of the reservation because of safety concerns. Thus, we could sell hot dogs, but we couldn't turn the money over to Harrah's, nor could we take it to the bank. Our only option was to close the unit until the catch-22 could be resolved.

When February of the new year rolled around, I began to believe that Lucky Dogs might not be so lucky. We received a call from our employee working the cart on the Hilton's *Flamingo* (the old *Queen*). U.S. Coast Guard inspectors had ordered the ship's captain to remove our wagon from the gaming boat; otherwise, the paddle wheeler would be forced to cease operations. By the time I arrived, our cart, cash register, and supplies were already on shore. The perishables were stacked next to the gangplank. Our equipment and register had been pushed several hundred yards to the *Flamingo*'s warehouse. Never before in the annals of U.S. history had the military been credited with a decisive victory over a hot dog stand. Outnumbered and defenseless, our employee had laid down her tongs and surrendered her position.

A Coast Guard inspector later explained that the abrupt action had been taken because the cart was on wheels. The cart had always been on wheels. For two years no inspector ever noticed this? In any case, the crisis was short lived. The Great Wienie War of '96 was over within minutes. No shots were fired. No dogs were tossed.

Just when everything appeared to be heading south for Lucky Dogs, Fortuna's wheel forcefully spun upward. In the course of 1996 we signed a national agreement with Coca-Cola. Then we opened in Harrah's Mardi Gras casino in Tunica, Mississippi. Shortly thereafter we were contacted by Euro-Disney. Through a special licensing arrangement Disney started operating five Lucky Dog carts at its theme park outside of Paris. They requested permission to sell wine from the wagons. P. J. requested permission to be our overseas quality control inspector. He planned on calling Jeno the Wino out of retirement as his assistant.

Not long after denying P. J.'s request, we heard from a prominent businessman in Tegucigalpa, Honduras. He was interested in bringing Lucky Dogs to the Central American country. I flew down to assess the potential. As I toured the capital city, I was amazed at the massive number of armed guards. Every service station had two men carrying sawed-off pump shotguns. The hardware store had a guard with a shotgun. Naturally, the doughnut shops were protected. The hotel I was staying in as well as the restaurant nearby had heavy security. Where there was money, there were guards. I was leery of trying to operate in such an environment. I was even more leery when I noticed a large flock of buzzards circling over the downtown business district. I took their hovering as an omen that perhaps we should pass on this opportunity.

Then, as I was waiting to catch my return flight home, a small, lean, dark-skinned lad walked up and pointed toward my shoes. He said something about "sixty lempiras." He repeated his statement. Suddenly, I realized that the kid was challenging me in Spanish, "I betcha sixty lempiras I know where you got dem shoes." Instantly, I realized that, third world or not, this town had potential. It had the type of grassroots entrepreneurship that it takes to make street vending succeed. Perhaps in a few years we would return and reevaluate the situation.

As amazing as it was that "Betcha I know where you got dem shoes" had spread south so rapidly from Mexico City, there was an even more astonishing bit of news. Doug, as president of Lucky Dogs, was selected the Louisiana, Mississippi, and south Alabama small business regional nominee for the 1996 Entrepreneur of the Year Award. This national award, sponsored by the Entrepreneur of the Year Institute, the Center for Entrepreneurial Leadership, Inc., *USA Today*, and the NASDAQ stock market, is considered the most prestigious honor that an entrepreneur can receive. If Vegas laid odds on the award, Doug, as owner of a Bourbon Street vending company, would have been a thousand-to-one shot to win. The crew, hearing about his success, suggested that we lock up the shop and go have a couple of beers in his honor. Some things never change.

While Doug was winning awards and we were making strides in expanding the business outside of New Orleans, Lucky Dogs in the Quarter seemed frozen in time. Subtle changes had taken place, but for the most part things had remained the same. The other day, for instance, Dan Myers was waiting to check in at the end of the night. Big Alice was next in line, but her eyelids were heavy from lack of sleep. Instead of standing at the counter, she decided to lie down on our flatbed dolly and rest until it was her turn. Myers assumed that she was asleep. He yelled out, "Hager, check me in next. The water buffalo's hibernating."

Like a flash, Alice bolted from the flatbed, grabbed Myers by the back of his neck, and began ramming his head into the Coke machine. Still not convinced that her co-worker had become sensitive to her feelings, she whirled him around and smashed his face into the pay telephone hanging on the wall.

Myers' eyes were crossed, his nose was flattened, and his head hurt, but he was still breathing. Before Alice could bounce him off the wall and clothesline him with a stiff forearm, Hager stopped the bout. Father Larry, who had been eagerly standing ready to administer last rites, disappointedly went back to unloading supplies from his cart.

The ruckus brought P. J. out of our elevator shaft where he had been sleeping. For over two years Smith had called the shaft home. His arthritis had gotten so bad that at times he could barely walk. His back was giving him trouble, and he had terrible swelling in his feet. He was physically unable to hold down a job, but no agency wanted to help him. Without money, he couldn't afford an apartment. Without an apartment, he would have to go back to the alley where he and Jeno once resided. But before doing that, he swore that he would commit suicide. I decided to make him Lucky Dogs' official volunteer security guard.

Our elevator was one of the old rope-driven early 1900s models. We seldom used it, so P. J.'s presence created no problem. He had a private door, a roof over his head, and the shop's bathroom and shower available to him. He also had friends to give him support. Smith had filed for disability through social security, but his request had been denied. We convinced him to hire an attorney and appeal. His petition became lost somewhere in the bowels of the system, but no one seemed to know where.

The noise created by Myers bouncing off of the Coke machine had awakened P. J. By the time he made it out of the shaft and to the kitchen, the match was over. He had missed it, but the following night he caught Myers in rare form. Dan came in drunk and was standing at the counter talking to Hager. He kept repeating over and over, "Pauline, you know I love you. Do you love me, Pauline? We've always been good friends. You know friends love one another, Pauline."

Hager was becoming frustrated. As Myers attempted to bring his tray of supplies to the counter, he waddled left, then right, then back, and finally he fell forward. The tray landed on the counter, but his container of quarter-inch diced yellow onions kept on going. It landed on the kitchen floor at Hager's feet. Onions spilled everywhere. All the while, Myers kept repeating, "Now, Pauline, don't you be mad. Don't you be mad at me, Pauline. Come on, let me see you smile." Then, in slow motion he would snap his fingers over his head and move his feet like a flamenco dancer.

Hager was fuming. Making matters worse, Myers was refusing to pay his bill. He insisted, "I won't give you a penny until you tell me that you love me and that we're good friends. Friends love each other, you know." Pushed to his limit, Hager grabbed a three-foot piece of metal pipe that was leaning against the kitchen wall and slammed it down on the stainless-steel counter three or four times. As he bashed the counter he screamed, "Myers, give me the f——ing money or I'll crack your damn skull open."

"Ohhh, temper, temper," Myers replied.

Hager came unglued. He was about to leap over the counter when P. J. stepped in and calmed him down. Paul regained his composure, and with P. J.'s help Myers was coaxed into paying his bill. With that accomplished, Father Larry ushered Dan out the front door, but Myers ran back in and shouted one last time, "I love you, Pauline. Now, don't you be mad. That'll only make your blood pressure rise." Hager bolted from the kitchen. Larry quickly ushered Myers outside.

The following night was Dan's last with the company. He reported to work sober and promised to stay that way until his shift was over. He did. But he still managed to get into hot water. As he worked his cart, he decided that if he just had some type of gimmick to attract attention, his sales might increase.

Then inspiration struck. He lay down in the middle of Bourbon Street near his cart. People started gathering around him. They assumed that he was suffering a heart attack and needed assistance. When the crowd grew to the size that he desired Myers jumped up, threw out his arms, and shouted, "Getcha eight inches of fun on a bun. Don't be a meanie—buy a wienie!"

No one was amused, including the beat cop. Hager called me at home. I had him push Dan in. Later, I asked Myers what had possessed him to do such an atrocious thing. "I had to do something," he declared. "You of all people should know that tourists don't feed on an east wind." I had heard the old saying that fish don't feed on a west wind, but I had no idea that easterlies affected the eating patterns of our out-of-town visitors. What I did know was that Myers needed some time off before he did something crazy enough to land him in Central Lockup.

Dan left because he had become too wild. Diabetes caused Father Larry to leave. By the time he received treatment, he was forced to lose his left leg just below the knee. Still, he hopes to return someday and work a cart. If that shouldn't pan out, he has an alternate plan. He intends to become the new "Chaplin of Bourbon Street." As he sees it, when the Reverend Bob Harrington left the street years ago to make a national name for himself, he left a religious void in the Quarter—a void that Larry feels is his moral obligation to fill.

He believes that God has blessed him with the talent necessary to spread "the word." He also figures that the same power has given him the skill to be proficient at gathering in tithes. I told him that he should be ashamed of himself. He replied, "I've never felt guilty about taking their money. If they're dumb enough to give it to me, then why shouldn't I be dumb enough to accept it? Besides, giving makes them feel good. To deprive them of such worldly happiness would be unchristian."

Like Myers and Father Larry, James Hudson also left the company, not by his own choice or ours. He had fought off a tire-wielding customer, a navy boxing champion, street punks, and obnoxious drunks. He was tough and victorious in every street bout except his last one. That one involved a delivery truck. The van struck the cart, then James. Hudson went flying. When he landed, his right hand was permanently damaged.

James always wondered how he would have stacked up against such great old-time vendors as Burt Richards and Bob McGregor. I always wondered how he would have stacked up in the ring against Frenchy. Personally, I think that he might have outsold Richards and McGregor and TKO'd the Canadian.

Stafford also recently left us. It seems that on his off days, he had been running bets for a local bookie. He noticed that some bettors never seemed to win, so he started pocketing their wagers instead of placing them. Then a hundred-to-one shot hit. The winner came looking for his money, but Stafford didn't have it. The man came back with an associate named Louie who gave George twenty-four hours to come up with the cash. Stafford instead came up with bus tickets. The last I heard, he, Julie, and the kids were Disneyland bound.

Everyone deserves a second chance. This principle even held true for Larry Griffiths. As soon as Larry got out of Charity Hospital, he came straight to the shop. When I arrived at work, I found him waiting for me by the front door. He asked, "Can we talk?"

I asked, "Are you armed?"

He was wearing a short-sleeved shirt tucked into his jeans. There was no pistol bulge that I could detect, so I agreed to listen. As a result of our conversation, I put him back out on a cart but warned him that if I ended up dead, our deal was off. Since his return he has been a model vendor. So much so that if we ever field a company softball team, Griffiths, sporting his red Wisconsin baseball cap, will have the honor of being its first head coach.

Barbara Huggins left us, but she has become the envy of every Bourbon Street vendor. In their opinion, she's hit the big time. This view is based on the fact that she landed a job working in a brewery. As they see it, what more could she possibly want, other than to be allowed to take her work home with her?

Big Alice is still around. For a while she was dating one of Hager's old boyfriends, but that didn't last. Word on the street has it that he called her a water buffalo. She supposedly threw him out of their apartment, without opening the door. It seems to have been for the best. This week she met a new love. Last night he proposed and she accepted. According to her, she's not getting any younger, and a girl has to think about her future. The blissful couple plan to leave the Quarter shortly after Mardi Gras and hook up with the carnival circuit in Illinois.

Campbell is still around, though as of late he has had his share of problems. He and Pepper had a spat. He threw an empty beer can at her. She threw him out of their apartment. At least she opened the door first. Jim said, "Hell, if I had really been mad, I would have thrown a full one."

Campbell has temporarily moved in with Joe Mayfield. Mayfield is the ex-vendor who in the 1980s stole one thousand dollars out of the safe and headed to Biloxi, where he spent it on booze and women. He is now sixty years old, suffering from emphysema and heart trouble, and in no condition to run. He's made partial restitution, so once again he is working in the shop. Where else can you rob a place and then be hired back as manager?

Smitty is now one of the senior members of our crew. No more ballerina slippers or hot pants for this man of modern fashion, though. His present wardrobe consists mostly of western attire—male western attire. Frankly, he has become one of our more stable vendors. Who would have ever thought it? It looks like he might be settling down. Just the other day he asked Hager if transvestites can get pregnant.

Social security, after almost two years of appeals, has finally admitted that P. J. is disabled. A few weeks ago he received a check for ten thousand dollars to cover the months that his claim had been denied. Upon receiving the money, he tried to move out of the elevator shaft, but no one would rent him an apartment because he didn't have a driver's license or an official state ID card. He was furious. I calmed him down by explaining that he was probably the wealthiest man in America living in an elevator. Besides, I informed him, with his newly acquired wealth he could afford to hire an interior decorator to really spruce up the shaft.

P. J. made it through the night sleeping in the elevator, and the following morning arrangements were made for him to move into an apartment. He has paid six months' rent, purchased a color television and a stereo, ordered cable, bought new clothes, and opened a bank account. He said, "Boy I wish Jeno could see me now."

P. J. did have one last request before moving out of the shop. He wanted us to promise that if anything should happen to him, we would have his remains cremated and sealed in an empty Thunderbird bottle. The container should then be tossed into the Mississippi River. In his words, "Let the current take me where it will."

Bill McCarty and Paul Hager are also still with us. McCarty is now sixty-five years old. He has never fully recovered from being hit by the car on Thanksgiving morning, 1994. As a result of the accident, he has a slight limp and he shuffles his feet instead of walking. He's old enough to draw social security, and working the street has actually become too rough for him; but thus far he has refused assistance. He claims, "I don't want to be a drain on the system." He has never received food stamps and never asked for a handout.

Paul Hager is still handling the night shift. His arm no longer has the zing that it once had, and as a result, his percentage of hitting annoying vendors with empty chili pots launched from the kitchen has dropped to a lifetime average of approximately .320. Other than that he hasn't changed. Paul will probably be with us until he retires. His co-workers have become his family, and he seems to thrive on the confusion of the shop.

Just when I begin to think that our modern vendors are completely different from those of earlier days, I discover I'm wrong. Recently, I installed a security camera in the kitchen to record the transactions that take place at the check-in counter at night when I am not there. The first day that it was activated, I put a sign up announcing that all proceedings were being taped. One of the vendors looked at the camera and shouted, "Hey, the red light isn't on. It's not working."

At that point the crew became fearless. One by one they made their way to the counter to exhibit their bravery. The first vendor, knowing that smoking is prohibited, stepped up and blew smoke rings while taunting, "Take a look at these puffs, Jerrrry." The second one had a girl with him that he must have picked up on the street. She lifted her blouse and said, "Baby, focus in on these hooters." The third vendor popped the tab on a can of beer and took a swig. Each vendor that followed did his own little thing. What they didn't realize is that not all cameras have a red indicator light to show that they are recording. The tape was capturing everything. It was shades of the wild crew of the 1970s.

The next afternoon I called all the vendors into the office. When I pressed the VCR's start button and said "Roll 'em," you could have heard a pin drop. To break the silence I asked, "Has anyone here ever read the *Iliad*?"

In writing what Ignatius would describe as "The Journal of a Working Boy," old memories have flooded back. I never believed that I would feel this way, but like Jim Campbell, I too miss the excitement of the seventies and eighties. I miss the street life of Decatur, Sally's unionization attempts, Kelly's nightly guzzling of Jack Daniels as he worked outside of the Famous Door. I miss David Garcia unable to pay his bill at check-in and always swearing that it would never happen again; and Frenchy stumbling into the shop drunk and trying to entice the rest of the crew to accompany him back to the Pair-of-Dice. I miss the carnies drifting in as their road shows closed for the season, and the spirited Vietnam veterans searching for their niche in society. But those days are gone. And with the passage of time has come change. Decatur Street is now an upscale, revitalized, integral part of the Vieux Carré.

Our crew has also changed. As a whole they lack the flamboyant medicine-show-style salesmanship so characteristic of Dan Myers and our earlier vendors. But they share with their predecessors an enthusiasm for working the street—as well as a few of the old hawkers' lines: especially the timeless "Getcha eight inches of fun on a bun." They,

The author in front of the entrance to the Forbidden
City, Beijing
Courtesy author and John J. Reardon

like those who came before them, also enjoy the freedom that working
the street offers and the zaniness of their surroundings.

A writer in a local newspaper in 1981 described Lucky Dogs as
"Tube steaks for the hungry. A bacchanal for the drunken. Nectar for
the Bourbon Street beehive. Hot dogs fresh from the womb of the
mother ship." As it was then, so it still is today. As for the future, For-

tuna has not yet revealed her master plan. Therefore, I will resist the temptation to speculate.

However, I can definitively state that the past twenty-six years at Lucky Dogs, at least for this "Working Boy," have been an incredibly exciting adventure—one that as yet has no end. In fact, just recently I was in Beijing, China, scouting the communist capital for future Lucky Dog cart locations. If all goes according to plan, we should open for business there in a few months.

As strange as some of the sights were in Beijing, none topped what I saw in front of our shop this morning. When I reported to work, a pony-tailed, blue jean–clad, barefoot, college-age guy was kneeling on the sidewalk in front of our building and bowing toward our open door. As he touched his hands to the sidewalk, he chanted, "Praise be to Ignatius." After the third bow he rose, put his hands together as if praying, and then politely nodded in my direction. Without another word he lifted his backpack from the sidewalk, threw it over his shoulder, and strolled off toward the river.

Then just a minute ago I received a call from our vendor at Jackson Square demanding my immediate assistance. It seems that a street entertainer, a clown, verbally assaulted him and then punched him in the face. Our vendor wants to press charges; but his only witness is a mime, and he's not talking. Making matters worse, a tarot card reader, whose table is set up near the cart, keeps shouting to the world, "I knew this was going to happen. I knew this was going to happen." The vendor is screaming back, "Dammit, if you knew it was gonna happen, then why in hell didn't you warn me!"

The tarot card reader won't shut up, and the mime won't speak. Before things get totally out of control, I had best put down my Big Chief writing tablet and report to the Square.

God I love the Quarter.